DRAWIN

PEOPLE AND WORK IN EVENTS AND CONVENTIONS

A Research Perspective

PEOPLE AND WORK IN EVENTS AND CONVENTIONS

A Research Perspective

Edited by

Thomas Baum PhD

University of Strathclyde, UK

Margaret Deery PhD

Victoria University, Australia

Clare Hanlon PhD

Victoria University, Australia

Leonie Lockstone PhD

Victoria University, Australia

Karen Smith PhD

Victoria University of Wellington, New Zealand

www.cabi.org

CABI is a trading name of CAB International

CABI Head Office
Nosworthy Way
Wallingford
Oxfordshire OX10 8DE
UK

Tel: +44 (0)1491 832111
Fax: +44 (0)1491 833508
E-mail: cabi@cabi.org
Website: www.cabi.org

CABI North American Office
875 Massachusetts Avenue
7th Floor
Cambridge, MA 02139
USA

Tel: +1 617 395 4056
Fax: +1 617 354 6875
E-mail: cabi-nao@cabi.org

A catalogue record for this book is available from the British Library, London, UK.

Library of Congress Cataloging-in-Publication Data
People and work in events and conventions : a research perspective / edited by Thomas Baum
... [et al.].
     p. cm.
   Includes index.
   ISBN 978-1-84593-476-7 (alk. paper)
1. Special events industry--Employees--Cross-cultural studies. 2. Special events--
Planning--Research. I. Baum, Tom. II. Title.

     GT3405.P46 2009
     394.2--dc22
                                                            2009001097

ISBN: 978 1 84593 476 7

Typeset by AMA Dataset, Preston, UK.
Printed and bound in the UK by MPG Books Group.

The paper used for the text pages in this book is FSC certified. The FSC (Forest Stewardship
Council) is an international network to promote responsible management of the world's forests.

Contents

Contributors

Charles Arcodia is Head of Event Management at the University of Queensland, Australia. He joined the university in 1996 after working in a number of industries and in private enterprise. He has held leadership positions in a variety of educational and business service contexts. Dr Arcodia completed his PhD in organizational citizenship and has an active research agenda in areas relevant to event management and broader tourism and leisure issues. His research interests include event management and administration, cultural diversity in hospitality and tourism management, and hospitality and tourism education. E-mail: c.arcodia@uq.edu.au

Chris Auld is a Professor and Dean (international) in the Griffith Business School, Griffith University, Australia. His research interests include volunteer management, board performance and governance in the non-profit sector, sport and leisure planning and management, and the impacts of major events. He is currently on the editorial advisory board of the *Annals of Leisure Research* and recently co-authored a research book entitled *Working with Volunteers in Sport: Theory and Practice* (2006), published by Routledge. E-mail: c.auld@griffith.edu.au

Tom Baum is Professor of International Tourism and Hospitality Management in the Department of Hospitality and Tourism Management, the University of Strathclyde, Glasgow, Scotland. Professor Baum has a BA and an MA from the University of Wales and a PhD from Strathclyde University. His research focuses on the study of people and work in the context of tourism and hospitality. He has published seven books and over 150 academic papers in this field. E-mail: t.g.baum@strath.ac.uk

Zuleika Beaven is a doctoral researcher into nascent musician entrepreneurship at Birmingham City Business School, UK, and lectures in Cultural Management at the University of Winchester. Previously she was a senior lecturer in

Arts and Event Management at the Arts Institute at Bournemouth, where her work focused on innovation in the cultural entrepreneurship curriculum. She holds bachelor's and master's degrees in arts management, and has a research interest in aspects of work in the cultural events industry. E-mail: zuleika. beaven@winchester.ac.uk

Graham Cuskelly is a Professor and Dean (research) in the Griffith Business School, Griffith University, Australia. His primary research and teaching interests are in sport volunteers, community sport development, and governance of non-profit sport organizations. He recently co-authored *Working with Volunteers in Sport: Theory and Practice* (Routledge, 2006) and *Sport Governance* (Elsevier, 2007) and is currently editor of *Sport Management Review*. E-mail: g.cuskelly@ griffith.edu.au

Margaret Deery is Professor in Tourism and Events Management at Victoria University, Melbourne, Australia, and a professorial research fellow in the Centre for Tourism and Services Research. She has worked with the Australian government-funded Sustainable Tourism Co-operative Research Centre and was Director of the Centre for Hospitality and Tourism Research. She has published widely in the area of human resource management, event evaluation and volunteer management as well as being the recipient of a number of research grants in these areas. E-mail: Margaret.Deery@vu.edu.au

Katalin Formádi is a tourism lecturer at the Tourism Department, University of Pannonia in Hungary. She holds a bachelor's degree in tourism economics and a master's degree in economics and sociology from the Corvinus University in Hungary; she is currently finishing her PhD in the sociology of professions from Corvinus University, Budapest. She has publications in the area of the health and wellness tourism and events sectors, including on the processes of professionalization and careers (Policy Press, 2008). She is an associated member (as a PhD representative) of the Executive Board of RN19 ESA (the Sociology of Professions Research Network of European Sociological Association). E-mail: formadi@turizmus.uni-pannon.hu

Joe Goldblatt, CSEP is Executive Director of the International Centre for the Study of Planned Events at Queen Margaret University, Edinburgh. He is a lecturer in the Tourism, Hospitality and Events Group. Dr Goldblatt is the author, co-author or editor of 19 books in the field of events management. He served as founding president of the International Special Events Society and was recently inducted into the International Festivals and Events Association Hall of Fame. E-mail: jgoldblatt@qmu.ac.uk

Clare Hanlon is a senior lecturer in the School of Sport and Exercise Science and member of the Centre of Ageing, Rehabilitation, Exercise and Sport at Victoria University, Melbourne, Australia. Dr Hanlon is a member of the editorial board for the *Bulletin of Sport and Culture* and an invited reviewer for refereed sport and event journals. Her publications in this related management field address human resource management in major sport events, and training needs of sport, tourism and recreation managers. E-mail: clare.hanlon@vu.edu.au

Maureen Harrington has a PhD in sociology from the University of California, Santa Barbara. After teaching at the University of Ottawa, Canada from 1988 to 1995 in the Department of Leisure Studies, she moved to Australia, where she has been teaching in the Department of Tourism, Leisure, Hotel and Sport Management at Griffith University, Australia. She has written on volunteering in sport, women's work, leisure and family lives, and gender and family leisure. Her current research is on family leisure and children's sport, healthy lifestyles and notions of risk. E-mail: m.harrington@griffith.edu.au

Russell Hoye is an Associate Professor in the School of Management, La Trobe University, Melbourne, Australia. Associate Professor Hoye is a member of the editorial board for *Sport Management Review*, the *International Journal of Sport Policy* and the *Australian Journal on Volunteering*, and current president of the Sport Management Association of Australia and New Zealand (SMAANZ). His most recent books include *Sport and Social Capital* (2008), *Sport Governance* (2007), both published by Elsevier, and *Working with Volunteers in Sport: Theory and Practice* (2006), published by Routledge. E-mail: r.hoye@latrobe.edu.au

Leo Jago is a Professor in Tourism at Victoria University, Melbourne, Australia, and Director of the Centre for Tourism and Services Research. He has degrees in engineering and economics, a master's degree in business and a PhD. Over the last 15 years, his research and publication interests have focused on event management and evaluation. He is an associate editor of the *Journal of Sport & Tourism* and on the editorial boards of a range of international journals, including *Event Management* and the *International Journal of Event Management Research*. E-mail: leo.jago@vu.edu.au

Chris Kemp is an Executive Dean at Buckinghamshire New University, UK. He is an expert in three specific areas: crowd and safety management, music and venue management, and music genre classification. Professor Kemp is widely recognized for his work on the management of crowds and his ceaseless endeavour to make events safer. He works with numerous organizations and government bodies, undertaking research projects and publishing their results. E-mail: Chris.Kemp@bucks.ac.uk

Adele Ladkin is Professor of Tourism Employment and Associate Dean for Tourism and Hospitality within the International Centre for Tourism and Hospitality Research, School of Services Management, Bournemouth University, UK. She holds an MSc and a PhD in tourism from the University of Surrey. Her publications are in the areas of career analysis and labour mobility in tourism and hospitality and the conference industry. Professor Ladkin is editor in chief for the *International Journal of Tourism Research*. E-mail: aladkin@bournemouth. ac.uk

Leonie Lockstone is a lecturer in Event Management at Victoria University, Melbourne, Australia. Leonie has pursued an interest in volunteer research since commencing her PhD thesis in 2000, entitled 'Managing the volunteer workforce – flexible structures and strategies to integrate paid and unpaid workers'. The thesis examined relations between paid workers and volunteers in the tourism sector, and the findings led to the development of an innovative and flexible framework to assist organizations in effectively managing these valuable human resources. In her current role, Leonie continues to undertake research on volunteering and has expanded her focus to include the events sector. Her other research interests include event management education, museum management and commemorative events. E-mail: leonie.lockstone@vu.edu.au

Vivienne S. McCabe is an Associate Professor in Hospitality Management at the University of South Australia. She holds a doctorate and a master's degree in business administration and professional qualifications of the Hotel, Catering and Institutional Management Association (HCIMA). Associate Professor McCabe has a passion for the convention and event sector, is an associate fellow of the Meetings and Events Association of Australia (MEA) and serves as a state and national judge of its industry awards. She is the lead author of the Australian text *The Business and Management of Conventions*. E-mail: mccabe@unisa.edu.au

Judith Mair is a postdoctoral research fellow in the Centre for Tourism and Services Research at Victoria University, Melbourne, Australia. She holds an MSc and a PhD in tourism, both from the University of Strathclyde, Glasgow. She has published in the areas of consumer behaviour and business events, and also event management education. E-mail: judith.mair@vu.edu.au

Catherine M. Matheson is a lecturer in Events Management at Queen Margaret University, Edinburgh. Her research interests lie within cultural policy, event-led regeneration and event strategies. Dr Matheson has published work on authenticity and Celtic music festivals and the heritage of festivals. Collaborative work has centred on events and cultural policy and consumer motivations within sporting events. Recent work has focused upon an evaluation of event-themed regeneration strategies and sports policy. E-mail: cmatheson@qmu.ac.uk

Roselyne N. Okech is an Assistant Professor in Tourism Studies at Sir Wilfred Grenfell College, Memorial University of Newfoundland, Canada. She holds a bachelor's degree in commerce and a master's in tourism administration from India and a PhD in tourism from KwaZulu-Natal University, South Africa. She has published in the area of tourism planning and management, appearing in *Anatolia* and *Journal of Human Resources in Hospitality and Tourism*. She is also a board member of ATLAS-Africa. E-mail: Rnokech@yahoo.com

Csilla Raffai is an assistant lecturer at the University of Pannonia, Hungary. She holds bachelor's and master's degrees in economy and tourism. E-mail: raffai@turizmus.uni-pannon.hu

Karen A. Smith is a senior lecturer in Tourism Management at Victoria Management School, Victoria University of Wellington, New Zealand. Her PhD from Nottingham Trent University in the UK investigated the management of volunteers in literary heritage attractions. She has published in the areas of event ticketing and distribution, film and literary tourism, and volunteer management, and has a forthcoming book *Managing Volunteers in Tourism: Attractions, Destinations and Events*, written with Kirsten Holmes and published by Elsevier. She is on the editorial boards of the *Journal of International Volunteer Tourism and*

Social Development, and the *Journal of Vacation Marketing*. E-mail: karen. smith@vuw.ac.nz

Sara St George is Head of Marketing & Development and Deputy Chief Executive at Lighthouse, Poole's Centre for the Arts, Dorset, UK. At the time of writing, she was a senior lecturer in Arts Education and Arts and Event Management at the Arts Institute in Bournemouth, UK. E-mail: saras@lighthousepoole.co.uk

Karin Weber is an Assistant Professor in the School of Hotel and Tourism Management, Hong Kong Polytechnic University, Hong Kong. Prior to joining the school in 2001, she taught in marketing and tourism at Monash University, Australia. A native of Germany, Karin received her Bachelor of Business (Hons) degree from Monash University, her MSc degree in hotel administration from the University of Nevada, Las Vegas, USA, and her PhD in services marketing from Griffith University, Australia. Assistant Professor Weber has published on a wide range of subjects in leading international tourism and hospitality journals and presented her research at international and national conferences. Her two major areas of research interest are services marketing and convention tourism/management. E-mail: hmkweber@polyu.edu.hk

Richard Wright is a principal lecturer and has been course leader for the BA (Hons) Arts and Event Management at The Arts Institute in Bournemouth, UK, since its inception in 1993. He has taught on vocational programmes in specialist art and design colleges for over 30 years, at Plymouth College of Art and Design and AIB, and has a particular interest in embedding employability in the curriculum through live event projects and work placements. E-mail: rwright@aib.ac.uk

List of Figures

List of Tables

Preface

The events and conventions sector represents a fascinating and challenging area in terms of the structure and dynamics of the employment environment it supports. It is a sector generally neglected in wider discourse and research into the labour process and employment analysis. Work and employment in the events and convention sector reflects a range of contextual and operational characteristics that impact on who works in the sector, the range of skills that they require and the conditions under which they undertake their work and, arguably, distinguishes work in the sector from other related areas. These characteristics include:

- The time-bound nature of events and conventions in terms of their organization and delivery, in so far as they are generally of short duration and may be one-off in a location or may reoccur, often on an annual basis.
- Peripatetic, in that many events rotate around a number of locations on a periodic basis.
- Diverse in scale, geographic focus and emphasis, encompassing both leisure and business events.
- Frequently events are highly dependent on volunteers for their organization and working contributions.
- Characterized by what might be called a 'petrol head', 'opera buff' or 'celebrity gazing' syndrome, in that many events attract employees and volunteers personally committed to the theme of the event in a way that impacts upon their expectations of conditions and remuneration.

Within this environment, events and convention work demand the delivery of a range of bundled skills, which may encompass technical, emotional, aesthetic, problem-solving and information-processing facets. This combination of skills, delivered in the complex contextual framework identified above, provides workplace challenges that are unique to the sector and demanding of further examination.

Events, as Mair rightly points out in Chapter 1 of this book, are no new phenomenon. Events, whether ceremonial, religious or sporting, have featured in all organized societies from earliest recorded time and continue to be an important dimension of contemporary living at a local, national and global scale. Clearly, alongside ancient events was to be found a level of organization and a requirement for workers to support such events, in their development and set up, delivery and post-event dismantlement. What is unclear is the status of those engaged in event organization in terms of their demographics, relationship to those leading the event, whether political or religious, or indeed whether they were free citizens or enslaved labour. Discussion of such ancient events in the literature today does not give us much indication of their organization or who the event workers were, although we may surmise answers to some of these quandaries – their frequent religious or political context means that the primary source for organization would have been within the respective religious or political elites or, indeed, both groups. Slave labour was commonplace in ancient societies, such as those in Egypt, Greece and Rome, so it is reasonable to assume a significant role for this class of workers at major events. Notwithstanding many evident differences between events in the ancient world and those with which we are familiar today, the nature of organization and work is likely to have included many tasks with which contemporary event organizers will be familiar.

Although employment in events organization, management and service delivery is clearly not a new phenomenon, its recognition as a discrete area of work, demanding specific skills, education and training, is relatively recent. One of the challenges in this regard is that events, in common with allied areas in leisure, tourism and hospitality, represent an amorphous and diverse field of economic, social and cultural activity, and the resultant employment likewise covers a wide range of activities and organizational/operational contexts.

Recognition of the discrete requirements of the events and convention sector has been manifest through the emergence of specialist educational programmes at vocational and university level in many countries and specialist publications and texts in event management and operations. At the same time, recognition has grown of the events management sector in employment terms, with moves towards professionalism at national and international levels.

Human resource, education and training themes in the context of events have attracted the recent interest of researchers because of the particular dynamics of work in the sector, coalescing mainstream 'conventional' employment with a wide range of time-bound, episodic work on both a paid and a voluntary basis. These dynamics present challenges in conceptual, theoretical, managerial and operational terms. This book is an attempt to bring together the main strands of research-informed debate relating to these challenges, drawing on experiences from a range of countries.

The book is organized into five parts. The first two chapters set the scene with respect to events and employment within the sector, focusing on a global review and an Australian case context. Subsequent parts consider education and career development in the events and convention sector, workplace flexibility in the context of events, recruitment and retention, and the management of people and work in events and conventions.

I   Setting the Scene

This part sets the scene, and Mair (Chapter 1) provides an overview of the events industry in an employment context. She details the growth of the global events industry and considers classifications of events in terms of size and type. Through examples of attendance numbers at a selection of mega and major events, Mair contrasts audience size with the numbers of people employed in both paid and volunteer positions. She introduces the increasing recognition of event management as a profession, a theme that is subsequently taken up in other chapters (see Part II). She highlights the diversity of work within the sector and concludes by discussing the broad range of employment opportunities on offer.

This diversity of event work is taken up by Arcodia in Chapter 2. He reports on an ongoing study of event management employment in Australia. Presenting data from a content analysis of job advertisements, he identifies the key skills and attributes of event managers. The chapter concludes by noting that while some skills are generic professional skills (such as communication, problem solving and leadership), others are more specific to the requirements of event management work (namely planning and organizational, marketing, financial and computer skills).

1 The Events Industry: the Employment Context

JUDITH MAIR

Victoria University, Melbourne, Australia

Introduction

This chapter sets the scene with respect to the global events industry and considers definitions of different types and sizes of events. It also examines human resource characteristics of the events industry, including consideration of some of the job functions and positions available in the industry, both paid and volunteer.

The Events Industry – a Dynamic and Growing Sector

Events have played an important part in human societies for thousands of years. Throughout history, people both ancient and modern have felt the need to mark particular dates and times with many kinds of ceremonies or celebrations. These range from the ancient celebrations of midsummer and midwinter to the wide range of religious festivals, royal coronations and other ceremonies throughout recorded history, and the contemporary celebrations that highlight birthdays, festivals and national days. Goldblatt (1990:1) notes that the need to celebrate is 'perhaps even more vital to the sustenance of the human spirit' than the physical needs of food, clothing and shelter. This serves to highlight the importance of events to the human psyche and underlines the emphasis that people have always placed on marking particular dates, seasons and life stages.

Historically, it may have been the case that attendance at events was a mandatory part of belonging to a particular community or religion, or at least was considered to be beneficial to the attendee. Organizing events was part of the 'job description' of religious leaders and royal courtiers and it is only comparatively recently that organizing events has been considered to be a job, or even a profession in its own right.

For most events, attendance is no longer compulsory but instead is at the discretion of the individual (exceptions may occur, however; for example, some corporate events are mandatory for employees, and within some political regimes, participation was, and still is, expected of ranks within the political establishment). Events catering to particular interests and enthusiasms are now commonplace – there is a huge variety of sporting events, special interest conventions, exhibitions and music festivals, as well as countless other events worldwide from which to choose, and understanding motivations to attend these different types of events is invaluable to the organizers in trying to maximize attendance.

Events can be fun in themselves, but they also add to the richness of the lives of those attending. Amongst other things, they can be entertaining, they can be competitive, they can be intellectually stimulating, they can engender community or national pride, and they can be representative of beliefs and faiths. They appeal to a broad range of people and they are becoming more and more numerous. Indeed, events have been described as '. . . one of the most exciting and fastest growing forms of leisure, business, and tourism-related phenomena' (Getz 1997:1). Globally, both non-profit and for-profit events have grown substantially to become a major area for investment, and the economic, social and environmental impacts of events are growing all the time. The industry is dynamic and exciting and offers tremendous opportunities both to those destinations that host events and to those who choose to work in this area. Few other industries are as diverse and difficult to define as the events industry and a glance at the wide variety of events that make up the industry will illustrate this point.

Event Classification

There is no strict classification of events that can be used to describe and analyse the events industry. However, there are certain classifications that are commonly used and the two main categories are by size and by type.

Classification by size

As has already been mentioned, events can be extremely diverse and range in size from local community festivals to the Olympic Games. There are a number of labels that can indicate the size of an event, but some of the most often used are mega-events, hallmark events, major events and local events. Within these types there are, of course, a myriad of different-sized events.

Mega-events
Mega-events are defined by Allen *et al.* (2005) as 'those that are so large they affect whole economies and reverberate in the global media. They include Olympic Games and World Fairs.' Additionally, Getz (1997:6) suggests that mega-events should have more than one million visitors, capital costs of at least US$500 million and a reputation as a 'must see' event. He goes on to say that 'mega events, by way of their size or significance, are those that yield extraordinarily high levels of tourism, media coverage, prestige or economic impact for a host

destination'. Mega-events are of such a large scale that they permeate into almost every aspect of life at the destination during the event – transport, retail, hospitality, even industry and healthcare. Mega-events require large numbers of people, working not only on the running of the event but also on the ongoing organization. This may mean working on the current event and also working on the bidding process for future events. During the event itself, vast numbers of volunteers are usually engaged to make the event run as smoothly as possible.

According to an economic impact analysis of the Commonwealth Games in Melbourne in 2006, 'over a twenty year period, the holding of the Commonwealth Games in Victoria is estimated to support 13,000 person years of employment in full time jobs and in 2006 create some 22,000 casual jobs' (OCGC, 2006:39). The same report showed that a study of the 2002 Manchester Commonwealth Games by the Manchester Council indicated that, with expected public sector investment of £277 million, there would be 6100 FTEs of employment created in Manchester and 17,000 jobs during the conduct of the games.

Hallmark events
Hallmark events on the other hand are not on such a huge scale. The defining characteristic of a hallmark event is that it takes place repeatedly in the same destination, to the extent that mention of the event automatically brings to mind the location where the event is held. Some hallmark events are very large, but most will not involve the huge numbers that attend mega-events. In fact, it can be argued that some fairly small events fulfil the criteria for being considered as hallmark events. Hallmark events are described as 'those events that become so identified with the spirit or ethos of a town, city or region that they become synonymous with the name of the place, and gain widespread recognition and awareness' (Allen *et al.*, 2005). Examples are the Oktoberfest (Munich), the Carnival (Rio de Janiero), Mardi Gras (New Orleans) and others such as the Edinburgh Festival. Getz (1997:6) suggests that 'Increasingly, every community and destination needs one or more hallmark event to provide the high levels of media exposure and positive imagery that help to create competitive advantages'. The people working on hallmark events are usually involved in a circular process – analysing the impacts and success or otherwise of past events, working on organizing the current event and planning for future events. Volunteers are often engaged to work at hallmark events, and as the event takes place repeatedly in the same destination, the same volunteers often return year after year.

Major events
Major events, by contrast, may on occasion actually involve more people than a hallmark event, and with examples such as the F1 Grand Prix, the Grand Slam tennis tournaments, Glastonbury Music Festival and a host of sporting grand finals it can easily be seen that these events are of major significance. They have enormous pulling power in terms of visitors, performers/competitors and media, and they generate a significant economic impact for their host destinations. Destinations work hard to attract major events, and to encourage them to return on an annual basis. Melbourne is the location of the Australian Open Tennis Championships, London plays host to the Wimbledon Tennis Championship

and the FA Cup Final, and Paris is the location for the finale of the Tour de France. These destinations often have to put a lot of effort into keeping these attractions – for example, Melbourne has been challenged for both the Australian F1 Grand Prix and the Australian Open Tennis Championship. The rewards of hosting these events are generally felt to be worth the effort in securing them, although they can be a source of financial concern, as the events themselves do sometimes lose money. The people who work on major events are often affiliated with the organization that stages the event – the Football Association or the Australian Tennis Association, for example. Organizing the annual major event for their association may be their full-time job, but it may be the case that people with other roles within the association (perhaps marketing or finance) will be involved immediately prior to and during the event itself. Major events are also a source of employment for casual labour (to work on food stalls, for example) and attract numbers of volunteers.

Local or community events

The final generic event size is local, also known as community events. These are small-scale events, often taking place over 1 or 2 days and usually involving the local community. Local community events may be defined as 'an activity established to involve the local population in a shared experience to their mutual benefit' (Berridge, 2007).They are generally organized and run by volunteers, with minimum financial assistance from the private sector. They are often held to showcase a particular local trade or community, or simply for fun. These local events can also be held with the purpose of increasing tolerance of a particular section of the community, or with an educational message. Additionally, sport is a common reason for holding a local event. Local events often have a strong fundraising element – perhaps raising money for a local school, sporting club or charity. These types of events often rely on the attendance of the local population as they are not always marketed outside the immediate vicinity. However, some hallmark events started out as small local events and have grown to represent much more. For example, the Notting Hill Carnival began life as a small-scale event with the aim of showcasing local talent and bringing together the community. It has now grown into a multi-million pound event, attracting large numbers of performers and a huge audience. Most local events do not have any full-time staff employed to put on the event, but rather rely on volunteers or sometimes part-time administrative assistance. Volunteers are essential to local events, both as members of the organizing committee and to help during the staging of the event.

Classification by type

Another common way of classifying events is by type of event rather than by size. There are sporting events, charity events, music events, arts events and cultural events, amongst others. This list is not exhaustive and there is no clearly accepted typology of events – Shone and Parry (2004) suggest leisure events, personal events, cultural events and organizational events (charitable, commercial, political and sales). Getz (2007), on the other hand, suggests cultural celebrations, political and state events, and arts and entertainment in one category; business and trade, and educational and scientific events in another category; sport competitions and recreation in a third; and, finally, personal events form a category of their own. Even where the overall event types are similar, there is little consensus as to how to group them. For example, Van der Wagen (2005) suggests a category of events including entertainment, art and culture. O'Hara and Beard (2006), however, suggest a category which they call 'music, arts and entertainment'. For Ali-Knight and Robertson (2004), the arts and cultural events are grouped together but entertainment events are not included. It appears that any grouping of event types is largely subjective and possibly not even very helpful. However, for the purposes of this chapter, some of the main event types will be discussed – sporting events, business events, music and entertainment events, and arts and cultural events. Other event types, such as charity events, political events and family events, are relatively self-explanatory and do not require further discussion at this point.

Sporting events

Sporting events are relatively easy to define. As the name suggests, these events are all held for the purpose of sporting competition. Sporting events are held all over the world, and the top events attract the world's best athletes. Some of the more famous international sporting events include the F1 Grand Prix competition, the European Football Championships and World Cup, the Rugby World Cup, the Grand Slam Tennis Tournaments and, of course, the Olympic and Commonwealth Games. Individual countries have their own major sporting events – for example, the FA Cup Final in England (football), the New York Marathon in the USA (and other marathons around the globe), the Melbourne Cup in Australia (horse racing), and the Tour de France in France (cycling race).

However, it is important to remember that sporting events take place at all levels – even the local Sunday football league matches, and Little Athletics competitions are sporting events. According to the Australian Bureau of Statistics, 7.1 million people in Australia attended at least one sporting event in 2005 (ABS, 2007a). That represents two-fifths of the Australian population over 15 years of age. In 2001, 462 million people attended organized sports events in the USA and Canada (Supovitz, 2005). This begs the question – why do so many people attend sporting events? According to Supovitz (2005:5), 'what makes sports events the world's most compelling entertainment form is the emotional capital the audience invests in the outcome of the contest'. This certainly differentiates sporting events from other types of events.

Getz (2007) suggests that sporting events can be characterized according to a number of potential factors:

- professional versus amateur;
- indoor versus outdoor;
- regular/scheduled versus one-off; and
- local, regional, national or international in scale.

Major sporting events are also characterized by particularly heavy sponsorship, from vast corporations such as Nike, Reebok, Motorola, IBM and Coca-Cola to slightly smaller companies such as Carling, ING, Barclays Bank and Timex. Supovitz suggests that corporations continue to sponsor sporting events because 'their customers, in record numbers, likewise continue to devote their dollars and emotions' (Supovitz, 2005:6).

Business events or, as they are sometimes known, the meetings, incentives, conferences and exhibitions (MICE) sector
According to McCabe *et al.* (2000), the business events sector is one of the fastest-growing and most lucrative areas of the tourism industry. It is estimated that 1.46 million conferences and meetings took place at UK venues during 2002 (BCVS, 2004). One of the key findings of the National Business Events Study in Australia was that, in 2004, business events generated annual expenditure of AUS$17.36 billion and created 214,000 Australian jobs (Deery *et al.*, 2005), and therefore it can be seen that this sector is a vitally important component of the events industry as well as the travel industry.

Meetings are generally smaller affairs, with fewer delegates, and can be held on company premises, in hotels, or in purpose-built meeting rooms. The term 'incentive' refers to a type of travel where a company pays for an employee to travel, sometimes to attend a conference or exhibition, sometimes for pleasure, as a reward for work-related performance. Conferences and conventions are generally understood to be large gatherings of like-minded individuals, who come together for professional or personal development purposes, for networking purposes and for educational purposes.

Exhibitions are well known and refer, of course, to large-scale showcasing of products and services. In the UK, research conducted by KPMG for the Association of Exhibition Organizers and the Association of Event Venues showed that the industry was worth £9.3 billion, with direct employment of almost 56,000 people, and with indirect employment estimated to be 136,000 (Berridge, 2007). Additionally, Europe as a whole now has over 15 million m^2 of exhibition space and a market share of 57%. This serves to underline both the current success of the exhibition sector in particular and the importance of business events to the economy. Exhibitions can be trade only, where attendees have to work in whatever industry is being showcased, or can be consumer or public, where anyone can attend. In the travel industry, the World Travel Market in London and the Internationale Tourismus Borse (ITB) in Berlin are examples of trade-only events, whilst The Holiday & Travel Show is a consumer exhibition. Other consumer shows includes hobby and special interest fairs, food and wine festivals (a growing area for events) and gardening shows. Probably the largest type of exhibition is the World Expo, held in various countries around the world. The most recent were held in Japan in 2005 and Shanghai in 2008.

Music and entertainment events
Music and entertainment events are able to attract some of the largest audiences of any type of event. Vast-scale events such as Live 8, which included ten venues, 150 bands and 1250 musicians, have demonstrated the pulling power of such events. The organizers estimated a global audience (in person and on television and the Internet) of 3 billion (Live 8, 2007). Of course not all music events

Table 1.1. Numbers attending events in Australia, 2005–2006. Data source: ABS (2007b).

Event	Number attending
Classical music concerts	1,508,100
Popular music concerts	4,035,900
Theatre performances	2,723,200
Dance performances	1,625,000
Musicals and opera	2,402,000
Other performing arts (variety shows, circuses, etc.)	2,655,000
Total	14,949,200

are on this scale – they range from small local bands performing in a pub to internationally acclaimed performers attracting crowds that can number into the hundreds of thousands. In terms of style, they range from pop and rock concerts to operas, concerts by symphony orchestras and performances by musicians from many genres. According to O'Hara and Beard (2006), music events can be defined by categories (e.g. jazz, blues, rock, dance, country, classical, world, gospel, etc.), by focus (whether they are niche events or whether they have wide appeal) or by geography (whether they are on a national, regional or local scale). Some examples of music events that target niche markets are opera (the Wexford Opera Festival in Ireland, as an example), jazz festivals (for example, Wangaratta Jazz Festival in Australia or the Isle of Bute Jazz Festival in Scotland), country festivals (such as Tamworth Country Music Festival in Australia or Creetown Country Music Festival in Scotland) and Celtic music events (the Mod or Celtic Connections in Scotland are both good examples). In Australia in 2005–2006, almost 15 million people attended at least one event in the performing arts arena (Table 1.1).

Arts and cultural events
According to Ali-Knight and Robertson (2004:4), 'The term "the arts" is often closely linked with festivals and special events, and the arts are seen to be an integral part of any celebrations of a country's history and culture'. Perhaps one of the best-known examples of an art and cultural festival is the Edinburgh International Festival. Edinburgh is home to around 15 national and international festivals, but the Edinburgh International Festival and the Edinburgh Festival Fringe remain world famous. The size and scale of the Edinburgh International Festival are well known and widely reported, but in conjunction with the other festivals held in the city, the Edinburgh City Council claims to make £150 million yearly from festivals (Ali-Knight and Robertson, 2004). Other substantial arts festivals around the globe include the Perth International Arts Festival and Toronto's Arts Week and International Film Festival amongst others.

Getz (2007) suggests that performing arts events and festivals can be defined by a number of characteristics:

- professional versus amateur;
- competitive versus non-competitive;
- mixed or single genre; and
- paid or free performance.

Also under the banner of arts and cultural events are religious events, examples of which would include the Mela (Hindu Festival), the Hajj (Muslim pilgrimage to Mecca) and visits by the Pope and other religious leaders to various towns and cities. Many cities also hold multi-cultural events, held with the aim of promoting tolerance amongst diverse communities.

People in the Events Industry

The 'events industry' is a growing global business as the role and impact of events in society is becoming more recognized than ever (Shone and Parry, 2004; Allen *et al.*, 2005) as an academic subject area, as a tool for promoting business, as a leisure time activity, as an income generator, as a source for urban regeneration, as a feature of tourist destinations, and as a career path.

(Berridge, 2007)

This indicates the importance of the sector within the broader economy and serves to highlight some of the characteristics of the sector.

Event Attendance at Mega- and Major Events

The biggest events that take place around the world are undoubtedly the mega-events. The 2000 Sydney Olympics and Paralympics had an attendance of 5.5 million (SOCOG, 2007). The 2006 Commonwealth Games in Melbourne had an attendance of over 2 million spectators and 5770 athletes (OCGC, 2006).

Major events that take place in Melbourne include, for example: the F1 Grand Prix, which in 2006 recorded 360,000 spectators over 4 days (Grand Prix, 2007); the Australian Open Tennis Championships, with an attendance of 550,550 over 2 weeks (Australian Open, 2007); the 2007 Australian Air Show, which had an attendance of 182,769 over 6 days (Australian Air Show, 2007); and the FINA World Swimming Championships, which had an attendance of 219,317 in total (State of Victoria, 2007).

Other internationally renowned major events include: the Edinburgh Summer Festivals (Edinburgh International Festival, Edinburgh Festival Fringe, Edinburgh Film Festival and Edinburgh Book Festival, amongst others), which recorded attendances of just over 2.5 million (EFF, 2007); the Notting Hill Carnival in London, with around 2 million spectators (Notting Hill Carnival, 2007); and the Munich Oktoberfest, with a massive 6 million visitors every year (Oktoberfest, 2007).

Ascertaining how many staff (both paid and volunteer) are associated with these events is harder than capturing audience attendance. There are several reasons for this, including the question of corporate confidentiality and also the fact that some staff can be employed all year round and others only for the period of the event itself. Additionally, economic impact analyses of events sometimes estimate employment numbers in terms of full-time equivalent positions which rely on the event but are not always necessarily directly employed at the event.

None the less it is possible to make some estimates of numbers of staff compared with numbers attending, as Table 1.2 shows.

Table 1.2. Numbers of staff compared with attendance numbers. Data sources: SOCOG (2007); BNET Australia (2008); OCGG (2006); State of Victoria (2007); EIFF (2007).

| Event | Attendance | Staff positions | | Ratio of staff to attendees |
		Paid	Volunteer	
Olympic Games, Sydney, 2000	5.5 million	2,400	47,000	1 staff per 111 attendees
Commonwealth Games, Melbourne, 2006	2 million	500	15,000	1 staff per 129 attendees
FINA World Swimming Championships, 2006	219,317	119	1,920	1 staff per 108 attendees
Edinburgh International Film Festival, 2006	58,161	103	133	1 staff per 246 attendees

It seems that the ratio of staff (volunteers and paid staff) to attendees varies dramatically depending on the event. The highest ratios were at the FINA World Swimming Championships, with 108 attendees for every staff member, and the Olympic Games in Sydney, with 111 attendees for every staff member. The lowest ratio was at the Edinburgh Film Festival, where there was 1 member of staff for every 246 attendees. This perhaps reflects the differing nature of the events – at FINA and the Olympic Games, large numbers of volunteer staff were used to direct members of the public to various events and both used a number of venues. However, in the case of events such as the Edinburgh Film Festival, which has a number of venues but a much smaller audience, such large numbers of volunteers are not required.

Event Management as a Profession

In tandem with the increasing awareness of the economic importance of events is the increasing recognition of events management as a profession. There are many reasons for this, but one of the most important is the increased numbers of event management training courses and degree qualifications. As employers recognize the importance of highly educated staff in the events industry, so the importance and recognition of these qualifications will grow. In addition, there has been growth in research into events and event management, to the extent that there are now a number of journals publishing papers in this area (such as *Event Management* and the *Journal of Convention and Event Tourism*) and a number of conferences dedicated to the academic study of events (the International Event Research Conference and the Global Event Congress, for example).

Goldblatt (2002:8) suggests that the events industry is ready to be accepted as a profession. He outlines three main characteristics:

1. The profession must have a unique body of knowledge.
2. The profession typically has voluntary standards that often result in certification.

3. The profession has an accepted code of conduct or ethics, and states that the profession of event management meets each of these qualifications.

Getz (2007:288) also agrees, although he only considers events management as a 'quasi-profession', explaining that event management can aspire to a quasi-professional status on a par with recreation and leisure managers but that, in his opinion, the typical absence of government licensing prevents full professional status. None the less he considers that the acceptance of event management as a profession is linked to the increasing numbers of graduates from various educational programmes as well as holders of designations from certifying professional associations.

Events Industry Workforce

Within the events industry there are huge numbers of people employed worldwide. It is difficult to ascertain the size of this industry simply because events form a part of so many other sectors and people working on events may not even consider themselves to be part of the events industry. Although there are many full-time event professionals employed in the industry, many events jobs are casual and/or part time and, as well as those employed, there are also vast numbers of volunteers in the events industry.

Events require staff to cover a broad range of positions, from director level all the way down to waiting and cleaning staff. Functional areas of work include executive, finance, administration, human resources, marketing, event management, maintenance/technical, catering, security and customer service (Westerbeek et al., 2005). Of course, only the largest annual events can afford to employ permanent staff for all these functions. Smaller and one-off events can outsource many of these functions to external contractors. This helps to explain why so many jobs in the events industry are short-term casual positions.

Another connected issue is the fact that many people who are involved in events participate on a volunteer basis. According to Goldblatt (2002:110), volunteers are 'the life blood' of many events and without volunteers these events would cease to exist. Some small local events are staffed and managed entirely by volunteers, although as the events get larger and more complex, paid staff are often brought in, or staffing functions outsourced to contractors to ensure the viability of the event. Nearly 47,000 volunteers were needed at the Sydney Olympics in 2000 (SOCOG, 2007), and they volunteered either in specialist roles (translators, medical volunteers, technical volunteers) or in more general roles (spectator services, transport and community information).

Motivations

Volunteers and paid staff have different motivations to work at events. According to Van der Wagen (2005), event employees are motivated by a wide range of factors, including finding hours compatible with study or other responsibilities, and getting work experience that will lead to career development and promotional opportunities. Volunteers on the other hand offer their services for free for a number of reasons. It would appear that motivations to volunteer at events differ depending on the nature of the event itself, but several themes do emerge. These include altruism, networking, social and career benefits, challenges, the prestige of the event, community pride and sharing the experience (Getz, 2007).

Employment Opportunities

One of the interesting areas for research in the events industry is the number of jobs that are coming under the events banner. According to Berridge (2007), there is now evidence of a shift in emphasis for jobs in events that in the past would have otherwise been seen as part of more established sectors such as hospitality and tourism. Some of these are jobs that previously (and to some people still do) belonged in other sectors, such as conference coordinator in a hotel, which is part of the hospitality industry and is usually in the conference and banqueting function, or events photographer, which used to be called 'wedding photographer' and refer only to that one type of event. Other jobs are completely new and have not previously been seen in any great numbers. Examples of these are events coordinators in schools, both state and private sector, and wedding planners (there have always been a few wedding planners but numbers are growing as weddings, like other events, become more complex and difficult to coordinate).

Students at a university in Victoria, Australia, were asked as part of an assignment to write about a job in the events industry that was being advertised at the time. The catch was that, in order to get the students to think laterally, the word 'event' could not appear in the job title. This was to stop students from simply putting 'event' into the careers website search engines. The task was completed by over 80 students and, interestingly, there were very few instances of different students choosing the same job. Many students wrote about positions such as conference organizer, account manager for professional conference organizers and catering manager at an exhibition centre, all of which are relatively standard jobs in the events industry. However, some of the jobs were less obviously related to events – examples included cruise shipping officer (although the job title appears unrelated to the events industry, the position description notes that the arrival of a cruise ship in port is considered as an event that needs organizing, and the advert asked for experience in event organization), charity campaign coordinator (again, although events is not included in the job title, further investigation showed that the successful applicant would spend much of their time organizing charity fundraising events) and entertainment coordinator (this job was available at a large casino and specifically required the successful applicant to organize functions and events at the casino, as well as manage the daily entertainment programme). Although hardly scientific in any sense, none the less the results of this assignment showed the breadth of positions available in the events industry. Interestingly, the fact that it was students (arguably the next generation of events employees) who assigned many of these positions to the events industry is some indication that, in future, positions in many diverse sectors of the economy may come to be accepted as part of the events industry.

Recent research (Lockstone *et al.*, 2008) investigated the trends in work-integrated learning opportunities for event management students in Australia, and compared this data to current job opportunities in the events industry in order to assess the type of industry work the students may choose to undertake upon the completion of their degrees. Sixty jobs advertised on a number of Australian career websites were examined. The most common job available at that time in the events industry was events coordinator, and the sectors advertising the most jobs were venues, associations and corporate employers. Associations had a sizeable percentage of jobs available on a contract basis, and for councils and the not-for-profit industry, half the jobs were permanent and half were contract. This suggests that venues, the events industry and corporate companies offered the best chance of full-time, permanent jobs, whilst not-for-profit companies and councils are currently offering more part-time, contract-based work. Of course this is only a snapshot of jobs in the events industry – one city at one specific time – but none the less this does indicate some of the general trends in the industry.

Conclusions

The events industry is large and diverse and is becomingly increasingly so. The most common way to categorize events is by size, using the terms 'mega-events', 'hallmark events', 'major events' and 'local events'. Although there is little consensus in categorizing events by type, none the less certain event types can be distinguished, such as sporting events, business events, music and entertainment events, and arts and cultural events.

There is increasing recognition of event management as a profession, thanks largely to the numbers of educational institutions offering courses in event management, and the corresponding increase in research in the events area. Jobs in the events industry are numerous, but it is important to recognize that not all jobs are full-time, permanent positions. In fact, in the industry, many events jobs are short-term, casual contracts that will build up work experience but will not provide continuity of employment. Partially for this reason, many events rely heavily on the good nature of their volunteer workforce, differentiated from employed staff by the fact that they are not paid for their service but also because they are motivated by different things – altruism and social reasons amongst others.

Finally, research is underlining the broad nature of employment opportunities in the events sector, and also is beginning to document a shift of positions from other industries to the events industry. Such studies constitute themes in the following chapters of this book.

References

ABS (2007a) *4174.0 – Sports Attendance, Australia, 2005–06*. Australian Bureau of Statistics, Canberra, Australia.

ABS (2007b) *4114.0 – Attendance at Selected Cultural Venues and Events, Australia, 2005–06*. Australian Bureau of Statistics, Canberra, Australia.

Ali-Knight, J. and Robertson, M. (2004) Introduction to arts, culture and leisure. In: Yeoman, I. (ed.) *Festival and Events Management: an International Arts and Culture Perspective*. Elsevier Butterworth-Heinemann, Amsterdam, The Netherlands, pp. 3–13.

Allen, J., O'Toole, W., McDonnell, I. and Harris, R. (2005) *Festival and Special Event Management*. John Wiley and Sons, Milton, Australia.

Australian Air Show (2007) Australian Air Show highlights. Available at: http://www.airshow.net.au/avalon2009/highlights.html (accessed 10 December 2007).

Australian Open (2007) Event guide/sponsors. Available at: http://www.australianopen.com/en_AU/event_guide/sponsors.html (accessed 10 December 2007).

BCVS (2004) *British Conference Venues Survey 2004*. Business Tourism Partnership, London.

Berridge, G. (2007) *Events Design and Experience*. Butterworth Heinemann, Oxford.

BNET Australia (2008) The Sydney challenge. Available at: http://findarticles.com/p/articles/mi_m0FXS/is_/ai_65650777 (accessed 25 Nov 2008).

Deery, M., Jago, L., Fredline, L. and Dwyer, L. (2005) *National Business Events Study: an Evaluation of the Australian Business Events Sector*. Common Ground, Altona, Australia.

EFF (2007) 2004 Festival economic impact study results. Available at: http://www.edfringe.com/story.html?id=923&area_id=48 (accessed 25 November 2008).

EIFF (2007) *Annual Review 2006*. Edinburgh International Film Festival, Edinburgh.

Getz, D. (1997) *Event Management and Event Tourism*. Cognizant Communication Corp., New York.

Getz, D. (2007) *Event Studies – Theory, Research and Policy for Planned Events*. Butterworth Heinemann, Oxford.

Goldblatt, J. (1990) *Special Events – the Art and Science of Celebration*. Van Nostrand Reinhold, New York.

Goldblatt, J. (2002) *Special Events – 21st Century Global Events Management*, 3rd edn. Wiley, New York.

Grand Prix (2007) Sponsorship opportunities. Available at: http://www.grandprix.com.au/default.aspx?s=sponsorship_opportunities (accessed 10 December 2007).

Live 8 (2007) The story so far. Available at: http://www.live8live.com/whathappened/# (accessed 3 December 2007).

Lockstone, L., Junek, O. and Mair, J. (2008) Experiential learning in event management education. In: Richardson, S., Fredline, L. and Ternel, M. (eds) *Proceedings of CAUTHE*. Griffith University, Gold Coast, Australia, CD-ROM.

McCabe, V., Poole, B. and Weeks, P. (2000) *The Business and Management of Conventions*. John Wiley & Sons, Brisbane, Australia.

Notting Hill Carnival (2007) Our facts. Available at: http://www.nottinghillcarnival.biz/aboutus/facts.php (accessed 10 December 2007).

OCGC (2006) *Economic Impact Study of Melbourne Commonwealth Games 2006*. Office of Commonwealth Games Co-ordination, Melbourne, Australia.

O'Hara, B. and Beard, M. (2006) *Music Events and Festival Management*. Music Business Education Supplement, Derrimut, Australia.

Oktoberfest (2007) The history of Germany's Oktoberfest. Available at: http://www.truebeer.com/The-History-of-Germanys-Oktoberfest_df_10.html (accessed 10 December 2007).

Shone, A. and Parry, B. (2004) *Successful Event Management: a Practical Handbook*. Thomson Learning, London.

SOCOG (2007) Sydney 2000 post-Games report. Available at: http://www.gamesinfo. com.au/postgames/en/pg001414.htm (accessed 3 December 2007).

State of Victoria (2007) *12th FINA World Championships Summary Report*. Sport and Recreation Victoria, Melbourne, Australia.

Supovitz, F. (2005) *Sport Events Management and Marketing Playbook*. Wiley and Sons, Hoboken, New Jersey.

Van der Wagen, L . (2005) *Event Management for Tourism, Cultural, Business and Sporting Events*, 2nd edn. Pearson Education Australia, Frenchs Forest, Australia.

Westerbeek, H., Smith, A., Turner, P., Emery, P., Green, C. and van Leeuwen, L. (2005) *Managing Sport Facilities and Major Events*. Allen & Unwin, Crows Nest, Australia.

2

Event Management Employment in Australia: a Nationwide Investigation of Labour Trends in Australian Event Management

CHARLES ARCODIA

The University of Queensland, Australia

Introduction

As the event industry grows and matures, it is important that high-quality personnel with the appropriate skills and attributes are employed. This will help to ensure professionalism in the field, equip managers with the necessary skills to deal with challenges and ultimately help to sustain the delivery of high-quality events (Harris and Jago, 1999). As Newell and Shackleton (2000:111) report, people are central to organizations: 'When we talk about "organizations" we are obviously talking about people who make up organizations, since by definition an organization cannot act. Continued success is dependent on attracting and retaining high-quality individuals who can respond effectively to … dynamic environments.' Conversely, employing individuals who do not meet job requirements can be detrimental to organizations as they may cause disruption to the workplace, increase training costs, and contribute to a loss of productivity and high turnover rates (Mathews and Redman, 2001).

It is therefore vital that relevant and effective skills and attributes of employees are identified for particular organizations and industries, and certainly for the emerging event management industry. Discerning the skills and attributes of event managers, however, may be as hotly debated within and between academia and in practice as reported for information managers (Snyman, 2001). Nevertheless, there is growing demand for greater collaboration between academia and event practitioners to increase the uptake of research findings and to produce graduates that are equipped with the skills to handle the challenges of the industry (Neale, 2000).

A small number of studies have responded to the above issues and have included the perspectives of practitioners in order to ascertain the skills and attributes of event managers. Harris and Jago (1999) provided a succinct overview of three survey-based studies that have been conducted in Australia.

Included in their review were the Perry *et al.* (1996) survey of 53 event managers that attended the Australian Events Conference in Canberra that year. These managers were asked to rank 19 pre-defined requisite knowledge and attributes, and they identified the following ten as being of importance to event managers: project management, budgeting, time management, relating to the media, business planning, human resource management, contingency management, marketing, sponsorship and networking. Perry *et al.* (1996) further reduced these knowledge and skill requirements into five main knowledge domains of an event manager. Listed in order of importance, these were: legal/financial knowledge, management knowledge, public relations/marketing knowledge, economic/analytical knowledge and ethical/contextual knowledge. When managers, however, were asked to list the essential attributes of good event managers, Perry *et al.* (1996) found the following in order of importance: vision, leadership, adaptability, high organizational skills, good communication skills, marketing skills and people management skills.

Royal and Jago's (1998) study of 42 special event practitioners in Victoria rated all their eight listed skills as being very important to their profession. They included in order of importance: planning, organization, sponsorship knowledge, marketing, human resource management, administration, public relations and finance skills. More than half the respondents also listed additional skills, the most common being: time management, leadership, flexibility, communication and people management skills (Royal and Jago, 1998).

Harris and Griffin's (1997) study of 84 event organizers in New South Wales found that most respondents classified their 11 pre-defined knowledge and skill categories to be of either significant or moderate importance to event organizers. These included: general management, planning and organization of events; event development and programming; finance; marketing; event operations; understanding of community expectations and support; event monitoring and evaluation; professional knowledge and event bidding; and feasibility analysis. Respondents did not mention additional skills (Harris and Griffin, 1997).

The above studies therefore show a level of consistency, with the appearance of several skills in all studies. Except for the work of Arcodia and Barker (2003), however, analysis of the skill and attribute requirements of event managers remained at the periphery of these studies, with the main foci being the development of training and education needs. This may account for the prevalence of learned skills in pre-defined categories and the appearance of personality traits when respondents answered open-ended questions. There has not yet been a nationwide study of the event management job market and skill requirements, and this is critical, given that Australian occupational standards for event management positions have yet to be established. This is despite the existence of Canadian, American and British occupational standards for several event management-related positions, such as 'special event manager', and the Australian National Training Authority (ANTA) having covered about 78% of Australian industries with competency standards by 1997 (Smith and Keating, 1997).

It is hoped that a nationwide study of event management job requirements will help provide further support to the current literature and contribute towards a broader-scale understanding of the event management job market, and thus

provide further leverage for the development of Australian occupational standards for event managers. To gain an indication of current employer requirements, a nationwide, ongoing study of job advertisements in event management
has commenced.

Research Methods

National studies of event management skills and attributes are difficult to conduct
because it is a rather disparate field, but as Getz (2000:11) states, this is common
amongst 'emerging fields or quasi-professions'. While an all-encompassing definition of events may not be possible (Jago and Shaw, 1998), for the purposes of
this study, events are defined as a 'unique form of tourism attraction, ranging in
scale from mega events such as the Olympics and World Cup Rugby, through
community festivals to programmes of recreational events at parks' (Getz, 1991,
in Tassiopoulos, 2000:10). It encompasses all event types listed under Arcodia
and Robb's (2000) three broad categories of events, including the meetings,
incentives, conventions and exhibitions (MICE) sector, festivals and events.
Therefore activities such as sporting events, community celebrations and conferences were included.

As a research-neglected recruitment medium, job advertisements provide
current and accessible data (Mathews and Redman, 2001). It is during the
initial recruitment phase that companies are able to specify the required skills
and personality attributes of event managers. Not only do job advertisements
contain information to attract appropriate individuals, they can also represent
occupational, organizational, industry and societal artefacts and can therefore
contain rich and insightful information (Rafaeli and Oliver, 1998). Yet only a
few job advertisement studies in tourism and leisure have been identified.
Crossley (1992) analysed recreation and tourism-related job advertisements
of a major US newspaper for a year to guide course development at the
University of Utah. Keung and Pine (2000) provided a longitudinal study of
hotel job advertisements listed in a major Hong Kong newspaper to indicate
changes in hotel recruitment over a 10-year period. The ANZ Bank has analysed the number of Internet job advertisements in major Australian cities on a
monthly basis since July 1999 (ANZ, 2002). These figures are combined with
the number of advertisements in major daily newspapers over the same time
period to predict changes in national employment growth (ANZ, 2002).
Arcodia and Barker (2003) conducted a study which specifically analysed the
content of 105 web-based job advertisements in event management. This study
identified a variety of skills and attributes which were relevant for the industry.

To provide a further analysis of required skills and attributes in event management, 1021 advertisements were analysed using content analysis, a commonly
used method in studies of advertisements (Crossley, 1992; Demets *et al.*, 1998;
Headrick, 2001; Mathews and Redman, 2001). For all advertisements, general
information was recorded when provided, including the job title, location and
industry type. Job and candidate specifications were classified into skills and personal attributes respectively, and were classified into more specific criteria that

emerged from the data. Pre-defined criteria were avoided, in order to allow employer requirements of event management personnel to emerge. The resulting categories were not mutually exclusive, for example marketing skills require communication skills. However, when a specific criterion was mentioned in an advertisement, it was thought to be important in its own right and was therefore recorded.

The advertisements were tracked, recorded and analysed for a 12-month period. An analytical framework was devised for the analysis of the advertisements themselves. The results reveal several interesting trends, including the plethora of relevant job titles, geographical concentration of the event management job market, and a series of skills and attributes sought of event managers. The results of this study will help establish a basis from which to develop a classification of event management skills and attributes required by the industry.

Findings and Discussion

Event management job titles

The range of job advertisements that include event management responsibilities in their descriptions, and which therefore can be linked to event management skills and attributes, is extensive. In the sample of advertisements, and the subsequent cataloguing of them, 355 different position titles were identified. Many of these job titles may be initially misleading because the titles do not appear to have an association with event management; for example international sales and distribution officer, media advisor, public affairs officer, sales coordinator, visitation executive, and youth project worker. However, a careful reading of the actual job descriptions lead to the identification that, indeed, such jobs either did have an event management focus or contained responsibilities in event management.

Geographical distribution

As mentioned, the job sections of the major Australian newspapers were analysed, and these included *The Courier Mail* (Queensland), *The Sydney Morning Herald* (New South Wales), *The Advertiser* (South Australia), *The West Australian* (West Australia), *The Canberra Times* (Australian Capital Territory) and *The Age* (Victoria). The majority of advertisements advertised positions located in the newspaper's state of publication. Each newspaper, however, also advertised some positions that were located in other states. The geographical distribution of the event management-related positions is not surprising, with the division generally following Australia's population distribution.

Event management skills and attributes

Two main elements of human capital can be discerned from job advertisements – skills and personal attributes. Skills are tangible and measurable and have been referred to as the visible competency component (Spencer and Spencer, 1993). As Perry *et al.* (1996) infer, knowledge and skills can be taught and through training and experience can be learned and developed. Personal attributes on the other hand are synonymous with the personal characteristics of an individual. They represent hidden and innate qualities, such as personal attitudes, traits and values, that are more difficult to develop and have been referred to as the invisible competency component (Spencer and Spencer, 1993).

Skills

Table 2.1 lists each of the skills for which the job descriptions were analysed. It shows both the number of advertisements and the percentage of advertisements that mention each skill.

The higher the skill in Table 2.1, the more times it was mentioned. From the analysis it can be seen that the skill that recorded the highest percentage of references in the job descriptions was organizational and planning skills, with just over 50% of the job descriptions requiring applicants to demonstrate this skill. Job descriptions mentioning this skill used terminology such as 'highly organized', 'highly developed planning skills', 'high-level capacity in strategic planning processes', 'excellent organization skills', 'demonstrated ability in strategically planning events', 'ability to handle multiple projects' and 'ability to handle and prioritize tasks in pressure situations to meet deadlines'.

While organizational and planning skills were mentioned in a considerably higher percentage of the job descriptions than the other skills, many of the other skills were mentioned in a considerable percentage of the job advertisements and therefore should still be seen as significant skills for event management employees. The next four most-mentioned skills were each cited in over 30% of the advertisements. General communication skills were cited in 38.52% of the advertisements. Team skills were cited in 37.8% of the job descriptions. Team skills required applicants to demonstrate such abilities as 'commitment to working collaboratively', 'working in a team environment' or 'understanding of the importance of a team'. Customer service skills were mentioned in 35.4% of the job descriptions. The advertisements requiring applicants to demonstrate customer service skills used terminology such as the ability to 'promote the organization's commitment to customer service both internally and externally', 'demonstrate commitment to an outstanding level of customer satisfaction' and 'demonstrate an excellent sales history with a strong customer focus'. Computer skills were required by 33.2% of the job advertisements. These advertisements asked applicants to demonstrate abilities such as 'relevant computer knowledge', 'strong computer skills', 'knowledge of, or competence in, a specific computer program', 'web skills', 'development and management of a website' or ' strong knowledge of computer hardware and software'.

The next five skills were each cited in over 20% of the advertisements and therefore can be considered as being reasonably important skills for event management employees to possess. The skill of building internal/external relationships was cited in 28.4% of the advertisements, and required applicants to demonstrate abilities such as 'building effective relationships with clients/stakeholders', 'finding new business opportunities', 'converting new business into long-term accounts',

Table 2.1. Advertised skill requirements (n = 1021 advertisements).

	Advertisements mentioning the skills	
Skill	n	%
Organizational/planning skills	507	50.60
General communication skills	386	38.52
Team skills	378	37.72
Customer service skills	355	35.43
Computer skills	333	33.23
Building internal/external relationships	285	28.44
Marketing skills	281	28.04
Leadership skills	278	27.74
Oral communication skills	234	23.35
Administration skills	218	21.76
Written communication skills	197	19.66
Sales skills	187	18.66
Analytical/evaluation skills	163	16.27
Budgeting/financial management skills	162	16.17
Presentation skills	160	15.97
Policy development and implementation	152	15.17
Fundraising/sponsorship skills	132	13.17
Media relations	96	9.58
Database management skills	89	8.88
Negotiation skills	82	8.18
Problem-solving skills	66	6.59
Bar and food-handling skills	62	6.19
Driving skills	54	5.39
Print production skills	47	4.69
Decision-making skills	43	4.29
Occupational health and safety	31	3.09

'nurturing relationships' and 'networking'. Marketing skills were mentioned in 28% of the job descriptions. Leadership skills were cited in 27.7% of the advertisements. These advertisements asked applicants to demonstrate abilities such as 'leading and managing a team', 'leading a team to achieve optimum outcomes', 'instilling confidence in others', 'selecting and supervising', 'staff management', 'rostering staff' or 'human resource management'. Oral communication skills, cited in 23.4% of the advertisements, required applicants to have 'excellent verbal communication skills', 'effective listening skills', 'the ability to give public or media presentations' or 'cold-calling skills'. Administration skills were mentioned in 21.76% of the job descriptions.

The remainder of the skills listed in Table 2.1 were mentioned in fewer than 20% of the advertisements. These skills, therefore, while important, do not appear to be as significant to event management-related positions as all of the above-mentioned skills. It must be pointed out, however, that while written communication skills were cited in fewer than 20% of the advertisements, it was only slightly below the 20% mark, recording a reference percentage of 19.66%.

Attributes

Table 2.2 lists the 16 personal attribute categories that emerged from the data. It shows both the number of advertisements and the percentage of advertisements that mention each attribute. As in Table 2.1, the attributes are listed according to the number of advertisements (percentage of advertisements) mentioning the skill. The higher the attribute in Table 2.2, the more times it was mentioned.

From the percentages listed in Table 2.2, it can be seen that attributes are generally mentioned in a considerably lower percentage of the job descriptions than the skills. As compared with the most highly cited skill, 'organization and planning skills', which was mentioned in just over 50% of the advertisements, the most highly cited attribute, 'motivation', was mentioned in only 22.8% of the advertisements. Position descriptions mentioning the attribute of motivation used terminology such as 'a self-starter', 'drive to succeed', 'hungry for success' and 'highly motivated'.

Other attributes that could be seen as relatively important to event management employees included flexibility, positiveness, friendliness and commitment/dedication. Position descriptions mentioning flexibility, cited in 16.4% of the advertisements, used terminology such as 'able to engage in occasional weekend work', 'a flexible approach and willingness to try new methods of working' and 'a flexible attitude'. A positive nature, also mentioned in 16.4% of the advertisements, asked for an applicant who would 'demonstrate high self-esteem', 'a can-do attitude', 'enthusiasm' and 'adopt a positive approach to issues/values/people's feelings'. The attribute of friendliness, cited in 14% of the position descriptions, asked for applicants with 'exceptional people skills', 'a friendly approach to customer service', 'a friendly nature', 'a warm personality' or 'a people-person attitude'. Commitment and dedication were cited in 10.5% of the

Table 2.2. Advertised attribute requirements (n = 1021 advertisements).

Attribute	Advertisements mentioning the attribute	
	n	%
Motivated	229	22.85
Flexible	164	16.37
Positive	164	16.37
Friendly	140	13.97
Committed/dedicated	105	10.48
Tenacious	97	9.68
Energetic	87	8.68
Respectful/mature/professional	81	8.08
Accurate	77	7.68
Creative	76	7.58
Dynamic	72	7.19
Independent	71	7.09
Innovative/strategic	58	5.79
Initiative	56	5.59
Sensitive	27	2.69
Trustworthy	20	2.00

advertisements. Job descriptions asking for this attribute used terminology such as 'a committed professional', 'committed to the innovative quality of services', 'an individual who is dedicated to the industry', 'commitment to a positive outcome', 'commitment to excellence' or ' a person who just gets on with it and gets it done'.

Conclusion

The event industry in Australia continues to sustain an excellent international reputation, but in order to maintain its position as a world class producer of events, it is vital to provide professional event managers who possess the skills and attributes the industry demands. As mentioned at the outset, the purpose of this study was to undertake an investigation of event management skills and attributes sought by Australian employers. Job advertisements were sourced from capital city newspapers and were recorded and analysed for a 12-month period.

Several skills and attributes of event managers have emerged. Some of these skills, such as communication, problem-solving and leadership skills, have previously been identified as being generic professional skills (Hearn *et al.*, 1994). Others, however, support previous findings of event manager's requirements, such as the importance of planning and organizational, marketing and financial skills (Harris and Griffin, 1997; Royal and Jago, 1998), and the emergence of computer skills as the highest-ranked practical skill requirement is a new but expected result.

Overall, personal attributes featured less frequently in the advertisements than skills. This may indicate that relatively greater importance is given to the latter. However, the listing of such attributes as motivation and positiveness adds another important dimension to the requirements of event managers. Further data collection and analysis are needed to ascertain the significance of these results and the relative ranking of the skills and attributes.

Event Management Employment in Australia is a long-term project that seeks to fill the current gap in labour trends data in the Australian event management industry. This is an ongoing study and it is hoped that it will contribute towards a broad-scale understanding of the event management job market by developing a classification of event management skills and attributes required by the industry.

References

ANZ (2002) Economic commentary: ANZ job advertisement series. Available at: http://www.anz.com/business/info_centre/economic_commentary/MC_anjobadv_seri

Arcodia, C. and Barker, T. (2003) A review of web-based job advertisements for Australian event management positions. *Journal of Human Resources in Hospitality and Tourism* 1(4), 1–18.

Arcodia, C. and Robb, A. (2000) A taxonomy of event management terms. In: Allen, J., Harris, R., Jago, L.K. and Veal, A.J. (eds) *Events Beyond 2000: Setting the Agenda.*

Proceedings of Conference on Event Evaluation, Research and Education. Australian Centre for Event Management, Sydney, pp. 154–160.

Crossley, J. (1992) Job announcement content analysis in commercial recreation and tourism. *Visions in Leisure and Business* 10(3), 25–35.

Demets, D.L., Woolson, R., Brooks, C. and Roger, Q. (1998) Where the jobs are: a study of *Amstat News* job advertisements. *The American Statistician* 52(4), 303–307.

Getz, D. (2000) Developing a research agenda for the event management field. In: Allen, J., Harris, R., Jago, L.K. and Veal, A.J. (eds) *Events Beyond 2000: Setting the Agenda. Proceedings of Conference on Event Evaluation, Research and Education.* Australian Centre for Event Management, Sydney, pp. 10–21.

Harris, R. and Griffin, T. (1997) *Tourism Event Training Audit.* Tourism New South Wales, Sydney.

Harris, R. and Jago, L. (1999) Event education and training in Australia: the current state of play. *Australian Journal of Hospitality Management* 6(1), 45–51.

Headrick, K.L. (2001) Want ads, job skills and curriculum: a survey of 1998 chemistry help wanted ads. *Journal of Chemical Education* 78(9), 1281–1282.

Hearn, G., Smith, B., Southey, G. and Close, A. (1994) Generic professional competencies: a review and analysis of the literature and implications for higher education. Working Paper Series. Queensland University of Technology, Australian Centre in Strategic Management, Brisbane, Australia.

Jago, L.K. and Shaw, R.N. (1998) Special events: a conceptual and definitional framework. *Festival Management & Event Tourism* 5(1/2), 21–33.

Keung, S.W. and Pine, R.C. (2000) Changes in hotel industry recruitment as reflected by content analysis of newspaper advertisement. *Asia Pacific Journal of Tourism Research* 5(2), 57–69.

Mathews, B.P. and Redman, T. (2001) Recruiting the wrong salespeople: are the job ads to blame? *Industrial Marketing Management* 30, 541–550.

Neale, M. (2000) Time for a new school of thought on degrees. *Marketing Event* Sept, 7.

Newell, S. and Shackleton, V. (2000) Recruitment and selection. In: Bach, S. and Sisson, K. (eds) *Personnel Management: a Comprehensive Guide to Theory and Practice*, 3rd edn. Blackwell Publishers, Oxford, pp. 111–136.

Perry, M., Foley, P. and Rumpf, P. (1996) Events management: an emerging challenge in Australian higher education. *Festival Management & Event Tourism* 4(3/4), 85–93.

Rafaeli, A. and Oliver, A.L. (1998) Employment ads: a configurational research agenda. *Journal of Management Inquiry* 7(4), 342–358.

Royal, C.G. and Jago, L.K. (1998) Special event accreditation: the practioners' perspective. *Festival Management & Event Tourism* 5, 221–230.

Smith, E. and Keating, J. (1997) *Making Sense of Training Reform and Competency-based Training.* Social Science Press, Wentworth Falls, Australia.

Snyman, R.M. (2001) Do employers really know what they want? An analysis of job advertisements for information and knowledge managers. *Aslib Proceedings* 53(7), 273–281.

Spencer, L.M. and Spencer, S.M. (1993) *Competency at Work.* John Wiley & Sons, New York.

Tassiopoulos, D. (2000) *Event Management: a Professional and Developmental Approach.* Lansdowne, Cape Town.

II   Education and Career Development

There is general agreement that the events and conventions sector offers excellent employment opportunities. Jobs are challenging and diverse, and the five chapters in this part suggest some variability in work across the sector. Jago and Mair (Chapter 6) suggest that business events offer better employment prospects, although anecdotal evidence suggests that event management students are often attracted to the glamour and media profile of major events, while Beaven, St George and Wright (Chapter 3) argue that cultural events employment has a very specific work ethic. The chapters also highlight commonalities: the complex nature of event work and employment, the varied routes into the sector, and the lack of clear career progression patterns.

Starting with education, Beaven, St George and Wright (Chapter 3) draw on their experiences teaching at the Arts Institute at Bournemouth, UK, to consider the challenges of developing employability in the cultural events sector. They draw together the findings of three research projects and begin by discussing the nature of cultural events work and employability. Then they examine the expectations of employers, the importance placed on graduates having gained experience, and how employers rate different approaches to embedding employability in the curriculum. Finally, they discuss how students themselves respond to various learning opportunities, and the value they place on practical project learning. The chapter has important lessons and guidance both for students preparing for a career in cultural events management and for educators designing curricula.

The next three chapters discuss the application of career theories to the convention and exhibition industry (Ladkin and Weber, and McCabe) and major events (Jago and Mair). They all discuss Arthur and Rousseau's (1996) theory of the boundaryless career, where the ownership and responsibility for careers is in the hands of individuals rather than organizations. The chapters by Ladkin and Weber (Chapter 4) and McCabe (Chapter 5) both observe that there is no clear route to career progression in the convention and exhibition industry, with careers paths being largely self-directed. Extending the boundaryless career model, they refer to McCabe and Savery's (2007) concept of 'butterflying' career patterns, where individuals move between different jobs and sectors as they build up human capital, expert knowledge, core competencies and professional expertise. Both chapters adopt the life and work history analysis technique but detail findings of research at different scales: Ladkin and Weber present aggregated data from a study of convention professionals in Hong Kong, while McCabe focuses on case studies of four individuals in Australia.

Ladkin and Weber's chapter examines the career profiles of managers working in the convention industry in Hong Kong. Their research supports the concept of 'butterflying' with no obvious career routes and skills and experiences developed through a range of sectors and levels of jobs. Nevertheless, although many convention professionals have developed their skills outside the sector, respondents strongly identified with and were committed to their careers in the convention industry.

McCabe's chapter continues these themes and she extends her previous Australian research on the career patterns of managers in the convention and exhibition industry by presenting four case studies. By mapping individuals' career profiles she clearly demonstrates the non-linear nature of career progression, with job movements encompassing intra- and inter-sector mobility, and horizontal, vertical and diagonal growth. She concludes with the implications for individuals and employers. Not least, individuals should be prepared to 'flutter' between jobs and sectors in order to build up their skills, competencies and human capital, and employers need to recognize these career patterns and incorporate them into their recruitment and retention strategies.

Jago and Mair (Chapter 6) also discuss the application of career theories, in this case to major events. They argue that, as pulsating organizations, the episodic nature of major events, and the need to expand and contract an organization and staffing over a short period of time, brings different challenges than the more constant work patterns found in the convention industry. They examine the impact of generational change on employment, focusing on the emergence of Generation Y in the workforce. They identify two key changes that have impacted on major events careers. First, the creation of an internal labour market by key staff rotating between different major event organizations and, secondly, the establishment of companies running multiple events.

The final chapter in this section considers events work in both conventions and cultural festivals. Formádi and Raffai (Chapter 7) offer an insight into the direction professionalization is taking in the field of event management in Hungary. They detail the skills, abilities and competencies required by event managers, the characteristics of event work and the role of professional associations. The state of professionalism in the Hungarian events sector is examined in relation to Greenwood's five attributes of a profession. They conclude that the process of professionalization is seeing the emergence of a recognized event management profession in Hungary, while, at the same time, there is also increased specialization within the profession.

3 Employability in the Cultural Events Sector: the Role of Specialist Degree Programmes

Zuleika Beaven,[1] Sara St George[2] and Richard Wright[3]

[1]University of Winchester, UK; [2]Lighthouse, Poole, UK; [3]Arts Institute at Bournemouth, UK

Introduction

Cultural events management is an area of study in post-compulsory education that is developing and expanding in the UK. The Commonwealth Games, European City of Culture 2008 and the Cultural Olympiad of the 2012 Olympics are examples of large-scale sustainable events which have raised the profile and significance of cultural events management as an academic discipline. As such, skills development and employability have become key issues in a sector which traditionally has not seen formal qualifications as a necessity, relying instead on a 'learn on the job' philosophy. However, with the sector now seen as one of the faster-growing areas of the economy (around 5% of the UK's Gross Domestic Product) (DCMS, 2002), the new generation of cultural managers must be ready.

According to the Sector Skills Council for the Cultural and Creative Industries, the creative and commercial success of live entertainment means the supply of skilled workers is already failing to match demand (DCMS, 2002). Their research predicts a need for 30,000 new recruits in the UK over the next decade. So how can cultural event management educators and students respond to meet the skills needed to support the growth of the sector? There has been a proliferation of specialist, vocationally orientated cultural event management courses in the UK, providing students with practical and theoretical education in preparation for work in the cultural sector through applying management theory to the leisure context. Essentially, specialist vocational courses exist to equip students with the skills and knowledge necessary for management work in the cultural events sectors, therefore student employability and the nature of learning and teaching to support this is a key concern.

This chapter draws together the findings of three research projects undertaken by the authors in order to discuss the perceptions of students, employers and cultural events workers about the nature of work in the sector and the role of experiential learning to support industry needs and graduate employability.

© CAB International 2009. *People and Work in Events and Conventions: a Research Perspective* (eds T. Baum *et al.*)

In doing this, it will be argued that cultural events work is a distinct profession with its own characteristics, that degree programmes should include significant elements of experiential learning in order to develop future cultural events managers' employability and that students of these programmes should have an explicit understanding of this process to support their learning. This discussion will be conducted with explicit reference to curriculum design and learning and teaching approaches on the BA (Hons) Arts and Event Management (BAAEM) programme at the Arts Institute in Bournemouth (AIB) in the UK. The chapter is aimed at both students preparing for a career in the field of cultural events management and educators designing programmes of study. Although the research projects referenced are UK-based, points of relevance to an international audience of cultural event management educators and students will be drawn out and discussed.

The chapter begins by setting the context for the nature of cultural events work and employability through reference to a study by Beaven (2003) set amongst music workers. Having established the special features of cultural events work, it progresses to the main focus, discussing both previously published (Beaven and Wright, 2006) and unpublished results from research examining the attitudes of cultural events graduate employers towards the importance of vocational training and transferable skills on employability. Finally, new findings from research by authors Beaven and St George are presented, which examine students' attitudes to the experiential learning approaches that they have encountered throughout their programme of study.

The Nature of Cultural Events Work and Employability

What makes work in the cultural events sector different from other event management employment? Summerton and Kay (1999) perceive the cultural events sector as being characterized by a very specific work ethic. The creation of artistic and cultural activity brings together 'changing coalitions of people' who work in a fluid and dynamic way, drawing upon an array of motives and goals that are personal to the individual. Despite the personal aspect of this approach, those working in the cultural events sector are still clearly linked in the pursuit of a common goal in support of this cultural activity.

This view is reinforced through the findings of a qualitative study investigating aspects of work in the area of music work and management (Beaven, 2003). In order to underline the practical implications for the reader, whether you are a student training to work in cultural events or an educator designing curricula, the findings of the study are considered in relation to notions of employability. The study involved conducting in-depth interviews with 20 people working in music; work undertaken included many elements of cultural event management such as venue management, fundraising, tour management, programming, concert management, marketing and promotion, and education. The subjects' work status included those in full-time, permanent work for an established organization, part-time workers, freelancers, sole traders, students and a combination of these. Interviews included discussion of the subjects' background and their routes into their current careers, considering both training and study, and participants were asked to characterize the nature of their work.

Analysis of the data suggested a variety of routes into the sector, including art form and managerial training. More specifically, 19 of the 20 subjects had at least one higher education qualification. Not surprisingly, most subjects expressed a great interest in music, some with a very specific sub-genre focus, and the majority (14) were involved in some form of amateur or professional practice.

Subjects were found to have a range of primary motivations for working in the sector, including support of artistic practice (either financial support through an activity not directly related to their practice or through entrepreneurial activity that directly generated bookings and opportunities to perform), substitution for artistic practice (this group is sometimes characterized as failed artists, but the research suggested more positive choice than some of the literature would suggest), non-artists with a belief in the value of the sector and a wish to contribute to it, and non-artists with the desire to work with creative people. For the present discussion, a particularly interesting group was clearly identifiable as being related to Summerton and Kay's (1999) 'chameleons', those working in more than one organization or setting, combining entrepreneurship or salaried work with study, practice or voluntary work in the sector. The analysis of the findings suggested that lack of job security was mentioned by many of the subjects, most of whom saw it as a feature of their working lives, with some suggestion that this contributed to a 'push' factor towards entrepreneurship.

What emerged from this study (Beaven, 2003) is a picture of cultural events showing a more complicated employment pattern and sector than the literature would suggest. Although the design of the research did not lend itself to any substantive conclusions, there is evidence of significant entrepreneurial activity. In addition, the complexity of career patterns and career development suggested by the study, where subjects may, in effect, be developing two parallel careers in tandem, calls for a flexible and sensitive approach to the provision of professional training. If employability is about graduates being ready to secure work of a suitable level within a reasonable time after graduation and being equipped to develop within their chosen career (Harvey and Knight, n.d.), then from the perspective of providers of cultural events management courses, this suggests a need for flexible delivery, offering support for advanced applied professional practice throughout careers and acknowledgement in the form of curriculum design that some students will be aiming towards entrepreneurial practice.

Extensive employability literature exists, including key contributions from the Learning and Teaching Support Network (LTSN) from Alison *et al.* (2002), Harvey and Knight (n.d.), Yorke (2004) and Yorke and Knight (2004a,b) in the form of accessible guides for the educator. With employability defined as a potential to gain and be successful in the students' chosen field, emphasis is placed here on practical measures that higher education institutions (HEIs) may take to support students in acquiring employability. The USEM approach (Yorke and Knight, 2004b), whereby employability is determined by the impact of the following elements on the student, is advocated as a way of understanding what leads to its achievement: Understanding (subject specialism); Skills (key skills, skilful practice); Efficacy beliefs (personal qualities that determine students' beliefs that they can make a difference); and Meta-cognition (learning how to learn, reflection on learning). Yorke and Knight (2004b:11–15) discuss five broad approaches as to how best to embed employability:

- employability through the whole curriculum (transferable skills);
- employability in the core curriculum (transferable skills);
- work-based learning (WBL) interspersed within the curriculum (sandwich courses, placements, work experience);
- employability-related modules (discrete skills modules, career modules); and
- WBL in parallel with the curriculum (part-time work as a learning opportunity).

They consider the need to avoid a 'one size fits all' approach and suggest that the size, context, student recruitment and envisaged labour markets influence embedding in the curriculum. With this in mind, the second section of this chapter will consider approaches to embedding employability in the curriculum that meet the expectations of employers in the cultural events management sector.

Developing Employability through Cultural Events Management Courses

Having set out our case that employability for cultural event managers (CEMs) must respond to the complex nature of work in the sector, we will now consider some specific approaches to embedding employability in CEM courses by drawing on findings from a survey of employer attitudes. The aim is to provide some insight for curriculum developers and students. The sample was obtained from two sources: a database of work experience providers and employers of graduates from the BAAEM course at the AIB, who were therefore known to the authors, and employers advertising jobs suitable for graduates in two of the primary publications (*Arts Professional* and *The Guardian*) used for cultural events job searches in the UK. Once the sample of 123 potential employers was in place, a four-page questionnaire, which used a combination of quantitative and qualitative questioning, was administered by post, with questions covering their attitudes to employing graduates and to hosting student work placements. The response rate was 51 (41.5%), with two invalid responses, so that n = 49.

Seventy-five per cent of all respondents consider an arts or event management qualification essential or desirable for those seeking employment in the cultural events sector, and the results suggest that gaining a specialist qualification is the single, most important step that someone wishing to enhance their employability in this sector might take. In addition, results clearly showed that employers surveyed placed considerable emphasis on experience, and had relatively high expectations that new graduates will have gained experience during their course. A suggestion here for cultural events educators is that curricula must go beyond Yorke and Knight's (2003) advocacy of 'knowing that' and 'knowing how' content to include elements of 'doing that' or perhaps 'done that and reflected upon it' if graduates are to most effectively promote their employability, and that students should pursue opportunities to gain experience during their programme of study. To underline the importance of this point, when respondents who recruit graduates with bachelor's degrees were asked how important it was for new graduates seeking to enter their employment to have experience of working on or assisting with events or arts projects, all said this was either desirable or essential.

We wanted to find out more about how strongly employers think experience supports employability and decided to use a scenario question in order to survey both respondents who had employed graduates in cultural events programmes and those who had not yet had the opportunity to do so. Employers were asked to imagine a situation where they are comparing graduate applicants of similar profile in all respects except that only one has any event experience. They were then asked to choose which of the following statements would most closely reflect their attitude:

- Experience is important to us, so I would strongly favour the graduate with direct vocational experience.
- Experience is important to us, and I would be inclined to be more interested in the graduate with direct vocational experience.
- We expect to train our graduate employees, so previous experience is less important than the ability to learn.
- For us, transferable skills are just as valuable in a graduate as direct vocational experience, so we wouldn't tend to favour the applicant with event experience.

Results showed that experience was highly valued by a large majority of employers, with 26% selecting the first statement (strongly favour experience) and 50% selecting the second (more interested in experience). Only 11% indicated that they would not tend to favour an applicant with experience (fourth statement). Analysis of the responses from those who had previously employed graduates indicates that significantly more of them would 'strongly favour' the graduate with direct vocational experience (35%, compared with 26% overall), suggesting that there was an expectation that a graduate employee would need less training.

The research investigated what employers actually meant by experience, and specifically whether they thought that the major experiential learning opportunities, such as work placements and project work that are embedded in many cultural events programmes, had value in supporting employability or, to consider this another way, 'counted' as experience when employers were considering job applications. The findings reflected the 'chameleon' nature of arts work, as more than four in five respondents considered volunteering and work experience as a valid experience, supporting employability. Student projects were less valued, although at 55%, the majority of employers would still consider this valid experience when considering an application for employment. For vocational courses with significant elements of practical live project work, there is potentially an issue about how students present their project work to employers. Further research might explore this, as some employers seemed to have concerns or queries about the level of experience that this allowed students to gain.

Whilst more than 80% of the sample recognized the value of student work placement as a means of gaining experience, once the responses had been adjusted to exclude those who were contacted because they were known to us as work experience providers, we found that only 55% of the remainder had hosted a student work placement (against 61% of all respondents). It is encouraging to note, however, that the majority gave 'never having been approached' as their reason, with only two (4%) respondents stating that this was not appropriate for their organization. All of those who had hosted students on work placement were asked an open-ended question about their perception of the contribution of these students to the organization. Responses are illustrative of the preconceptions of hosts and of the value they place on a range of qualities. Whilst 43% of those responding to this question either said that students had met their expectations or gave a neutral response, and 3% reported being disappointed (specifically by low literacy levels), 54% reported that their expectations were exceeded. Comments included: 'I have been very impressed with their self-confidence and flexibility', 'Bright, perceptive, articulate', 'They can pick up new information and skills quickly', 'Pleasantly surprised by the high level of ability' and 'Good at networking, creating partnerships, liaising with other agencies'.

This takes the research on from vehicles for developing employability to the specific attributes that cultural event employers expect from staff. To test attitudes to the importance of subject knowledge, employers were asked to rate as 'essential', 'desirable' or 'unimportant' a set of 14 given areas of vocationally specific knowledge, skills and experience. There was a significant interest in graduates with subject knowledge: 'securing licensing' was the only area seen as unimportant by more than half the respondents. Clearly there are useful pointers to curriculum content for vocational courses to be drawn from these results, with over three-quarters of respondents agreeing that the following are essential or desirable: project management, work with audiences or customers, hands-on production experience, budgeting, work with performers or artists, promotion and PR, fundraising and development, and marketing planning. This is entirely in line with the USEM model (Yorke and Knight, 2004b) and is an endorsement of the approach of embedding experiential learning opportunities, such as the production of live events, into the curriculum.

Open-ended responses to questions about most important, evident and lacking skills suggest employers choose to make little distinction between the importance of direct vocational and transferable skills within the 'basket' of competencies they look for in graduates – however, when asked to compare vocational experience with transferable skills, the former was strongly favoured. Less emphasis is placed on subject-specific IT applications, but the need to be self-supporting through use of word processing applications is clearly, and unsurprisingly, entrenched.

The View from the 'Sharp' End: Students' Perceptions of Experiential Learning

So far, this chapter has considered the role that major experiential learning opportunities can play in developing the employability of students of cultural events management. In this final section, focus is shifted from the general to the specific, and the response to these learning opportunities from the perspective of a group of students on the BAAEM degree at the AIB is explored. The approach to teaching on the BAAEM is based largely on learning by experience from arts events and festivals. The course includes an assessed work placement with an arts or event management organization, and specifically requires students to manage the conceptualization, planning, funding and delivery of a minimum of three live event projects during their degree, including a sophisticated and complex final major project undertaken by a pair of students, which might involve an international exhibition, a mid-scale festival, a regional tour or a London fashion show.

In recent years, the emphasis at AIB has shifted from a mature and proven approach to competency training to a conceptualization of live events project work as an integral part of a sector-focused, risk-promoting curriculum. This re-imagining of the curriculum has allowed employability to be embedded through creating a real, not simulated, environment for students to learn. A dual approach has been taken to the curriculum for arts management students:

- At the broader level, a synergistic, whole-course approach to learning has been developed, which embeds the concept to support employability across units and draws on the established creativity, risk-taking and 'learning by doing' elements of live projects to support the concept.
- At the level of learning and teaching methods, the established learning approaches of the practical, live project units have been transferred to reinvigorate learning in explicitly management-related units.

So how do students perceive this approach and what contribution do they feel it will make to their employability? To explore this further, Beaven and St George conducted a study in 2008 with final-year undergraduates on the BAAEM. A short, confidential questionnaire was administered to all 23 students in the cohort and, in addition, in-depth interviews were conducted with five of these students, asking them to reflect back on their learning experience from project work since beginning their degree (in reporting this qualitative data, the students involved provided written consent for their first names to be disclosed). Issues of experiential learning through practical project work assignments, the cultural entrepreneurship focus of the programme and the related issue of risk-taking by students as part of their course were investigated.

Findings suggested a high degree of reflection upon learning approaches and a perceptible course culture which valued learning by doing and risk-taking as a valuable part of project work. Dani, now a final-year undergraduate, has spent time reflecting on her experience of running a music festival at the end of her first year of study:

> I would never had gone to university to do an academic course and that was just a fantastic first year, because it was learning by doing stuff and that was so important for me… When you do anything practical, like when you are typing on a computer and you don't think you are learning where the keys are but all of a sudden you're not looking at them when you are typing – and that was what happens [with project work]; you just tend to absorb it.

Although Dani and other members of her cohort have talked about this as being 'thrown in at the deep end' – a demanding experience requiring long hours of independent work – they recognized this intensity of engagement supported deep learning. Josh acknowledged that the critical engagement with tutors and peers that happened when pitching project concepts for approval was a valuable learning experience.

> I think the pitches brought up a lot of problems. To start with everyone was in a dream world, thinking everything was running nicely, and then we had the presentations and the tutors were ripping our ideas apart – and we were ripping the ideas apart as well, as we went through the pitches realizing this couldn't work and that couldn't work … I felt it was risky and I felt personally responsible, and that made it more exciting. All project work for me needs to have a certain element of risk.

Students Rachel and Joe agreed that being thrown in at the deep end, which they juxtaposed with being 'spoon fed', enhanced their learning. Here Joe talks about the specific example of having to work within a limited budget.

> We really had to haggle, to cut things. There were no extras; we had to make the signs at home the night before – 6 hours of painting. But I enjoyed it because you have to make it happen, and you've learnt from every paint stroke in a little way. I do really think that you benefit from it.

Rachel, who characterized herself as someone who would not have been comfortable to take risks or volunteer for challenging work when she arrived on the BAAEM, summed up the experience of project work as a journey from feeling under pressure to realizing that she had grown and developed as a cultural events manager.

> I'd not done any events before and personally it sounded like something I couldn't do… I was really worried that no one was going to come and it would be really embarrassing with artists and so on… and there was a lot of trying to prove to tutors that we could do it. The risk was definitely worthwhile. If you spoon feed it, we don't gain as much experience…. It has made me more confident and made me look at other people and see how they work and think there is no reason why I can't do that. Everyone can do it. [Another student] said to me 'You've come a long way', and if it had been an easier project, I wouldn't have learnt so much.

Some students are starting to see their work as more than a response to the educational requirements placed on them. Many students have established a mind-set which recognizes the value of the skills they are developing and independent, student-centred learning, so it is not uncommon for students to continue organizing and managing live arts and events projects in their own time. This is a significant feature of the course which has direct impact on student employability, and the belief of the curriculum designers is that this approach to experiential learning is a catalyst for active learning by students. It is this very approach which supports the needs of the sector and provides a very real and relevant learning experience for students. As Joe said:

If daddy gives you a Rolls Royce at 17, it's way different from your own first Ford Escort – even though it is not necessarily as good, you've worked for it. If we want to go and work in festivals or in theatre, you've got to do amazing things.

Conclusions

In this chapter the findings of several research studies have been drawn together to throw some light on the challenge for educators and students of developing employability in the cultural events sector. The complex nature of work in the sector and what this means for employability have been considered, and it has been shown that the employers surveyed place considerable emphasis on experience and have relatively high expectations that new graduates will have gained experience. Relatively good news for courses with work placement or sandwich elements is that more than 80% of responding employers suggest they would value work-based learning as a valid way of gaining acceptable experience, and, encouragingly, this figure is higher for those employers who have had contact with BAAEM students, including as placement hosts.

Of concern, however, is the relatively poor consideration of the value of experience gained through student projects, despite the rich range of challenging and successful projects being undertaken by students on many cultural events programmes. This suggests a significant challenge for both education providers and students, including the need for greater dialogue with the sector and careful consideration of how to 'package' project work to potential employers.

Finally, it has been highlighted that, when asked to reflect, students themselves place great value on the learning opportunities offered by challenging and risk-orientated practical project learning.

References

Alison, J., Harvey, C. and Dixon, I. (2002) *Enhancing Employability: a Long Term Strategic Challenge*. Higher Education Academy, York, UK.

Beaven, Z. (2003) Employment and work orientation in the cultural sector. *Employment Relations Record* 2, 61–69.

Beaven, Z. and Wright, R. (2006) Experience! Experience! Experience! Employer attitudes to arts and event management graduate employability. *International Journal of Event Management Research* 2, 17–24.

DCMS (2002) *Creative Industries Factfile*. Department of Culture, Media and Sport, London.

Harvey, L. and Knight, P. (n.d.) *Helping Departments to Develop Employability*. HEFCE (ESECT)/LTSN, York, UK.

Summerton, J. and Kay, S. (1999) Hidden from view: the shape of arts work and arts organizations in the UK. In: *Proceedings of AIMAC '99 Arts and Cultural Management Conference*. AIMAC/Helsinki School of Economics and Business Administration, Helsinki.

Yorke, M. (2004) *Employability in Higher Education – What It Is – What It Is Not*. LTSN, York, UK.

Yorke, M. and Knight, P. (2003) *The Undergraduate Curriculum and Employability*. LTSN, York, UK.

Yorke, M. and Knight, P. (2004a) *Employability: Judging and Communicating Achievement*. LTSN, York, UK.

Yorke, M. and Knight, P. (2004b) *Embedding Employability into the Curriculum*. LTSN, York, UK.

4 Career Profiles of Convention Industry Professionals in Asia: a Case Study of Hong Kong

ADELE LADKIN[1] AND KARIN WEBER[2]

[1]Bournemouth University, UK; [2]Hong Kong Polytechnic University, Hong Kong

Introduction

This chapter uses empirical data collected as part of an ongoing research project exploring the careers of individuals working in the convention industry in Asian convention destinations. Taking Hong Kong as a case study, the chapter examines the career profiles of people working in the convention industry through an exploration of cumulated human capital. By exploring the human capital behind jobs in the convention industry, an understanding of the skills required, where they were acquired, and the experience gained over a person's career can be obtained. The intention is that through the exploration of career profiles the chapter can provide a better understanding of how convention and exhibition industry professionals develop their careers, and to highlight the characteristics of the labour markets for this profession. Hong Kong was selected as a case study due to its importance as a world-class convention destination within Asia.

Careers in the Convention Industry

There is little doubt that the conventions and exhibitions industry is an important sector of business tourism. The industry has undergone significant growth since the late 1980s, and is increasingly recognized by governments and national tourism offices as a highly lucrative market (McCabe, 2008). Asia as a region has made considerable attempts to capitalize on this market, with extensive investment in infrastructure giving many of Asia's cities enviable convention and exhibition facilities. In Hong Kong, the Hong Kong Convention and Exhibition Centre is currently undergoing refurbishment at a cost of HK$1.4 billion. Beginning in 2006, the renovation will be completed in 2009 and will result in a total exhibition space of 83,000 square metres. The venue consists of six exhibition halls, two convention halls, three foyers, two theatres, 52 meeting rooms, four restaurants and two underground car parks (Hong Kong Convention and Exhibition Centre, 2008). AsiaWorld-Expo, built in December 2005, adds a further 70,000 square metres of exhibition space, located next to Hong Kong International Airport.

The conventions and exhibitions sector is seen as providing excellent employment opportunities. Labour is required in a range of different ways, beginning with the building of the facilities, through to the management and operational elements of running a successful conventions venue. Employment opportunities exist in many different organizations, for example, convention and exhibition centres, within large hotels and corporate organizations, convention bureaus, public sector events departments and private companies that specialize in professional conference organization. The type of employment opportunity in the industry is also varied and includes sales, marketing, food and beverage, accountancy and coordination roles.

The variety of employment opportunities largely stems from the fact that the sector is highly labour intensive. Furthermore, it is the quality of the labour that influences customer service, which in turn can give competitive advantage. As a consequence, appropriately educated and trained labour is essential for the success of the convention and exhibition industry. Despite the recognized value of labour and the wealth of employment opportunities, to date there is little understanding of careers in the sector, which provides a rationale for research in this area.

In addition to the practical value in exploring the careers of convention service professionals, the topic can also contribute to the current theoretical debate concerning careers in general. In recent years, there has been discussion on how the traditional concepts of a career based on organizational structures and an organized line hierarchy are in decline (Eaton and Bailyn, 2000). These are increasingly being replaced by the concept of a multi-dimensional career that develops beyond the boundaries of a single organization or occupational setting (Collin and Young, 2000). The term 'boundaryless career' has been used to describe the type of career that places the ownership of careers primarily in the hands of individuals rather than institutions (Arthur and Rousseau, 1996), playing down the role of organizational structures for career development (Weber and Ladkin, 2008). In a boundaryless career, the career is no longer constrained by the boundaries of an organization (Arthur and Rousseau, 1996). New models of work organization have also emerged, as has the issue of age and different career paths of 'Generation X' (McCabe, 2008).

Despite the dearth of research into careers in the convention industry, some interesting work undertaken on the convention and exhibition industry in Australia provides an insight into both the theoretical and practical elements of careers in the industry. On the theoretical side, McCabe and Savery (2007), through an examination of labour mobility in the industry, identified 'butterflying' as a career pattern. This research explored the job movements of those working as professional conference organizers, and employees in hotels and convention venues, purpose-built convention and exhibition centres, and convention and visitor bureaus. Tracing the careers of the sample revealed that rather than having one particular career route through different sectors, the respondents 'flutter' between sectors according to opportunities and personal choice, building human capital as they go. The 'butterfly' pattern can be identified as an extension and development of the boundaryless career model (McCabe and Savery, 2007).

On the practical side, McCabe and Savery (2007) and McCabe (2008) explored career development in the industry. McCabe and Savery (2007) examined career progression through the sectors and by job function and responsibility, and also the impetus for job moves. McCabe (2008) assessed the career planning and development strategies of individuals. The sample of 126 employees revealed that the industry is dominated by well-educated females who follow a variety of career routes. Personal career planning and development strategies were also explored to ascertain how individuals advance their careers. The findings revealed that strategies relate to both the internal and the external environments. The practical implications for current and future employees in the industry included the importance of networking and the need to continually develop skills over their careers. For the employers, issues related to recruitment and retention were identified (McCabe, 2008).

Given the value of human capital to the successful continued development of the industry, a further understanding of careers in the industry would be beneficial to both the individual, in terms of career choice, opportunity and development, and the industry, in respect of how to attract, build on and retain human capital.

Life and Work History Research

This research collects work history data from a sample of people working in the convention industry in Hong Kong. The collection of work history data has its origins in the life history approach, the developments and use of which have been well documented (Dex, 1991). There are two main ways of collecting work history data, either longitudinally over time or through the use of memory recall. The merits and difficulties of each of these are described in full by Dex (1991), while Ladkin (1999) discusses the collection of work history data using the memory recall method. In terms of data analysis, the work history data enables career profiles to be created, which may be explored in aggregate form or as individual work histories (Weber and Ladkin, 2008).

Work history data can be collected on many aspects of a person's working life. Data can be quantitative in nature, for example the number of jobs a person has held, the length of each job, and how many times they have moved jobs within the external or internal labour market. Work history data can also be qualitative when gathering data on career choice, ambition and personal career motivations. A combination of both approaches gives a full picture of all the elements that comprise a persons working life over time, with the detail being constrained by the reliability and effectiveness of human memory.

Career Profiles and Human Capital

The use of career profiles in research is not new. A career profile is the result of collecting information on individuals' work histories, which gives a picture of a person's career profile over time through the collection of work history data. When individuals are asked about their working lives, the information they provide can be used to create a detailed picture of their work history. What these career profiles provide is a picture of the development of human capital. Human capital can be defined as an individual's education, skills and experience (Ghodsee, 2005). Of course, human capital is not only developed according to an individual's choice and career opportunities, but it is also influenced by structural opportunities provided by the industry at any given time. The structural opportunities in an industry provide the framework for any occupation, and individual ability and ambition determine how people make choices within the structural opportunities (Ladkin and Weber, 2006). Therefore, the reasons behind all career patterns include both organizational influences and those related to the individual in terms of career choice, opportunities, job satisfaction and personal motivations. In the broadest sense, careers are concerned with a person's working life and are the outcomes of structural opportunities made available to an individual, for example the size of the industry, organizational structure and knowledge requirement, and human ability and ambition.

In the present research, career profiles are considered in aggregate form to provide information on educational qualifications, job patterns over time, career commitment and career decisions. Qualitative responses are also explored from individual responses regarding career motivations.

Methods

Using the memory recall method an online survey of convention industry professionals was undertaken between January and March 2008. The sample for this study comprised industry professionals from key convention destinations in Asia, namely Hong Kong, Singapore, Thailand and Malaysia. An e-mail list of these industry professionals was compiled from two major sources: membership directories of the key industry association and web sites of key industry players. Following this, an introductory e-mail was sent to all 693 contacts on the list, together with a link to the online survey. A total of 112 responses were received. Following elimination of incomplete questionnaires, the final sample size was 104 respondents, giving a response rate of 15%. In view of the potential non-response error, a follow-up was conducted with industry professionals who did not complete the survey. Reasons for them declining to participate were primarily related to privacy concerns, given the detail required for the career analysis, and time constraints.

The information presented here details the results for the Hong Kong sub-sample only. The personal e-mail addresses of 246 industry professionals in Hong Kong were identified; a total of 53 responses were received, giving a response rate of 21%. Following elimination of incomplete questionnaires, the final sub-sample for Hong Kong comprised 51 respondents.

Based on a review of pertinent literature on career development, a self-administered questionnaire was developed. It was pre-tested extensively in terms of structure, layout, wording of the questions and proper online data collection/storage, drawing on the assistance of three academics and three industry professionals. The final online survey was posted on a designated university web site. The sample was invited via e-mail to participate in the study and provided with the URL to access the questionnaire. The first e-mail and subsequent follow-ups were sent in early January 2008, mid-February 2008 and early March 2008, respectively.

The questionnaire consisted of three distinct sections. In section 1, respondents were asked about their background in terms of key demographics (age, gender, education and nationality) and their current employment. Section 2 enquired about respondents' career history, with a specific focus on respondents' last five positions. Details ascertained included previous jobs' industry sector and level of responsibility, the duration of each job, whether job changes required relocation, and whether any action had been taken to move out of the industry. Section 3 centred on respondents' career motivations, career decisions, career identity, job challenges and career satisfaction/commitment. For sections 1 and 2, the questions were closed questions that required respondents to choose the appropriate box. Although this approach to a certain extent limits available choices, it was taken to keep the questionnaire to a minimum length and aid speed of completion. For section 3, where value judgements were required (for example, in relation to job satisfaction and commitment), a seven-point Likert scale was used. The quantitative data were analysed using SPSS, with specific data analysis techniques discussed together with respective study findings. The remaining questions were open-ended and required respondents to enter qualitative comments in textboxes. Owing to the relatively simple and small number of comments, they have been presented in their raw form where appropriate.

Results

Demographic profile of the sample

The majority of respondents were female (57%, Table 4.1). The largest group of respondents (31%) was in the 36–45 years age group, followed by respondents in the 26–35 years age group (30%). The majority of respondents were Hong Kong/Mainland Chinese nationals (73%). In terms of educational attainment, more than half of respondents had attained an undergraduate degree, with another quarter of respondents having completed postgraduate education.

Although there are no formal direct entry points into the conventions industry, the sample displays high levels of education, with three-quarters of the sample being educated to degree level or above. Further analysis revealed that in terms of the type of undergraduate degree held, 31.4% were in business subjects.

Table 4.1. Demographic profile of the sample (n = 51).

Demographics	No. of respondents	%
Gender		
Female	29	56.9
Male	20	39.2
Age		
21–25	6	11.8
26–35	15	29.5
36–45	16	31.3
46–55	10	19.6
56 and older	3	5.9
Nationality		
Hong Kong/Mainland Chinese	37	72.6
British	5	9.8
Canadian	3	5.9
American	2	3.9
German	1	2.0
Malaysian	1	2.0
Educational background		
High school	3	5.9
Diploma	7	13.8
Undergraduate degree		
Business	16	31.4
Other discipline	13	25.5
Postgraduate degree	12	23.5

Current employment

The sample's current job titles pointed to many respondents being in senior positions in the industry, with almost half of respondents having a job title of CEO (3), Director (8), General Manager (3), Deputy General Manager (2), Managing Director (4), Deputy Managing Director (1) and Senior Vice President (2). A further 17 respondents were in middle-management positions. The length of employment in the convention and exhibition industry ranged from 3 months to 49 years. As the sample had captured a number of respondents in senior positions, this provided a valuable opportunity to explore the career paths of those who had reached top-level jobs in the convention industry.

Job patterns

The results presented refer to how the respondent's employment has changed over time. Viewed in aggregate form they show the various jobs that have been undertaken prior to current employment. Although they cannot indicate individual career paths, looking at job positions in this way gives an indication of the

Table 4.2. Career path by industry sector.

Job area	Present job	Previous job	Job 3	Job 4	Job 5
Independent professional conference organizer/meeting planner	2	1		2	
Conference organizer – association		2			
Conference organizer – corporate	1		1		
Exhibition organizer	30	12	4	2	2
Conference venue	1	2	1	1	1
Purpose-built convention and exhibition centre	4				
Convention bureau		1			
Government – state/federal convention and events department	1		3		
MICE industry supplier	7	7	1	1	1
Other – in MICE industry	4	2		1	
Other – not MICE industry		20	15	12	8
Sample size	50	47	25	19	12

sectors where people have gained prior skills and experience. Two aspects are considered here: industry sector and level of responsibility. In both cases the sample size declines as you move back over time, reflecting the fact that not all respondents will have held five jobs. Table 4.2 shows the career paths of the sample by industry sector.

In terms of industry sector, the sample is dominated by those currently in the exhibition sector, a trend that follows through in the previous jobs. Industry suppliers also feature as the current job and previous job sector. There are small numbers of respondents in the current and previous jobs for a whole range of different industry sectors. Although there is clearly a variety of jobs held over time, the dominant finding shown in Table 4.2 is the large number of respondents who have come to the sector from outside the MICE industry. There is clearly no specific route into the industry, with experience being generated in a wide variety of sectors. Whether this is a structural feature due to the relative immaturity of the industry warrants further investigation.

Table 4.3 shows the career paths of the sample by level of job responsibility. As the sample is dominated by respondents in senior positions, it would be expected that more junior roles would have been undertaken prior to these higher-level jobs. Although many of the respondents' previous jobs were also in senior roles, this is indeed the case, with a dominance of those who have previous jobs in managerial or executive roles. The dominance of respondents whose prior jobs were outside of the convention industry is evident here.

The exploration of job findings indicated above points towards a dominance of experiences gained outside the industry. Further investigation revealed those jobs outside the conventions sector to come from a wide variety of different industries. The dominant sectors were administration, general management and marketing, with research and development, consultancy, human resources, IT, sales, hotel and resort work, publishing, and food and beverage outlets also

Table 4.3. Career path by level of responsibility.

Job area	Present job	Previous job	Job 3	Job 4	Job 5
Principal/CEO/Managing Director	10	3	1	1	1
Partner	1				
Director	9	7	3	2	1
Executive	3	2	3		2
Manager	15	12	2	1	
Supervisor	0	0			
Operations	1	0		1	
Other	12	24	14	12	6
Sample size	51	48	23	17	10

featuring. The skills and experiences of those in the convention industry are clearly developed in a range of different labour markets. Further analysis of the specific jobs within the industry indicated a dominance of the sales and marketing functions.

Career identity and career commitment

Despite the fact that the majority of the respondents had come from outside the conventions industry, they appeared to strongly identify with their career in the convention and exhibition industry, as shown in Table 4.4.

This strong identification is demonstrated by the mean scores relating to cognitive identification (statements 2 and 3), affective identification (statements 4 and 8), evaluative identification (statements 1 and 7), and behavioural identification (statements 5 and 6). Resulting from respondents' strong career identity,

Table 4.4. Career identity.

Statement	Mean[a]	Std Dev.
1. My career in the convention and exhibition (C&E) industry is positively judged by others	5.40	1.3
2. I identify myself with my career in the C&E industry	5.36	1.4
3. Being a professional in the C&E industry reflects my personality well	5.06	1.3
4. I like to think about plans for advancing my career in the C&E industry	5.00	1.2
5. I work for my career in the C&E industry more than what is absolutely necessary	4.84	1.4
6. During the holidays I'm not ready to work for my career in the C&E industry	3.92	1.8
7. Sometimes I'd rather not say that I'm a professional in the C&E industry	3.22	1.8
8. I think reluctantly of my career in the C&E industry	2.54	1.4

[a]All variables were measured on a seven-point scale, with a value of 1 indicating 'strongly disagree' and a value of 7 indicating 'strongly agree'.

Table 4.5. Career commitment.

Statement	Mean[a]	Std Dev.
I'm very committed to my career	5.60	1.2
I'm satisfied with the:		
success I've achieved in my career	5.22	1.3
progress I've made towards my overall career goals	5.28	1.4
progress I've made towards meeting my goals for:		
income	4.84	1.5
advancement	5.24	1.4
developing new skills	5.12	1.2

[a]All variables were measured on a seven-point scale, with a value of 1 indicating 'strongly disagree' and a value of 7 indicating 'strongly agree'.

a high level of commitment to their career in the industry was reported (mean = 5.6, measured on a seven-point Likert scale; Table 4.5), with equally high levels of satisfaction both in general and with various aspects of their career (advancement, skill development), and to a lesser extent with their income. Further testimony to the professionals' commitment to their industry is the fact that 90% of respondents had not taken any action to move out of the convention and exhibition industry into another industry sector during their careers. Of those who had considered moving to a different industry sector, a variety of sectors were stated as being possible, including cosmetics, event marketing, government and publication relations, IT and publishing.

In an attempt to further understand the reasons for the commitment to the profession, the research sought information on career motivation for entering and remaining in the industry. Reasons for entering the industry were varied but typically referred to the dynamic nature of the industry and the challenges it presents. Taking directly from the qualitative comments provided by respondents, examples of the reasons stated include:

- It is a very interesting and challenging industry.
- Challenging and dynamic.
- Creative with many opportunities.
- Dynamic, interesting and provides chances to meet people from different industries.
- It is a fun and interesting industry and I wanted to meet lots of different people.
- Not a 9–5 office environment.

The comments presented above represent what many felt were the main reasons they entered the industry. Two common themes are evident. One is that the profession is perceived to be interesting. It is not viewed as a boring job where tasks are repetitive and mundane but one in which the working days might be varied. This leads to the second theme, which is that the job is challenging. Owing to the varied and interesting job nature, industry professionals have to be prepared and ready to react to the many different challenges that can arise.

Again taken from the qualitative comments, reasons for wishing to remain in the industry include:

- Change (never routine), people, challenging in many areas, travel required.
- Daily challenges and seeing plans come to fruition and mostly success.
- Ever-changing working environment and challenges in work nature. Good career to move up to director and shareholders level.
- Exciting and planning ahead. Sense of belonging to the company.
- Fun, fast-growing and dynamic economic environment in Asia and China makes the job very challenging and enjoyable.
- I enjoy working with like-minded people who work hard, play hard, are creative, well organized and result oriented. I continue to enjoy meeting interesting and influential people and leaders from all around the world, including the ones that I worked with…
- Job satisfaction, recognition of contribution by the immediate supervisor/ company, promotion available…
- You will never get bored in this industry. Able to learn different industry, see the latest products, services and trends. Meet with lots of vendors and professionals from different industry.

The reasons that people remain in the industry are similar to the reasons they entered in the first place, with the added theme that the job is very satisfying. Similarities in the reasons as to why people were attracted to and remained in the industry indicate that initial perceptions often proved correct. For people who enjoy their working environments, the reality of working in the industry lives up to expectations.

These and other comments indicated that respondents feel very positive about their chosen career in the convention industry. It is viewed as an attractive industry and one that can offer many exciting job challenges and opportunities.

Conclusion

The exploration of the career profiles of convention industry professionals in Hong Kong presented in this chapter reveals a number of issues relating to the development of human capital and labour markets.

First, although there are no specific educational qualifications required for the industry, a degree-level education is held by the majority of the respondents, specifically in the area of business. Although it is not known if having a degree assists with employment opportunities in the industry, it would appear that higher-education qualifications are commonplace. Further research is required to ascertain the value of education to the convention industry and, with the increase in events-related degree courses, to explore if they are seen as a valuable attribute for career development.

Secondly, in relation to developing human capital within the industry, evidence suggests there are no obvious career routes and that skills and experiences are developed through a range of different sectors and levels of jobs. This research supports the concept of 'butterflying', identified by McCabe (2008) in the context of Australian conventions professionals. Furthermore, there is strong evidence to suggest that those working in the industry have developed their skills outside of the conventions industry, indicating that generic skills and experience relevant for the industry can be gained in a range of different labour markets. Whilst this provides a wealth of career development opportunities for those interested in developing a career in the industry, the lack of a defined career route may act as a deterrent to choosing the conventions industry as a career. Further research is required to test this assertion. In addition, as evidence suggests that careers in the convention sector are boundaryless, this has implications for how long people may remain in the industry. Evidence from the career commitment suggests that people are committed to their profession, but it is not possible to ascertain from the present research how long the respondents may remain in their chosen profession. What is clear, however, is that the industry provides a wealth of career opportunities and is therefore considered by many as an attractive industry to enter.

Thirdly, in terms of the ability of the conventions industry to attract and retain individuals to the sector from other labour markets, evidence from the Hong Kong sample indicates that those who enter the industry are very much committed to working in the sector. Although individuals move jobs to gain knowledge and skills to build their human capital, they are committed to the profession. The perceived attractiveness of the industry combined with the lack of specific skills requirements indicates that the labour markets from which to attract employees are large and varied. How best to develop the careers of people in the industry in order to retain high-quality labour is a subject for future research.

References

Arthur, M.B. and Rousseau, D.M. (eds) (1996) *The Boundaryless Career: a New Employment Principle for New Organizational Eras*. Oxford University Press, New York.

Collin, A. and Young, R.A. (2000) The future of careers. In: Collin, A. and Young, R.A. (eds) *The Future Career*. Cambridge University Press, Cambridge, pp. 276–300.

Dex, S. (1991) *Life and Work History Analysis: Qualitative and Quantitative Developments*. Routledge, London.

Eaton, S.C. and Bailyn, L. (2000) Career as life path: tracing work and life strategies of biotech professionals. In: Morris, T. (ed.) *Career Frontiers: New Concepts of Working Lives*. Oxford University Press, Oxford, pp. 177–201.

Ghodsee, K. (2005) *The Red Riviera: Gender, Tourism and Postsocialism on the Black Sea*. Duke University Press, London.

Hong Kong Convention and Exhibition Centre (2008) Fast facts. Available at: http:/www.hkcec.com (accessed 17 November 2008).

Ladkin, A. (1999) Life and work history analysis: the value of this research method for hospitality and tourism. *Tourism Management* 20(1), 37–45.

Ladkin, A. and Weber, K. (2006) Career profiles of tourism and hospitality academics. Presentation at 24th EuroCHRIE Congress: in search of excellence for tomorrow's tourism, travel and hospitality. Thessaloniki, Greece, 25–28 October.

McCabe, V.S. (2008) Strategies for career planning and development in the convention and exhibition industry in Australia. *International Journal of Hospitality Management* 27(2), 222–231.

McCabe, V.S. and Savery, L.K. (2007) 'Butterflying' a new career pattern for Australia? Empirical evidence. *Journal of Management Development* 26(2), 103–116.

Weber, K. and Ladkin, A. (2008) Career advancement for tourism and hospitality academics: publish, network, study and plan. *Journal of Hospitality and Tourism Research* 32, 448–466.

5 'Butterflying' Career Patterns in the Convention and Exhibition Industry

VIVIENNE MCCABE

University of South Australia, Australia

Introduction

The end of the 20th century and the beginning of the 21st century have seen many changes to the work environment and to careers within the work organization. The evolution of the 'new economy', with its characteristics of independent work activities and dynamic changing technologies, has provided not only opportunity and flexibility but also insecurity and uncertainty within the work environment. This has impacted upon a career (Arthur *et al.*, 1999).

Within the convention and exhibition industry the concept of a career is a relatively new phenomenon and is a result of the exponential growth worldwide of this blue chip sector of the events industry. Since the late 1980s the rapid expansion of the sector has provided many new employment opportunities. The industry is considered to be an attractive career option for many new and potential employees, who see employment within the sector as an opportunity to undertake a range of varied job activities and responsibilities. Work is considered dynamic and challenging and to provide the potential for rapid career progression and excellent career prospects (McCabe and Savery, 2007). Despite the worldwide rapid expansion of the industry there is still minimal formal information as to how potential entrants and existing employees can develop and progress their career within this dynamic, fast-developing sector.

The challenge for individuals who seek a career in the convention and exhibition industry is to establish what potential career paths are available, identify how to progress their career and determine if there are key employment areas that are important. Employers need to establish whether there are certain key factors that relate to a career in the industry. If the industry is to ensure its long-term sustainability, there is a need to understand the phenomenon of a career in this sector.

The purpose of this chapter is to explore the career patterns of individuals in the convention and exhibition industry. Given that the sector is an emergent service industry within the 'new economy', it is useful to determine the format and structure of a career in the sector. This chapter will therefore identify the concept of a career and some of the established models of a career, discuss the impact of a career on an individual and review the role of a career within an organization. Results from a study of career patterns and profiles found within the contemporary convention and exhibition industry in Australia will be outlined and illustrated through the use of four case studies, with the potential implications for both the individual and the organization discussed.

Careers, Career Theory and Models of a Career

According to Arthur *et al.* (1989:8) a career is 'the evolving or unfolding sequence of a person's work experiences over time'. Despite changes to the contemporary work and organizational environment of the 21st century (decline of the industrial age; emergence of the information age with its flat, lean and global organizations; the demise of the traditional hierarchical or organizational career model; changes to the psychological contract), a career is still very much part of an individual's life. There are a number of aspects contained within the sequence of a career. These include career direction, goals, barriers, motives, mobility, success, failure and human capital accumulation (Riley and Ladkin, 1994). A career contains all the activities that an individual faces during his/her working life. It includes the structure and sequence of jobs as well as motivations and feelings behind each career opportunity, together with any particular constraints (McCabe and Ladkin, 2002).

Individuals and their careers have an impact on, and can affect, an organization and its workings. One way an organization can achieve and accomplish its tasks is to motivate staff through career opportunities (McCabe and Ladkin, 2002).

A career is also linked to the structure and function of labour markets. In rapidly changing conditions an individual must be more flexible in managing his/her career, often without having a definite career path. At the beginning of the 21st century the trend in a career is one of a dynamic, developing entity (Arthur *et al.*, 1999), where the individual is expected to manage and formulate his/her own career whilst, at the same time, taking into consideration the internal and external environment. An individual's career behaviour, its progression and development, and the role of the organization within that individual's career can take a variety of different forms. These can be linked and influenced not only by factors such as age, gender, education, the individual's place in society and the external environment but also by models of a career.

The career model established in the mid- to late 20th century was formed on the stable conditions of the industrial state (Arthur *et al.*, 1999). Its basis was on a traditional hierarchical or organizational career, where the emphasis was on career planning and hierarchical progression within an organizational bureaucracy. In this model an individual's career was developed through employment within one to two firms. It was a static not a dynamic environment, with managers being given little flexibility. An individual's career progression was upwards and not sideways (Sullivan, 1999).

Changing patterns in the work environment at the end of the 20th century have now seen work organizations becoming flat, lean and global (Arthur *et al.*, 1999). With the demise of the traditional organizational career model and the emergence of the 'new economy', the approaches and themes that supported the traditional career have changed (McCabe and Savery, 2007). This has impacted on both careers and career models. Career patterns have become more difficult to define, with individuals following a self-directed career where they take control of their own career path, which is no longer confined to one or two organizations.

The new careers of the 21st century are now based on the assumption that an individual's job security is anchored not in an organization but in his/her own portfolio of skills and personal employability (McCabe and Savery, 2007). This has led to the identification of new career models such as portfolio careers (Handy, 1994), protean careers (Mirvis and Hall, 1996) and boundaryless or intelligent careers (Arthur *et al.*, 1999). The current career models have embraced some of the concepts from the traditional career and placed them within the contemporary situation of the 21st century. According to Gunz *et al.* (2000), an individual is expected to have 'several careers' in a lifetime. The focus is now one of an individual taking action and managing his/her career (Arthur *et al.*, 1999). It is very much self-directed.

Careers and Individuals

A number of factors can influence an individual in their development of a career. As identified earlier, these can include age, gender, place in society and the external environment. An individual's age, for example, and where they see themselves in the career life cycle can impact on their goals, career mobility and the development of their potential. Ladkin (2002) identifies that individuals tend to identify the progress of their career in relation to where they are at a particular stage of their life, for example mid-life.

A further aspect that impacts on the development of a career is the acquisition and accumulation of human capital as it can affect an individual's marketability in the labour market. According to Parker and Arthur (2000), a number of core competencies are required in the development of an individual's human capital. This is particularly the case in boundaryless or intelligent careers, where individuals move freely between firms and rely on a range of technical and general core competencies that are seen to be transferable between companies (Gunz *et al.*, 2000). The core competencies of 'Knowing Why', 'Knowing How' and 'Knowing Whom' (Arthur *et al.*, 1999; Parker and Arthur, 2000) have been identified as particularly important to a boundaryless or intelligent career (Gunz *et al.*, 2000).

Another aspect of a career is how to develop and accumulate professional expertise. In order to develop professional expertise an individual needs to be provided with important experiences or be able to take advantage of new knowledge and skills (Van der Heijden, 2001). This may be achieved, for example, by a series of rapid career changes. The continued development of an individual's core competencies and professional expertise can also influence and affect future career choice, adaptability and commitment.

The career of individuals in the 21st century has also been impacted by societal changes which have resulted in increases in employment mobility. The new generation of career individuals are highly job mobile and have different work and career values to their predecessors (Kaye and Jordan Evans, 1999).

There are also a number of external factors that relate to the industry sector which can influence the pattern of an individual's career. These include the size of the industry sector, the size of organization within the industry sector, the number and geographical dispersion of organizations, and the management structures found within the organization. These factors can provide a tension between what an individual wants of an organization in terms of his/her career and what the organization can provide.

Careers and the Organization

Within an organization, a career involves the establishment of a psychological contract or set of expectations that are held by the employer and employee. In the contemporary work environment of the 21st century there have been significant changes to the psychological contract between the organization and the employee. It is now seen as one of performance in exchange for continuous learning and marketability (Alteman and Post, 1996; Hall and Mirvis, 1996, both cited in Sullivan, 1999). According to Van der Heijden (2002), the new psychological contract involves job enrichment and the development of competencies, with an individual's promotion being seen as much more opportunistic and with performance being rewarded by both responsibility and accountability.

Changes within organizational structures have also occurred, with less emphasis now being placed on vertical movement but more on the intrinsic job factors. As a result employees grow in expertise and receive greater challenges and responsibility within their current job. Organizations now require their employees to be adaptable and provide loyalty, knowledge and skills. In return employees expect to be rewarded for their knowledge and skills and be allowed the freedom to make their own decisions.

New models of work organization have also been developed, such as network organizations and professional service firms (Morris, 2000), the latter being based on the boundaryless or intelligent career model. These knowledge-intensive or human-asset-intensive firms are prevalent in the convention and exhibition industry in such organizations as professional conference (PCO) or meeting manager organizations. Such models of work organization can impact on the career and potential career pattern of an individual employed within such an organization.

The convention and exhibition industry is fragmented and demonstrates a predominance of small businesses. There are few major players, apart from the international and national hotel groups and purpose-built convention and exhibition centres, together with a small number of national conference/meeting management organizations. This raises two questions. The first question relates to the impact of such potential career and work models on the structure and format of an individual's career pattern and progression within the industry. The second question relates to the mobility of individuals. It also brings into question whether industry employers are aware of these patterns and their potential implications on the short- and long-term human resource needs. In an ever-increasing global marketplace there is a need to continue to maintain and develop high levels of professionalism and quality of service, to ensure key staff and work teams are retained within the sector in order to benefit from their expertise.

Career Patterns in the Convention and Exhibition Industry

Research undertaken in Australia (McCabe and Savery, 2007; McCabe, 2008) has provided a range of revealing information on the career patterns of individual managers and supervisors in the convention and exhibition industry. Through the use of a structured, self-administered questionnaire and a range of techniques, such as life and work history analysis, information that related to occupational mobility and career history (Ladkin and Riley, 1996; Arthur *et al.*, 1999; Ladkin, 1999) was gathered from individuals. Information sought included type of job, job sector of current and previous employment, job levels and responsibility, sequence of jobs held and frequency of job movement, together with a range of demographic data.

The self-completed survey instrument used four types of measurement scales (nominal, ordinal, interval and ratio). Nominal scales and a checklist investigated an individual's career progression by job sector and area of job responsibility over their last eight jobs. A range of eight jobs had been established in previous studies (Ladkin and Riley, 1996; Ladkin, 2002) as a potential norm. The use of the technique of life and work history analysis provided a methodological approach to obtaining both quantitative and qualitative data of an individual's detailed career history. According to Ladkin (1999), life and work history analysis is an established method of data collection used within the social sciences to examine work histories in conjunction with labour market analysis. For example, in relation to career management, the technique can provide quantitative data in the form of the number of job moves as a measure of labour mobility. Though the method has a potential weakness in that it depends on the quality of an individual's recall, Ladkin (1999) identifies that this can be overcome through the careful use of survey techniques and data collection methods. It has been used in a number of studies by Ladkin (1999) as an appropriate methodology for studying the career paths and labour mobility of hotel general managers.

The target population for the research survey was managers and professionals who worked in the convention and exhibition industry in Australia. They were employed in hotels and other venues, purpose-built convention and exhibition centres, meeting manager or professional conference organizations, convention and visitor bureaus, exhibition organizations and other industry suppliers. McCabe (2008) identifies that the sample frame for the survey was obtained from two sources. The first source was through the Meetings and Events Australia (MEA) national conference, which had the potential to provide a sampling ratio of 45% of its membership. The second source was through the use of a postal survey of 132 four- to five-star hotels with convention and exhibition facilities in Australia, identified from the Facilities Guide/Meeting Planners produced by Convention and Visitor Bureaus in each Australian state capital city. McCabe and Weeks (1999) have previously identified residential venues and hotels with convention and exhibition facilities as an important sector of the convention and exhibition industry in relation to the number of staff employed and the potential career opportunities. Probability sampling was used in both instances (McCabe, 2008). From a potential 484 respondents employed in a range of sectors of the industry (such as hotels and convention venues, professional conference organizers, purpose-built convention and exhibition centres, and convention and visitor bureaus) a statistically valid response rate of 26% (n = 126) was obtained.

Detailed data of the job sectors that an individual had worked in on his/her career path/progression, together with the identification of the individual's job responsibility areas, were presented in McCabe and Savery (2007). As such, this chapter will illustrate, through the use of four case studies, some of the key findings in relation to an individual's career progression apparent from the main research results. The results presented do have some limitations. The first is that the research focus is on the convention and exhibition industry in Australia; it does not include the incentive or special events sectors or countries outside Australia. A further limitation relates to the distribution of the survey instrument, which does not represent the total convention and exhibition industry in Australia.

Results from the overall study revealed that the convention and exhibition industry in Australia is dominated by females (74%), who are highly educated (through vocational and tertiary-level programmes) and who primarily work full time (98%). The industry attracts and retains employees of all age groups. Whilst the predominant group is 26–40, the older age group (individuals in age group 50 plus) is well represented. Though there are many job sectors within the industry, respondents were primarily employed in hotels and convention and exhibition venues and conference and exhibition organizations. They held a wide range of job levels, from managing director, general manager to director, manager, assistant manager and coordinator roles (McCabe and Savery, 2007).

The research provides evidence that, in relation to the profile of a career in the convention and exhibition sector, individuals gain experience in a range of job sectors both within and outside the industry (McCabe and Savery, 2007). For example, PCO or meeting manager organizations, hotels and venues, purpose-built convention and exhibition centres, convention and visitor bureaus, specialized government departments and other convention and exhibition organizations such as audio visual suppliers and specialist technology companies. It is also clear that it is the residential and non-residential sector of hotels, venues and clubs that dominates as the main area of the industry in relation to job opportunities. This is illustrated in the cases presented in Figs 5.1, 5.2 and 5.4, where each individual's first point of entry to the convention and exhibition sector was through employment in the functions/banqueting department of a venue. Having then gained career experience in other sectors of the industry, they returned to the venue sector to take up convention and exhibition-related senior management positions. At the same time, conference organizers – association and in-house – or PCO/meeting manager organizations also provide another key industry employment sector in which to gain career experience, as seen in Fig. 5.3. It is also apparent that a large number of people move into the sector having begun their careers in areas outside the industry.

Career structure – job function and responsibility

Within the convention and exhibition industry, the structure and form of a career is seen to demonstrate horizontal, vertical and diagonal growth. Having entered the convention and exhibition industry, career progression for an individual can involve diagonal job shifts, in terms of industry sub-sector and/or functional responsibility within that sub-sector. Individuals undertake horizontal moves across sectors (intersectorial movement) and diagonal, intrasectorial mobility of job function. This is evident in Fig. 5.1 – the career profile of a convention and exhibition sales and marketing director. In this example the individual had undertaken three job roles in banqueting operations in different venues (horizontal, intersectorial mobility) prior to a diagonal, vertical career move to a further two

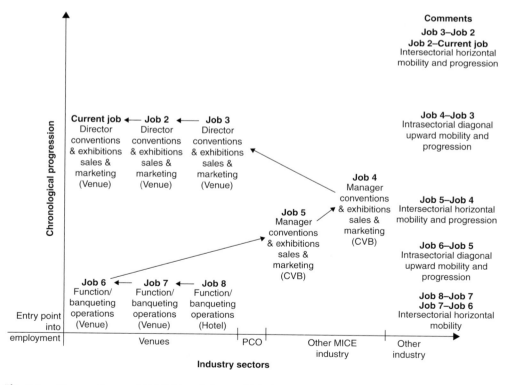

Fig. 5.1. Convention and Exhibition Sales and Marketing Director.

roles in sales and marketing within convention and visitor bureaus. A further intrasectorial, diagonal, vertical move to the role of director of sales and marketing for conventions and exhibitions in a venue was then undertaken; this was followed by subsequent intrasectorial movement to other similar roles within the venue sector.

Figure 5.2 provides an example of an individual who commenced his/her career outside the convention and exhibition industry and whose first three job roles involved inter-industry, diagonal, functional mobility (first role outside the sector, second role within the venue sector, third role involved a further inter-industry move to another industry prior to returning as a convention and exhibition organizer in a PCO firm – Job 5). Jobs 4 and 3 had involved intrasector, diagonal, functional mobility, whilst vertical movement (intrasectorial) had been undertaken in the progression to the individual's current position as general manager of a convention and exhibition venue.

In Fig. 5.3 the individual had commenced their career outside the convention and exhibition industry, but on entering the industry had remained within the PCO sector, progressing their career through a series of diagonal, horizontal and vertical moves in different, small, PCO-type organizations, to his/her current role as principal in a large PCO organization.

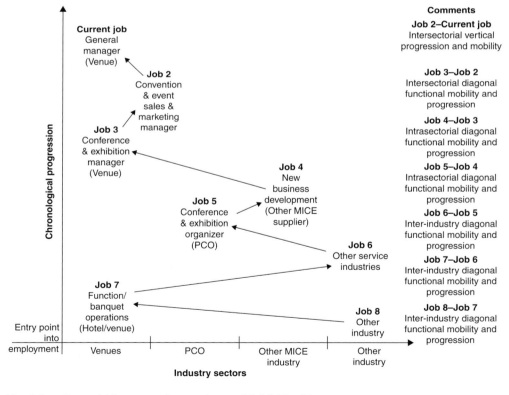

Fig. 5.2.   General Manager – Convention and Exhibition Venue.

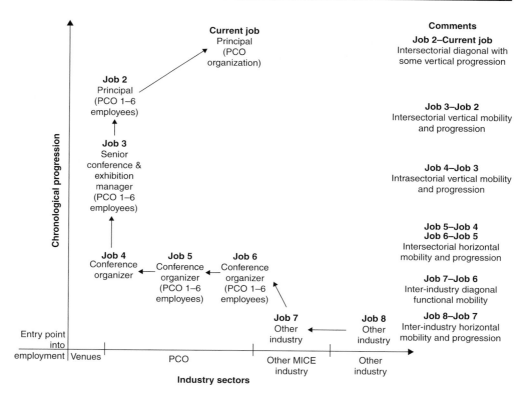

Fig. 5.3. Director/Partner Professional Conference Organization.

For some employees, such as a convention services director in a hotel or venue, career progression may be more structured and formalized, with a clear vertical progression. This is illustrated in the case study in Fig. 5.4, where the individual commenced his/her career in a venue but then left the industry to gain experience in other industry sectors. Having once returned to the venue sector, a clear path of vertical career progression had occurred through undertaking roles as a function/banqueting manager in two different-sized venues prior to gaining a position as director of convention and exhibition services in a large hotel/venue.

Further data presented by McCabe and Savery (2007) provide evidence that there is no clear route of career progression to a particular job, with an individual's career structure and movement seen to go in numerous directions. For example, an individual employed within a PCO or meeting manager organization may have previously worked in sub-sectors within the sector, such as in associations, as an in-house corporate conference organizer, in a venue, in other areas of the convention and exhibition industry (e.g. audio visual supplier) or in a convention and visitor bureau. The initial job shift into the convention and exhibition sector may have been from a job in another industry. As such, individuals move amongst the sectors of the industry in the pursuit of their careers, as illustrated in Figs 5.2 and 5.3.

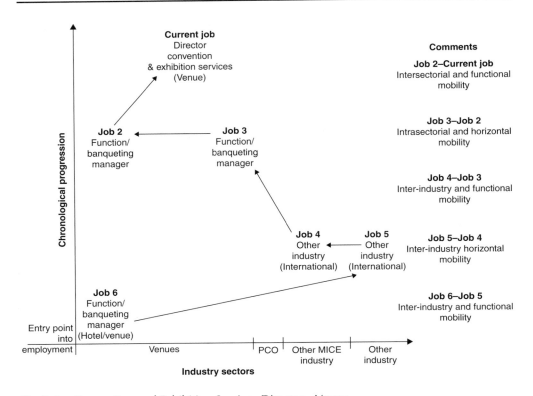

Fig. 5.4. Convention and Exhibition Services Director – Venue.

As an individual pursues a career in the convention and exhibition industry, his/her movement among the sectors of the industry can be identified as 'butterflying' (McCabe and Savery, 2007:112), with, in many instances, no clear path of career progression. The 'butterfly' movement is similar to a butterfly flitting from one flower to another, with 'tasting the nectar' seen as 'the individual building up human capital, gathering expert knowledge through the development of core competencies and professional expertise' (McCabe and Savery, 2007:112).

As an individual follows the 'butterfly' approach and 'flutters' from one sector to another or from one job type to another within a sector, he/she pursues the functional responsibility aspects of career progression. For example, roles in banqueting and function operations, conference and exhibition organizer, new business development, venue convention services manager, and conference and exhibition sales and marketing may have preceded and been undertaken in the career progression to a position of general manager of a convention and exhibition organization, as illustrated in Fig. 5.2 – career case study of a general manager in a convention and exhibition venue.

It would appear that there are therefore multiple directions by which an individual can pursue his/her career progression in the convention and exhibition industry. The process of undertaking diagonal, vertical and horizontal job movements provides the individual with valuable learning opportunities and the potential to increase personal competency ('tasting the nectar'). For the employer there is a potential benefit in acquisition of the new employee's existing skills and competencies.

The structure of a career in the convention and exhibition industry is therefore one of horizontal, vertical and diagonal growth as individuals develop their skills and knowledge in accordance with their goals. Movement is intersectorial, within the industry, as in the case of PCOs, and within a sector (intrasectorial), as found in residential and non-residential venues. It is also clear that hotels and venues play a dominant role in enabling an individual to gain experience in the sector.

Career mobility

The second issue in respect of career patterns relates to the career mobility of individuals in the convention and exhibition industry. It focuses on and explores the type of mobility that a career within the industry might involve.

In undertaking a job change or move into or within the convention and exhibition industry, it is the individual who initiates the job change. Nearly 90% of job moves within the industry are initiated by individuals (McCabe, 2008). This confirms that individuals follow self-directed careers and clearly manage and control their own careers. An individual may enter the convention and exhibition industry after a range of other jobs in an unrelated industry or as a new or young employee. Many people, therefore, have held only three or four jobs in the sector before they undertake a management/supervisor role.

In the progression of a career in the convention and exhibition industry, individuals use both internal (movement into another job role within an organization) and external (movement into a job in another organization) mobility, and use a range of career-planning strategies to assist them in this mobility. Strategies such as networking, regular scanning of job advertisements in the newspaper and on the Internet, recognition of the potential for chance opportunities and keeping up to date with potential opportunities within the organization through colleagues and via internal bulletins are among those that have been identified (McCabe, 2008). It seems that individuals both search their present organizations and look at other employers when they want to move job.

Individuals change jobs approximately every 2 to 3 years, though there is some evidence of individuals who change job less frequently. What is apparent is that to reach their current positions less than 50% of individuals have held more than four jobs within the convention and exhibition sector (McCabe, 2008). Indeed some of these managers and supervisors may not have direct overall experience in the sector prior to their current positions. They may, however, have brought with them, in their 'kitbag of skills', generic core management skills and competencies. According to Van der Heijden (2001), changing jobs frequently is not always detrimental but can increase an individual's level of employability, and assist them to build networks and gain competence and experience. It is also a way to build up professional knowledge and skills.

A job move within the convention and exhibition industry may or may not always involve relocation to another city or area. In Australia, the close geographical proximity of convention and exhibition organizations within, for example, the main capital cities could mean that individuals within the industry are aware of the opportunities in other firms and other firms are aware of the bright stars in their competitors (Gunz *et al.*, 2000).

The final issue that relates to an individual's career mobility is job/sectorial and functional mobility. It is now recognized that it is highly likely that a large proportion of people will have several careers in their lifetime (Gunz *et al.*, 2000), with nearly all careers crossing multiple boundaries (Arthur *et al.*, 1999). In order to progress a career in the convention and exhibition industry, there is a need to gain experience in a hotel or venue either in operations or in a sales and marketing capacity. Once in the industry, individuals take a range of operational and functional roles in order to build up their skill base and reach their current career positions.

The situation in PCO organizations is different. Individuals in PCO firms have the tendency to only have one job within the industry prior to joining the PCO firm. PCO organizations could be considered as professional services firms (Gunz *et al.*, 2000). The levels of mobility of senior staff in these organizations could impact on the high levels of commercial secrecy required of firms who rely on the knowledge of key senior staff with regard to the intimate details of their clientele (Gunz *et al.*, 2000). As a result these organizations may need to retain the expertise of their key senior managers.

In summary, there is a clear indication of levels of mobility in the careers of individuals in the convention and exhibition industry. This mobility is self-directed, occurs every 2 to 3 years, with individuals using both the internal and external job market in their search for a career move. An individual's career mobility will also be across job sectors and may involve functional mobility. In the pursuit of a career, individuals demonstrate extensive intra- and intersectorial, inter-industry and geographical mobility, spending, on average, 2–3 years in a job. Any international experience is primarily gained in Europe, but movement also occurs within cities and states within Australia.

Implications for the Individual and Convention and Exhibition Organizations

The information presented to date has a number of implications for both the individual and employers in the convention and exhibition industry. For the individual the information that relates to career patterns and potential career progression within and between the industry sectors is a useful tool to assist both entrants and existing employees in determining a potential career path and pattern. Entrants into the industry should also recognize the role that hotels and venues play in the provision of career opportunities in the sector and the value of gaining experience in either operations or sales and marketing. In undertaking careers in the convention and exhibition industry, individuals should also be prepared to 'butterfly' in order to 'taste the nectar' and build up their 'kitbag of skills' and competencies to ensure they are both applicable and transferable between companies and within specific industry contexts. They need to ensure the currency of their human capital.

Employers in the industry should not view the movement of individuals into and within the various sectors of the industry as detrimental. New employees can bring a range of core skills, competencies and know-how. The movement of individuals between jobs in the various sectors may be to ensure that their level of employability and currency of human capital is maintained. For PCO organizations, however, there may be a more specific need to retain senior staff to ensure the retention of the organization's specific knowledge (for example, client-specific characteristics) and know-how. As such, PCO and similar organizations could introduce strategies to assist the retention of key senior staff.

Information on career mobility and how people move within the industry in order to progress their careers is important for employing organizations. It provides information on the use of the labour market and how individuals progress and develop their careers. It has implications for the recruitment of new employees. For example, a potential employer should not expect to see a linear progression in the career profile of a job applicant but should be prepared to recruit individuals who have undertaken job moves both within and outside the industry (McCabe, 2008). The potential employer should recognize that the job applicant may bring a range of transferable skills that are highly desirable for the organization. A further implication is in relation to staff retention. For example, in order to retain managers or supervisors, small businesses within the convention and exhibition industry should seek to provide training and development opportunities for these individuals in order to retain their knowledge and skills within the organization. The provision of such training and development would enable these individuals to update and maintain the currency of their human capital and ensure their long-term employability.

As previously identified, the convention and exhibition industry is predominantly made up of small to medium-sized enterprises that operate in a highly competitive environment. There may be benefits from the levels of job mobility and the recognition by individuals and the industry of the importance of networks. As a result, the convention and exhibition industry could benefit at one level from ongoing experimentation, innovation, and collective learning and entrepreneurship by individuals. The professional and social networks developed could minimize the search and switching costs of the potential labour mobility. The levels of labour mobility within the structure of the industry and the use of networks to project-manage events could be a strength.

This chapter has explored the career patterns of individuals in the convention and exhibition industry, a key sector of the overall events industry. Given that the sector is a new industry within the 'new economy', it is important to determine the format and structure of a career in the sector and identify whether new patterns of careers have emerged. The notion of 'butterfly' progress as a career pattern in the convention and exhibition industry is important to the understanding of careers within the sector and to the long-term sustainability of the industry.

References

Arthur, M.B., Hall, D.T. and Lawrence, B.S. (1989) *Handbook of Career Theory.* Cambridge University Press, Cambridge.

Arthur, M.B., Inkson, K. and Pringle, J.K. (1999) *The New Careers: Individual Action and Economic Change.* Sage, London.

Gunz, H., Evans, M. and Jalland, M. (2000) Career boundaries in a 'boundaryless world'. In: Peiperl, M.A., Arthur, M.B., Goffee, R. and Morris, T. (eds) *Career Frontiers: New Conceptions of Working Lives.* Oxford University Press, Oxford, pp. 24 –53.

Handy, C. (1994) *The Empty Raincoat: Making Sense of the Future.* Arrow Books Ltd, Random House Australia Pty Ltd, Sydney.

Kaye, B. and Jordan Evans, S. (1999) *Love 'em or Lose 'em: Getting Good People to Stay.* Berrerr-Koehler Pub. Inc., San Francisco, California.

Ladkin, A. (1999) Life and work history analysis: the value of this research method for hospitality and tourism. *Tourism Management* 20, 37–45.

Ladkin, A. (2002) Career analysis: a case study of hotel general managers in Australia. *Tourism Management* 23, 379–388.

Ladkin, A. and Riley, M. (1996) Mobility and structure in the career paths of UK hotel general managers: a labour market hybrid or bureaucratic model? *Tourism Management* 17, 443–452.

McCabe, V.S. (2008) Strategies for career planning and development in the convention and exhibition industry in Australia. *International Journal of Hospitality Management* 27(2), 222–231.

McCabe, V.S. and Ladkin, A. (2002) Career motivation and commitment in the conventions and exhibitions industry: exploratory evidence from the UK and Australia. In: Jago, L., Deery, M., Harris, R., Hede, A.-M. and Allen, J. (eds) *Proceedings of the Events and Place Making Conference.* UTS: Australian Centre for Event Management, Sydney, pp. 144–174.

McCabe, V.S. and Savery, L.K. (2007) 'Butterflying' a new career pattern for Australia? Empirical evidence. *Journal of Management Development* 26(2), 103–116.

McCabe, V.S. and Weeks, P. (1999) Convention services management in Sydney four to five star hotels. *Journal of Convention and Exhibition Management* 1(4), 67–84.

Mirvis, P.H. and Hall, D.T. (1996) Psychological success and the boundaryless career. In: Arthur, M.B. and Rousseau, D.M. (eds) *The Boundaryless Career: a New Employment Principle for New Organizational Eras.* Oxford University Press, New York, pp. 237–255.

Morris, T. (2000) Promotion policies and knowledge bases in the professional services firm. In: Peiperl, M.A., Arthur, M.B., Goffee, R. and Morris, T. (eds) *Career Frontiers: New Conceptions of Working Lives.* Oxford University Press, Oxford, pp. 138–152.

Parker, P. and Arthur, M.B. (2000) Careers, organizing and community. In: Peiperl, M.A., Arthur, M.B., Goffee, R. and Morris, T. (eds) *Career Frontiers: New Conceptions of Working Lives.* Oxford University Press, Oxford, pp. 99–122.

Riley, M. and Ladkin, A. (1994) Career theory and tourism: the development of a basic analytical framework. *Progress in Tourism, Recreation and Hospitality Management* 6, 225–237.

Sullivan, S.E. (1999) The changing nature of careers: a review and research agenda. *Journal of Management* 25(3), 457–484.

Van der Heijden, B. (2001) Encouraging professional development in small and medium sized firms: the influence of career history and job content. *Career Development International* 6(3), 156–168.

Van der Heijden, B. (2002) Prerequisites to guarantee life-long employability. *Personnel Review* 31(1), 44–61.

6 Career Theory and Major Event Employment

Leo Jago and Judith Mair

Victoria University, Australia

Introduction

The field of major events has grown enormously in recent years and has been seen by many as offering attractive employment opportunities. Despite this, however, the field has not provided much in the way of career options. This chapter explores the relevance of career theory to the field of major events and examines the impact that generational change is having on the sector, namely the emergence of Generation Y in the workforce. It has been found that the key characteristics of careers are changing in all sectors of the economy, and the advent of Generation Y into the workforce is expediting these changes. The chapter also examines how the very nature of major events, in particular their episodic nature, affects career options for staff working in this sector.

Background

Since the 1980s, the event sector in many parts of the world has experienced meteoric growth. Whilst so much of the attraction for host destinations of staging events relates to their potential economic impact, it is now recognized that events also have a very important social dimension and can result in 'psychic income' for local communities. In relation to the above-mentioned growth rate of events, demonstrations of this growth can be seen in the exponential increase in the number of events on offer, the academic journals that have been produced, event associations, conferences and education programmes on offer.

In 1999 there were only four Australian universities that offered specializations in event management (Jago and Harris, 2001). Since that time, most Australian universities involved in hospitality and tourism education now offer event programmes, and these have become some of the most popular courses in terms of numbers of applicants and entry scores in those particular institutions.

Indeed, for many of these institutions, increased demand for event management programmes has more than offset the general decline in demand for places in tourism management programmes. It should also be noted that many technical and further education institutions now offer programmes in event management. Similar increases in numbers of event management courses, at both further and higher-education level, are to be found in both Europe and North America. This huge increase in demand for event management training highlights the fact that many people see prospects for careers in the events sector.

There is common agreement that the event sector is divided into two main components, namely business events and major events. Much of the glamour and media profile in the event sector relates to major events, and based on discussions with students in event management courses since the late 1990s, the majority of them aim to pursue careers in this division of the market. Although there appears to be much less interest in the business events component of the sector, business events provide many more employment options, particularly in relation to full-time and regular part-time positions. Research recently carried out into the career opportunities for event management students at an Australian university indicated that, along with venues, the corporate and association meeting sectors provided the best opportunities for full-time, permanent employment (Junek *et al.*, 2008).

In the business events component of the events sector, much of the employment is found in venues, either convention centres or hotels specializing in business events. Given that business events involve ongoing business, there is a raft of full-time employment opportunities as well as many regular part-time and casual positions. Whilst this part of the event business may not have the glamour of major events, it is certainly possible to develop long-term careers in this sector, as businesses within the sector have clearly defined career structures (McCabe, 2008).

It should also be noted that many event positions are not advertised under this heading; for example, there are positions within large accounting organizations, schools and car dealerships that are clearly event related, but they tend to be listed in the newspaper as related to marketing or other more traditional fields of employment. This illustrates that event-related jobs are not always seen to be part of the events industry and that candidates pursuing careers in event-related jobs may not consider themselves to have a career in the events industry itself.

Career Theory

Whilst careers have traditionally been thought of as 'a sequence of work positions of increasing responsibility and seniority over time' (Adamson *et al.*, 1998:251), there has been a more recent push to take a much broader perspective. Traditionally, organizations were very hierarchical in structure, with most having a large number of 'steps' upon which employees could aspire to climb. During the 1980s, however, there was a strong push for flatter organizational structures (*inter alia* Arthur *et al.*, 1999), and as a consequence, many organizations dispensed with large sections of their middle management. Whymark and Ellis

(1999:117) state that there are very few occupations which offer 'jobs for life' and, indeed, that 'organizations are no longer comfortable with employees who are equipped only to perform narrowly-defined job roles'. Therefore, the traditional view of the career as a hierarchical progression within one company is no longer relevant in today's job world.

This change, which resulted in a reduced number of levels within organizations, prompted employees to re-think their views in relation to careers; given the reduced number of organization levels, fewer staff could now consider the prospects of a management position and thus workplace satisfaction has to be derived in other ways, such as via an increased breadth of experience. In the past, careers tended to be based on moving up the corporate ladder, which relied on the goodwill and support of supervisors. Nowadays, there is much more acceptance of the view that individuals take more responsibility for their own careers and the basis upon which such careers are judged. Increasingly, careers are seen as a means of personal development for the individual (Shepard, 1984). There is now recognition that 'the chronological component of career theory [be] de-emphasized in favour of the situational' (Adamson et al., 1998:255). The relationship with employers is becoming shorter term and there are more opportunities for lateral development instead of simply moving up the hierarchy of the organization.

There have been many attempts to define the new career paradigm. Arthur and Rousseau (1996) wrote on the 'boundaryless' career, one which, by their definition, spans a range of possible career forms which defy traditional employment assumptions. According to Adamson et al. (1998:253), 'The term "career" can be defined simply – it implies a route which one is following, a route which has both direction and purpose'. Careers are now built from experiences with a number of organizations, and options for self-employment, consultancy and temporary employment can all be woven into a recognizable career pattern (Whymark and Ellis, 1999). The traditional career offered security of employment – new career patterns offer security that will be anchored not in a particular organization but in the portable skills or employability of the individual (Mallon, 1998).

There has been a clear move away from the traditional notion of carrying out your job role to the best of your abilities and waiting for promotion and towards the notion of using work experience to improve 'employability' and 'marketability'. Van der Heijden (2002:44) defined employability simply as 'the capability of being employed in a job', but the word seems to have a broader meaning – not just being able to get a job but being able to succeed against the competition by having a range of diverse, yet relevant, work experience on a curriculum vitae (CV). According to Adamson (1997:256), new organizations are seeking staff with a 'rich CV' instead of simply a 'good CV', whereby these proactive staff will probably have worked in a range of 'work and non-work activities', including periods of time away from the organization, provided that there has been a learning period in the time away.

> The new career message therefore no longer necessarily implies a long-term relationship between employer and employee but rather a series of mutually beneficial transactions based on both organizational and individual needs.
>
> (Adamson, 1997:256)

In moving away from the very rigid hierarchical career structures of the past, there are substantial opportunities to do things quite differently and in a much more flexible manner. Since the sign of career success is less likely to be movement up the hierarchy, there is potentially less attachment to individual employers and more opportunities to take time out for personal and professional development. Indeed, Van der Heijden (2001) considers career mobility to be one of the best ways for employees to enhance their career prospects. She highlights four positive effects of career mobility: 'It increases employees' employability, it helps employees build their own networks, it permits transfer to a more powerful function in an organization with better prospects and [it allows] employees to gain a wider spectrum of experiences and competencies' (p. 158).

Generational Changes in the Workplace

There are now four main generations in the workplace, and the fact that each generation has different characteristics poses some interesting challenges for managers. There are a variety of labels for each generation, and although there is some dispute over the exact dates that are apportioned to each generation, the most commonly used distinctions (Eisner, 2005) are 'Traditionalists' (born before 1945), 'Baby Boomers' (born between 1945 and 1964), 'Gen X' (born between 1965 and 1980) and 'Gen Y' (born after 1980). Theory suggests that each generation can be characterized by the social context in which people grow and develop interests, which influences their norms, values and beliefs (Baruch, 2004). Baruch (2004) goes on to suggest that this in turn influences their career aspirations, career choice and career progress.

Some of the changes identified in the manner in which employees relate to careers can probably be attributed to generational change. Research that has been undertaken on different generational groups indicates quite clearly that there are substantial differences in attitudes and behaviours between generations. For example, Generation Y (Gen Y) employees are likely to have some experience in the workplace already, having worked part time throughout their education (unlike the older generations) and are therefore much more likely than their older colleagues to have firm ideas about what they expect from a job (Broadbridge et al., 2007). Broadbridge et al. (2007) also suggest that Gen Y is more likely to be interested in the fast track, feeling that once they have received a degree or other qualification, this equips them for higher roles. Employers on the other hand, who are generally from the Traditionalist or Baby Boomer generations, are less likely to be in agreement with such sentiments, as, anecdotally, employers seem to prefer experienced workers over those straight out of university. According to Martin (2005), Gen Y is characterized by independent, entrepreneurial thinkers who relish responsibility, demand immediate feedback and expect a sense of accomplishment hourly. This snapshot illustrates both the opportunities offered by this generation and the challenges associated with managing them.

Broadbridge et al. (2007), whilst highlighting that there is little previous academic work on the characteristics and work expectations of Gen Y, stress the importance of understanding this, as Gen Y now forms a substantial percentage of the workforce (up to 30% in the USA according to Eisner, 2005). A further interesting point to consider in relation to Gen Y is that, in the USA, two experienced workers now leave the workforce for every one who enters it (Eisner, 2005). Assuming that such statistics are likely to be replicated in other Western, developed countries, the importance of understanding generational differences becomes clear. In addition, the move towards the 'boundaryless' career (Arthur, 1994), and the fact that relationships between employers and employees are now more transactional and short term, suggests that, for this generation, the notion of 'career' is entirely different. Baruch (2004) terms it the multi-directional career, as opposed to the linear career of the Baby Boomers. He suggests that people now expect an organization to serve them, rather than the other way round.

Amar (2004) suggests three main sources of work motivation for Gen Y – the job, the outcomes of the job (rewards, etc.) and the organizational system (policies, practices, culture and image of the organization). He also notes specifically that job security is not a substantial motivator for this generation – they do not expect long-term employment. In their study into the employment of Gen Y in the retail industry, Broadbridge *et al.* (2007) report that their findings support these three main sources of motivation. Barron *et al.* (2007) reported that Gen Y favours achieving a work–life balance over high rates of pay, and this, when combined with the apparent entrepreneurial nature of Gen Y, may lead to the creation of more small businesses and fewer large organizations.

Barron *et al.* (2007) examined the situation in the hospitality industry and concluded that the hospitality industry needs to work hard to counter any negative images of the industry that Gen Y might have formed whilst working part time during their studies; these negative images were reported to have negatively affected students' perceptions of a future career in hospitality management. It is entirely possible that the experiences students have of working at events whilst still studying (possibly low pay, food and beverage-type roles) may also exercise a negative influence on their choice of a career in the events industry. At the same time, however, the literature seems to support the view that Gen Y is more willing to move jobs in order to experience new challenges (Baruch, 2004; Martin, 2005; Barron *et al.*, 2007; Broadbridge *et al.*, 2007), and for the major events industry this may be seen as positive. Moving from event to event may provide the new challenges and new directions that Gen Y is looking for, whilst still providing the responsibility and sense of accomplishment that is sought by this generation (Martin, 2005).

The Application of Career Theory in the Events Industry

A number of identifiable trends that represent new and different ways of working can be discerned, many of which are relevant to, and can be observed in, the events industry. McCabe (2008:227–230) suggests the idea of 'butterflying', in that 'the butterfly movement is similar to a butterfly flitting between one flower and another tasting the nectar'. Her research shows evidence of this type of movement between jobs in the business events industry, and it is even more likely that this would also be the case in the major events industry. She suggests that there are high levels of intrasectorial, intersectorial and inter-industry mobility within the business events area and proposes that such mobility should be seen as 'healthy for the industry', as individuals may bring highly transferable skills to the organization and may provide 'cross-fertilization of ideas, innovation and experimentation'.

Mallon (1998:361) described the portfolio career, where someone undertakes 'bits and pieces of work for different clients'. The self-employed nature of the portfolio career may not be suited to everyone, but she does note evidence that this type of career is growing in popularity. In terms of the events industry, there are a number of small and medium-sized businesses involved in supplying services to events and in the organization of events, and a number of these business owners fit into the portfolio career bracket.

The concept of the 'flexpert', as someone who is both flexible and in possession of expertise (Van der Heijden, 2002), is also relevant to the events industry. Such people, who according to Van der Heijden (2002:46) 'are capable of acquiring more than one area of expertise within adjacent, or radically different fields', abound in the events industry, which is anecdotally famous for its challenges and variety.

Finally, the notion of organizational groups, for example groups of people who work seasonally in different areas yet manage to make a full-time career of it (for example those who work in the ski fields in winter and at beach resorts in summer), is also a useful one to consider in relation to the events industry. There are people who have expertise in running events – perhaps they are flexperts – who are therefore in demand at various times around the year to work on a number of different event projects.

Within the tourism industry and more particularly in the hospitality industry, research has indicated that an internal labour market exists (Ladkin and Riley, 1996:445) and that, within these domains, career mobility is encouraged, so that 'looking outside rather than within [the organization] becomes a normative process'. This reflects the intersectorial and intrasectorial mobility described by McCabe (2008) and is likely to apply within the major events sector as well. A successful example of this type of internal labour market is evident in Silicon Valley, California; Arthur and Rousseau (1996:29–32) suggest that 'this type of intercompany milieu underlies the success of industry regions like the Silicon Valley' and go on to suggest that movement of employees between organizations allows the 'unbounded knowledge transfer of new processes and problem solving' in the Silicon Valley region. Arthur and Rousseau (1996) propose that this is one of the reasons why industries are so often clustered in geographical regions. There were many factors that led to the development of the events industry in Melbourne but the availability of a pool of experienced and trained staff was an important factor in the success of Melbourne's events industry.

Careers in Major Events

In the major event component of the event sector, all events are classed as episodic, even though this is not strictly correct based on the definition of the term 'episodic', which according to the *Concise Oxford Dictionary* means 'occurring at irregular intervals'. Although most mega-events, such as the Olympic Games, World Cup Soccer and the like, tend to be staged in a single destination only once, most major events tend to be staged on an annual basis at a particular location, which strictly speaking could not be classed as irregular.

The fact that major events by their very nature are staged infrequently poses a huge challenge in terms of attracting the calibre of staff needed to stage a high-quality event. In conventional organizations, the staffing levels remain fairly constant throughout the year and peak periods are managed by employing a small number of part-time or casual staff. The high level of employment stability in terms of the conventional organization means that suitable staff can be attracted and developed over time, to meet the needs of the individuals as well as the organization. Career structures are put in place to maximize the long-term benefits for both individuals and organizations. Major events, however, are termed 'pulsating' organizations (Hanlon and Jago, 2004) because of the manner in which they start with a very small number of staff and build to large numbers of staff and volunteers at the time of the event, and then shrink back to their original size soon after the event has concluded. This pulsating effect makes the management and staffing of major events so much more difficult than is the case in conventional organizations and means that it is much harder to attract the type of staff that the organization would wish to attract.

For even the largest of the major events that are staged on an annual basis, there is rarely more than a handful of staff who are employed on a full-time, continuing basis. For the vast majority of these events, increased labour in the run up to the event and during the event is provided by employees on short-term contracts, casuals and volunteers. According to Hanlon and Jago (2004), pulsating organizations tend to have very flat organization structures for most of the year and expand in the event period by adding teams reporting to a small number of continuing, full-time staff. As a consequence of this flat structure, there has not tended to be much opportunity for full-time staff to seek promotion as part of a long-term career in the sector. For many of the smaller major events, there is only a single part-time director for most of the year, and additional manpower is provided largely by casual employees and volunteers during the peak event periods.

Given the situation outlined above, it has not generally been possible for major event organizations to offer their small number of continuing employees any form of career structure. This has meant that many do not stay long term in the sector as, despite the passion that many have for the sector, there has not traditionally been much opportunity for them to develop over time.

Key Changes in Relation to Careers in Major Events

Since the late 1990s, there have been some substantial changes to the field of major events, which have had quite an impact on the potential for continuing employment in the sector and for the introduction of career plans as are found in most non-pulsating organizations. The first of these changes is the phenomenon of key staff rotating between different major event organizations, so that there is continuing year-round employment available, but across a number of organizations rather than within a single organization. The second change is the growing incidence of companies being established to run multiple events. A key outcome of both of these changes has been that they have provided mechanisms via which staff in the sector can develop more substantive longer-term careers and thus provide a basis to encourage experienced and well-credentialed staff to remain in the sector.

Over the last decade in particular, the event field has become more highly professional and there has been wide recognition of a skill set required by key event staff if major events are to realize their potential. Given these required skills, and the fact that they cannot be developed within the confines and time-frame of a specific event, it has been necessary to build what could be described as an internal labour market (ILM). In other words, it has been necessary to encourage the development of a group of key event staff with well-developed skills and expertise who are effectively employed by the sector and move from one event to another. These staff take the key driving roles within a particular event organization and take the lead in bringing on the additional staff and training them to ensure that the event functions well. For most industries, an ILM is required if the sector is to flourish. For example, a requirement for the information technology (IT) industry to develop in a particular economy is to have a pool of experts in IT who can move between companies to underpin their development. These experts help train others in the sector and can build their own careers by moving to more senior positions in larger organizations. This same approach has been adopted in the major events sector. A difference in the major events sector, however, is that the timelines are much shorter and moves are 'forced' in the major event organizations that are 'one-offs' in a particular destination, such as the Olympics, rather than annual events.

Early examples of this phenomenon were seen in Australia after the staging of the Olympics in Sydney in 2000. As a result of working on the Olympics, many staff built key expertise in various aspects of the Games and became 'hooked' on the event experience. After the Sydney Olympics, these staff moved to other major event organizations, such as the organizing committee for the Athens Olympics. In the 8 years since the Sydney Olympics, a core of the staff trained for the Sydney Olympics has moved from one event to another and their expertise has been exploited in a range of settings. These staff have effectively used this opportunity to create careers across a range of organizations.

Even though the development of an ILM within the major events sector has provided a mechanism for long-term careers for key event staff, this important opportunity will not be fully exploited until the sector becomes less fragmented and recognizes the need to take a sectoral approach to developing staff. The short-term nature of the sector has acted as an inhibitor to this opportunity. In other sectors where operations tend to be more constant over time, it is much easier for industry associations to form, which can provide a platform for the sharing of knowledge and staff. The pulsating and short-term nature of the major events sector has worked against the formation of associations of like organizations, although this is changing.

The other approach that has been adopted to get around the staffing consequences of the episodic and short-term nature of major events has been the formation of larger organizations that take on the management of a range of individual major events. This development tends to take out the cyclical nature of the major event sector by having a range of events that are staged by a single organization at different times of the year, so that staff within the organization can move from one event to another in a seamless fashion. This provides the basis for the long-term employment of major event expertise, which can then be rotated between events. From the event perspective, it means that there is a pool of qualified staff available to manage the event without the requirement to recruit in a tight labour market, not knowing whether anyone may be attracted, especially if the employment opportunity is short term. For staff working in the sector, this development provides them with a more stable career opportunity as well as the chance to work on a range of events without having to change employers. The critical mass of event staff that can be employed by these organizations means that there can be staff with complementary skills and the opportunity for individual staff to build expertise across a range of activities. As these organizations are larger and provide ongoing employment, there is ample opportunity for careers to be fostered.

Conclusion

Expectations in relation to careers are changing and there is now reduced expectation that one will spend extended periods in a single organization, moving up a hierarchical structure. It is becoming more commonly accepted that one must manage one's own career and that this will probably entail moving from one organization to another on a regular basis, and acquiring skills and experience that will make one more employable over time. A result of this change, or perhaps a driver of this change, has been the changing needs and expectations of Gen Y. This generation, which is often termed the 'me generation', wants more immediate gratification and does not tend to see merit in a long-term involvement with a single organization. There is a trend for this generation to take sideways moves in terms of employment and to take time out of the workforce for other personal development activities such as travel.

The traditional career model was problematic for major events as it did not provide many opportunities for people to develop careers in the sector owing to the pulsating effect and the fact that employees felt compelled to remain with a single employer. With the changed career structure, where it is acceptable to move from one company to another, acquiring skills and experience along the way, there are now more options for longer-term careers in major events. As the need for an internal labour market in the sector becomes more widely acknowledged, there will probably be a greater range of flexible employment options. The advent of larger organizations that manage a range of events has also helped in providing more regular employment opportunities in this sector.

References

Adamson, S. (1997) Career as a vehicle for the realization of self. *Career Development International* 2(5), 245–253.

Adamson, S., Doherty, N. and Viney, C. (1998) The meaning of career revisited: implications for theory and practice. *British Journal of Management* 9, 251–259.

Amar, A.D. (2004) Motivating knowledge workers to innovate: a model integrating motivation dynamics and antecedents. *European Journal of Innovation Management* 7(2), 89–101.

Arthur, M.B. (1994) The boundaryless career: a new perspective for organizational enquiry. *Journal of Organizational Behavior* 15, 295–306.

Arthur, M.B. and Rousseau D.M. (1996) A career lexicon for the 21st century. *Academy of Management Executive* 10(4), 28–39.

Arthur, M.B., Inkson, K. and Pringle, J.K. (1999) *The New Careers: Individual Action and Economic Change*. Sage, London.

Barron, P., Maxwell, G., Broadbridge, A. and Ogden, S. (2007) Careers in hospitality management: Generation Y's experiences and perceptions. *Journal of Hospitality and Tourism Management* 14(2), 119–128.

Baruch, Y. (2004) Transforming careers: from linear to multidirectional career paths. *Career Development International* 9(1), 58–73.

Broadbridge, A., Maxwell, G. and Ogden, S. (2007) Experiences, perceptions and expectations of retail employment for Generation Y. *Career Development International* 12(6), 523–544.

Eisner, S.P. (2005) Managing Generation Y. *SAM Advanced Management Journal* Autumn, 4–15.

Hanlon, C. and Jago, L.K. (2004) The challenge of retaining personnel in major sport event organizations. *Event Management* 9(1/2), 39–49.

Jago, L.K. and Harris, R. (2001) Event education in Australia: demand versus supply. Presentation at Asia Pacific Tourism Association 7th Annual Conference, Manila.

Junek, O., Lockstone, L. and Mair, J. (2008) Experiential learning in event management education: do industry placements in degree courses complement jobs available in the events industry? In: Richardson, S., Fredline, L. and Ternel, M. (eds) *Proceedings of the 18th Annual CAUTHE Conference*, Griffith University, Gold Coast, Australia, CD-ROM.

Ladkin, A. and Riley, M. (1996) Mobility and structure in the career paths of UK hotel managers: a labour market hybrid of the bureaucratic model? *Tourism Management* 17(6), 443–452.

Mallon, M. (1998) The portfolio career: pushed or pulled to it? *Personnel Review* 27(5), 361–377.

Martin, C. (2005) From high maintenance to high productivity. *Industrial and Commercial Training* 37(1), 39–44.

McCabe, V.S. (2008) Strategies for career planning and development in the convention and exhibition industry in Australia. *International Journal of Hospitality Management* 27, 222–231.

Shepard, H.A. (1984) On the realization of human potential: a path with a heart. In: Arthur, M.B., Bailyn L., Levinson, D.J. and Shepard, H.A. (eds) *Working with Careers*. Columbia University Press, New York, pp. 25–46.

Van der Heijden, B. (2001) Encouraging professional development in small and medium-sized firms. The influence of career history and job content. *Career Development International* 6(3), 156–168.

Van der Heijden, B. (2002) Pre-requisites to guarantee life-long employability. *Personnel Review* 31, 44–61.

Whymark, K. and Ellis, S. (1999) Whose career is it anyway? Options for career management in flatter organization structures. *Career Development International* 4(2), 117–120.

7 New Professionalism in the Event Sector and its Impact in Hungary

KATALIN FORMÁDI AND CSILLA RAFFAI

University of Pannonia, Hungary

Introduction

The growing recognition of the role of events as motivators for tourism and catalysts for destination competitiveness has led to a subsequent growth of this sector, which has implications for human resources and on the professionalism of this field. Equally there has been an increase in the need for qualified personnel who are able to create, organize, coordinate and manage events, but, as is generally the case with such newly emerging sectors of the economy, the provision of training for such personnel has lagged behind demand. The absence of a developed professional culture means that there is also huge variation in the qualification level of persons managing events. However, although it has been widely argued that event management is, in fact, a profession (Goldblatt, 2005; Harris, 2005; cited in Van der Wagen, 2007), what it means to be a profession and the concept of professionalism itself are shifting phenomena. In this exploratory research we provide an insight into what direction professionalism is taking in the field of event management in Hungary. Interviews were undertaken with professional associations and a survey was conducted with event-organizing companies, and the responses form the basis for the discussion that follows. The level of professionalism is examined on the basis of criteria articulated in classics such as Greenwood (1957) and more recent approaches (Evetts, 2006). The research reveals what the industry sees as the skills, abilities and competencies required for event managers.

Professionalization

Professionalization may be defined as a process by which occupations gain their standing as a profession by identifying attributes which separate professional work from that of other kinds. According to the structuralist–functionalist approach, a system of norms outlines the boundaries of a profession and the profession/occupation continuum is based on a set of criteria. The most cited list of professional attributes is that of Greenwood (1957, cited in Hall, 1994:44 and Auster, 1996:14), which defines professions as possessing:

1. A systematic body of theory.
2. A professional authority over clients.
3. Formal and informal community sanction.
4. A regulative code of ethics regarding appropriate professional behaviour.
5. A professional culture (norms, symbols, language).

As professional affiliations are not stable – first, because of the dynamics of personal careers and, secondly, owing to the transformations of professions – the occupation/profession continuum is used to define levels of professionalization.

The new discourse of professionalization develops a more flexible theoretical approach, which can be used in diverse working contexts and examines both the occupational/organizational level and the individual level (Evetts, 2006). Evetts groups the various forms of knowledge-based, service-type jobs into two types of professions. The first are characterized by managerial control of work, hierarchical structures of authority, accountability and standardized work practices, and are mainly based on occupational certificates or training and are thus more formal and objective in their organization. The second type is structured in a more innovative, flexible way, involving more independence in decision making and a more collegial form of authority, and is based on trust on the part of both the client and the employer. Work is based on the relevancy of education, training and occupational socialization processes (Evetts, 2006). We will turn this distinction into two types, reshaping Evetts' categories into organizational and entrepreneurial ones. With this distinction we refer to the new kind of employment described by Voß and Pongratz (2001) under their 'entreployee' concept, which opens up a new, integrative interpretation of the terms 'occupation' and 'profession'. There is a shift away from the Taylorist distinction between managing ('profession') work and implementing ('occupation') work: 'to free up the usual boundaries of the traditional employee in the workplace in nearly all dimensions – time, space, content, qualifications, cooperation – and enhance their own responsibility through strategies of increased flexibility and "self-organization" in the workplace' (Voß and Pongratz, 2001:241).

In this new approach, self-control on the job, i.e. a high level of independence and influence over one's own activities, becomes very important. The higher level of autonomy in day-to-day work (in controlling resources, time, etc.) has an impact on the commitment to the job and the employee's motivation. Flexibility and self-control have another impact on the issue of work–life balance, as the life world is more subordinated to work, or in another approach is more twinned with it. The entreployee needs self-rationalization and self-determination to an extent in daily life and with regard to work schedules. Nevertheless, this usually involves an increased work load, as well as the necessity to use resources from the private sphere (both material and temporal) (Formádi, 2008).

Research Approach

The aim of this chapter is to examine the state of professionalization in the field of event management in Hungary, and to define the professional characteristics of an event manager and to examine the work characteristics from the new approaches to characterizing professions, such as self-control, flexibility and autonomy. A mixed methodology of semi-structured interviews with professional associations and a survey of managers of Hungarian event companies provides an insight into the objective characteristics of this relatively new profession, which has developed in Hungary since the 1990s.

Tourism employment in general, and the field of event management in Hungary in particular, is an under-researched field of study. The main research question is to identify to what extent professionalization has been formulated and organized by the sector itself – the event managers/event businesses and event-related professional associations – in order to promote the field. Simultaneously with a survey, semi-structured interviews were designed to examine the role of event-related professional associations in the process of professionalization. Event management falls under the rubric of commercialized professionalism, in which the actors try to emphasize the importance of the field, strengthen the status of the field and gain recognition as a profession by the public. As the power of a profession is relevant and witnessed in other fields, promoting professionalism is challenging for the event management field too. The state is less directly involved in this process, as constructing professionalism is promoted more by the event companies and the professional associations involved. It assumes that commercialized professionalism is promoted by its members (Hanlon, 1998).

However, professionalization should not only promote the sector but there is also a need to serve as a regulatory order for protecting the quality of services and the interests of both the employees and the client. Referring to Boyce, Hanlon directs attention towards new forms of commercialized professionalism:

> Professionalism is being subjected to reforming pressures that contribute to shifts toward entrepreneurial professionalism in which the possession of managerialist and entrepreneurial skills is increasingly valued by the professionals themselves, the professional practices are repositioned around a more business-like focus.
>
> (Boyce, 2008:87)

This is rather refashioning traditional professionalism, not rejecting it.

Event sector in Hungary

In order to examine professionalism in the context of Hungarian event management, we will now examine the size and scope of this sector. This is a rapidly growing and increasingly professionalized field, with all events now being seen to require professional planning and management. In quantitative terms, the event management sector is measured on the basis of the number of planned events of various types. In Hungary, statistics are mainly focused on international conferences, exhibitions and cultural festivals (see Hungarian Convention Bureau, 2006, 2007), which show an unbroken increase in number. In 2007 the number of conferences and international fairs grew by 12% compared with the previous year (485 conferences, 32 fairs in 2007), although the intensity of annual growth halved. The exhibition market size is also growing; members of the Association of Hungarian Exhibition and Fair Organizers hold approximately 85% of the whole exhibition market, which means a yearly average of 80 exhibitions and trade events. There are more than 3000 festivals in Hungary, which attract 18–20 million visitors from Hungary and abroad.

The vast majority of event management companies were founded between 1995 and 2007. The exact size of the event industry is unknown, owing to the many fly-by-night events with *in situ*, uncertified organizers. However, there is more exact information on professional congress/conference organizers (PCOs), the professional event management companies and festival organizers, through their professional memberships, an indication of their longer existence and professional quality. There are approximately 130 festival organizers and 40 event companies, one-third of which are PCOs specializing in educational and scientific events and two-thirds of which organize business events (meetings, consumer and trade shows). The Hungarian Tourism Joint Stock Company registered and qualified 30 PCOs in 2006, in contrast to 1990, when there were only six PCOs. There has been a tendency towards organizing private events such as weddings, parties and socials through professional event managers, which is a new type of event business in Hungary. It must be noted that in many cases the profiles of the companies are not very precise; for economic reasons, a company may use their free capacity to organize recreational and entertainment events, balls and ceremonies, in addition to business meetings and international conferences.

Methodology

The primary data are based on semi-structured interviews with all Hungarian event-related professional associations and a questionnaire completed by managers of event businesses in Hungary. Respondents were answering as individuals but within the context of their working experience and as a representative of their organization. The sample size consisted of six professional or representative organizations and 25 event companies, of which 16 were PCOs, four exhibition organizers and five festival organizers. As will be discussed later, the size of the industry is only estimated, owing to the rapid changes of organizers. The sample size covers about half of the PCOs, one-quarter of the exhibition organizers and only a very small percentage of festival organizers, as festivals are organized by more than 1000 non-governmental organizations (NGOs), local communities or event companies, the exact number of which is constantly changing.

The primary research was extended by collecting secondary data available on the Internet, in order to measure professionalization on the institutional–educational level. The Internet research provided general information on the educational institutions specializing in event management (the programme structure, the activities, etc.) and also on the NGOs (the mission, the foundation, the future goals, etc.).

The data collection period lasted between December 2007 and February 2008. The research focused on the professional characteristics of event managers, borrowing from the sociology of professions and the process of professionalization. The use of semi-structured interviews encouraged respondents to comment openly and freely. The nature of the questions ranged from the empirical to those seeking to establish opinions about the characteristics of professionalization. The survey of managers of event companies provided information on the employees' educational backgrounds, which were followed up by a discussion about work characteristics of an event manager. In analysing the interviews, ATLAS.TI qualitative analysis software was used. The interviews were transcribed and then coded. A few of the codes stemmed from a prior knowledge, whereas most of the code list emerged as open and *in vivo* coding. Given the relatively small sample, the notion of statistical significance was not always the best test of the rigour and reliability of the research; however, some of the quantifiable answers were coded and the quantitative data was analysed with SPSS software.

Characteristics of the sample

In the following section we would like to envisage the major actors in the field of event management – the event companies and the professional associations – in Hungary. The short introduction of actors is a result of primary research and secondary analysis of professional associations' data.

Event companies
The surveyed event companies (including PCOs and festival and exhibition organizers) are mainly small enterprises with an average of one to five employees. During events the companies usually work with part-time, temporary employees. The number of full-time employees (five to seven people) is somewhat higher when it comes to festival management, in contrast to the event companies specializing in conferences or other areas. Cultural institutions commissioned to arrange regional cultural programmes alongside festival organizations employ an average of 15–20 permanent workers.

Professional associations
In Hungary, there are several professional associations that represent the event management field at national level, and they are divided on the basis of the type of events their members organize. They have different influences and power, based on the length of time they have existed and the number of members. Nevertheless they are eager to compete for the prestige of event management and for the professional designation, and so they emphasize the relevance of competence and the educational needs of event managers. Table 7.1 shows the professional associations representing Hungarian event managers. During the

Table 7.1.   Professional associations representing Hungarian event managers.

	Date founded	Membership		Advantages of membership claimed	Code of ethics	Main objectives
		When founded	2008			
Hungarian Festival Association	2002	50	130	Information exchange, counselling, identity and recognition	In progress	Interest groups, support members, lobbying, promotion
Hungarian Art Festival Association	1990	18	42	Prestige, identity and recognition	In progress	Lobbying, promoting the festivals, international status, to strengthen professional competence, create a quality system for festival organizers
The Association of Open Air Theatres	1997	7	9	Lobbying, exchanging experience, trust	Exists	Study tours abroad, professional development
The Hungarian Association of Event Managers	1992	15	110	Interest group, ethical standards, networking, lobbying, education, professional development, bonuses for the members	Exists	Recognition of event management as a profession
The Hungarian Association of Exhibition and Fair Management	1989	4	13	Networks and collegiality, exchanging experience, interest group	Exists	Coordination of the activities of members, cooperation, training, nurturing international relations
The Hungarian Association of Folklore Festivals	1991	No data	25	Networks and collegiality, exchanging experience	No data	Interest groups, lobby

interviews, the associations' representatives expressed their views on what advantages membership brings to the members and explained the main objectives of the associations.

These associations play a significant role as a network for their members, the event companies, as well as serving the overall goals of event managers. Two-thirds of the event companies contacted were members of at least one event association. The reasons for joining these associations are diverse, but the respondents recognize the claims indicated in Table 7.1. These suggest that the main aims of these associations are: advocacy lobbying for recognition and professional identity, standard setting, avoiding competition, sharing the enhancement of communication between event managers, the facilitation of an exchange of experience and information, promotions, providing education, organizing training courses, fora and networking.

The low level of membership compared with the total number of event companies is due to the fact that the associations exercise strong control over the members (usually every second to third year the members are audited and monitored) to maintain quality and prestige. In some cases the applicants have to fulfil several criteria – for instance the Hungarian Event Managers Association requires a reference event and nomination by three members of the association. The final decision on new membership rests with the committee. The most influential associations are the Hungarian Association of Event Managers and the Hungarian Festival Association, not only measured by the number of members but also on the basis of lobbying activity. The former has an essential role in promoting event management as a new professional field and emphasizes the competence level of event managers and the educational needs. The latter is elaborating a quality system for evaluating festival organizers and monitoring festivals.

It must be stated that not all event companies are exclusively committed to one association, and a few of them are members of two professional associations. Nevertheless, event companies specializing in a particular type of service (e.g. PCOs, exhibition-designers) tend to ally in specific associations. As part of a big association such as the Hungarian Event Managers Association or, in case of cultural events, the Hungarian Festival Association, they can play a more effective role. There is a general trend towards the Hungarian Event Managers Association becoming stronger, and within the associations specialized sections are being formulated (e.g. exhibition-designers, meeting venues).

The responding event companies seemed to suggest that professional memberships are considered to provide a positive value, as they promote and support members and act as a guarantee for quality service. Besides the positive message of being a member, it provides advantages such as opening up new business opportunities and cooperations. It is observable that, as a sign of market integration, cooperation is evolving between event managerial services and suppliers providing services indispensable to event management (for example between PCO and party service, illumination technology, stage management businesses, hotels, etc.).

Results

In this section we present the results of our research, which envisages the characteristics of event management jobs from various perspectives and explores the state of professionalization in the event management sector in Hungary.

Event management jobs

There is debate over whether the event management profession can be classified as a homogeneous group, owing to differences in the level of required skills within the sector, which appear across the country. Presumably the level of professionalization is mirrored by the existence of event positions/jobs. It must be noted that the title of the job – with more or less the same tasks – may differ not only by country but sometimes also by businesses as well. As the European Centre for the Development of Vocational Training's (CEDEFOP, 1998) research has shown, the field exhibits a variety of roles and job titles, such as festival manager, event manager, meeting planner, convention coordinator, corporate event planner, programme director, event marketer, etc.

Skills and abilities

In the field of events, various skills and experiences are found to be very important factors in being a good professional, in addition to formal educational background. During the research, the managers of event companies revealed the important skills, abilities and competencies required for the daily operations of event managers in general. We were also interested in finding out how difficult it is to find appropriate employees with the aforementioned skills. The survey respondents evaluated the list of skills and abilities according to a five-point scale with 1 representing the highest and 5 the lowest score. Table 7.2 presents the most required skills, which are, in order of importance: problem-solving ability; conflict-resolution skills; team spirit and ability to work with different people; good communication skills; self-management skills, such as punctuality, time management and flexibility; creativity; networking and human capital; decision-making ability; IT skills; and adaptability.

Former practical experience in the field of events was also seen to be an advantage; however, event management job experience in a foreign country is rated as less important for a candidate. This could be explained by the international differences in business culture, the applied practices and differing legal frameworks between the countries. Intercultural capability, project-developing skills and understanding of tourism operations such as planning, implementing an event, marketing and accounting are rated as important but not essential.

Among these skills, the respondents suggested that it is easiest to find a candidate with appropriate IT skills, followed by adaptability and good communications skill. Most difficult to find are candidates with relevant human capital (networking) skills and qualified, determined employees with former experience who are able to make decisions and have appropriate project-management skills. There were other special requirements mentioned by the event managers: attention to detail and accuracy, loyalty, intelligence, a positive attitude, integrity, continuous improvement and innovation. These skills are very often required to address everyday tasks, but they are not certified in any way. In several cases these are based on past experience, gained and also practised over the years on the job.

Table 7.2. Required experience, abilities and skills of event managers.

Experience, abilities and skills	Importance[a]		Difficulty to find[b]	
	Mean	Standard deviation	Mean	Standard deviation
Problem-solving ability	1.25	0.91	3.06	1.30
Conflict-resolution skills	1.45	0.99	3.11	1.30
Team spirit, ability to work with different people	1.45	0.94	3.00	1.06
Good communication skills	1.47	1.02	2.88	1.11
Self-management skills, such as punctuality, time management, flexibility	1.50	0.94	3.18	0.95
Creativity	1.50	1.27	3.00	1.00
Networking, human capital	1.60	0.88	3.65	1.22
Decision-making ability	1.65	0.81	3.29	1.04
IT skills	1.85	1.04	2.06	0.96
Adaptability	1.90	0.71	2.94	1.05
Former practical experience in the field of events	2.00	0.98	3.22	1.19
Intercultural capability	2.05	0.82	3.22	0.87
Project development skills and understanding of tourism operations, such as planning and implementing an event, marketing, accounting	2.45	1.27	3.65	0.78
Self-marketing and presentation skills	2.55	0.94	3.06	0.65
Good foreign language knowledge	2.75	1.25	3.06	0.93
Event-managing job experience in a foreign country	3.85	1.06	4.44	1.35

[a]1 = most important to 5 = least important experience, abilities and skills.
[b]1 = the easiest to find someone with the given skills to 5 = the most difficult to find someone.

Professional background of event managers

Event management jobs in Hungary require at least a General Certificate of Secondary Education. The share of secondary or higher education in event management jobs is about equal: almost 50% of responding event managers possess secondary qualifications, the rest have an academic degree, having completed a bachelor's or master's programme. Managers with tertiary qualifications are mainly experts in science subjects. Among event managers, the most commonly spoken foreign languages are English and German. The level of conference managers' linguistic knowledge is higher than that of others, such as the festival organizers. Only a few event managers speak conversational Italian, Spanish or Russian.

It is interesting to note that all managers interviewed consider computer literacy indispensable, but not many were able to point to specific software programs appropriate for making processes and projects more transparent and comprehensible. They only apply a few standard programs (for example, all used Word, Excel and the Internet), whereas fewer than five mentioned Microsoft Project or Access. In the case of tasks that require a higher level of technical IT knowledge, they turn the task over to IT experts (publisher, graphic designer, etc.).

To explore the sources of professional development, the event managers evaluated their event companies' practices for allocating money to finance training for employees. According to the survey respondents, this is not relevant among Hungarian event managers, as only three of the event companies spent a significant amount of money on training in the previous year. Instead of training, for the majority of event managers, professional meetings and forums are the primary sources of new technical knowledge, other skills and up-dating information. They also attribute great significance to journals, newsletters, the Internet, professional fora and conferences organized by the event associations. The respondents were asked to highlight any deficiency of skills and competences; the majority identified marketing and PR skills, followed by the improvement of language skills.

Characteristics of event work

Owing to the small size of event enterprises, a two-level hierarchy model usually exists in Hungary: the managerial and implementation levels. The general manager of the event business usually coordinates and manages the actual events with the help of assistants (called event managers or event assistants), in addition to fulfilling general financial and administrative roles. Regardless of job title or hierarchy level, the field is characterized by great independence in time management. It means that the working time is mainly flexible, with some restrictions given by the management (usually as the event dates are approaching more restrictions apply, including the daily work time), but otherwise the employees decide on the time schedule. Generally, flexibility means working more hours than the official 40 hours per week in these jobs. Only one-fifth of the respondents (mainly the assistants) work according to rigidly fixed times without any flexibility. Four-fifths of the employees reported that they work flexitime. Those who reported longer working hours also reported that they experienced independence and autonomy in their jobs. Despite the fact that the respondents reported more autonomy, almost 90% of them report to their superior (the general event manager) either daily or weekly. It shows that the levels of independence and autonomy are interpreted subjectively, depending on the person. The major restrictions are based on quality control mechanisms which monitor individual decisions. Independence and autonomy are considered to be important factors as the implementation-oriented work involves more self-management and self-control. Subjectively interpreted, autonomy offers more possibilities to manage the work–life balance of the employees.

Discussion – the State of Professionalization in the Event Sector

Promoting professionalism is as challenging for the event management sector as it is in other professions. Furthermore, in Hungary, the state is less directly involved in this process; instead, constructing professionalism has started on the side of event managers/businesses, with the help of professional organizations. Commercialized professionalism in the field of event management is solely promoted by its members (Hanlon, 1998), but, by the same token, professionalism should serve as a regulatory order for protecting quality of services and the interests of employees and clients, a process in which the professional organizations take a significant role. The occupation/profession continuum helps to define the progress of professionalization. In general, event planning has moved away from the 'rule of thumb' way of organizing of the past, towards a professionalized process of creating and sustaining events by applying a well-defined methodology and guidelines. The state of professionalism in the Hungarian events sector can be related back to Greenwood's professional attributes.

The existence of a systematic body of theory and education

A complex theoretical knowledge behind the relevant skills is required for professional work. Parallel with strengthening the body of knowledge, the transfer of knowledge has started to develop and become more widespread, and the event research field is continuously expanding. More and more scientific conferences, research journals, publications, case studies and practices are devoted to this field, to provide a deeper understanding of events' contexts and characteristics.

The Hungarian event management sector is experiencing ongoing professionalization, and highly values continuing education and on-the-job training, because institutionalized educational programmes specializing in event management have only recently been established. Entry paths to the event business through experience were quite common in the past. Since the late 1990s, there has been a significant growth in event-related courses. All of the Hungarian higher-education institutions with tourism programmes (nine institutions in a number of locations) provide opportunities for students to major in event management or deal with event management at least as an elective course. In a couple of academic institutions, students have been able to enrol in master's courses in event management, beginning in late 2008.

Traditionally, the first generation of event courses comprised individual subjects within wider tourism, hospitality and leisure programmes. They often emphasized the MICE (meetings, incentives, conferences and exhibitions) aspect of events, and focused on the management of meetings and conferences in the context of the tourism industry. New courses have been developed with a wider focus, encompassing the full spectrum of event types. These courses focus on providing education and training for future event professionals. Generally built around a management core, they cover areas such as marketing, management, human resource management, destination/regional development, finance, administration and operations, together with event-specific modules such as event planning, production or risk management.

A wide range of further-education institutions also instruct students in event management, especially in the capital city. These are independent adult-training courses organized by educational or training institutions. Among the educational programmes there are specialized courses for wedding planners, party service providers and conference planners, etc., which range from 2-day wedding seminars up to 3-year academic programmes in event management.

Professional authority

According to the classical approach, the profession should have professional authority over field-specific knowledge and skills and also with regard to clients. In Hungary, event management has developed into a separate and prestigious profession in the last 15 years. Nevertheless it was not registered as an independent activity on the list of the Central Statistical Bureau until 2008. The Hungarian Event Management Association has put a lot of effort into getting event management acknowledged as a profession in its own right in the Occupational Classification System and in the branch-based Classification System of Economic Activities. Before 2008, the profession was classified as an item under the categories of travel counselling and travel management. The amalgamation of event management and travel management had no sound logical basis, as they have become entirely separate activities over the course of time. Formerly, in Hungary, event management companies had to meet government requirements applicable to travel management. In accordance with government orders, companies were obliged to employ a person who was responsible for the given activity and possessed the necessary certificates prescribed. In travel management examinations, the expertise in event management was not tested, which meant that candidates having accomplished the course were not necessarily competent in this field. It is also true the other way round: event managers do not necessarily need knowledge of travel management. It also seemed futile for event managers to have financial reserves, like the travel agencies, simply due to their position in the classification mentioned above.

Another deficiency is that event management is not listed in the National Educational Register, so the institutions have created a certificate confirming the completion of the actual event management course or they provide a certificate for a registered course organically related to event management, such as protocol or travel management, etc. Because of the lack of governmental licensing in the field of event management, the accreditation of educational programmes or training courses is done by professional bodies (e.g. event-related professional associations).

Professional authority has another implication for the level of consumer or client acceptance and trust. As a guarantee of quality, professionals try to keep their authority over the clients by identifying the importance of competencies and the relevance of practical field-related knowledge and the market. In practice it means that the client simply follows the professional advice of an event manager, such as in proposing pre- or post-conference programmes, menu plans, programming advices, protocol, etc. This authority over the clients is based on trust and confidence, which is usually built up over a long period (thus the longer the business has existed, the better), and on the references of the event managers. In these terms, there is a lot of spontaneous use of event-programming services. Event services are developing continuously as they become more specialized, and professional authority is strengthening in a parallel process.

Sanction of the community

The third attribute is that a profession must have the sanction of the community. It means that professions are licensed or certified by state agencies, so only those who are authorized and have the appropriate and required training can use the title of a profession. Practical experience is not enough to legally practise any profession; the sanction of the professional community is required, in the form of state licensing or a higher degree. Another aspect of community sanction is the professional confidence that the client shares information with the professionals – in this interaction the professionals feel privileged that the client shares the information in order to protect the client's interest and rights or solve any uncertainties, and in this way the client reaffirms the authority of the professional.

At the early stage of development, the body of knowledge needed to manage and coordinate events was not a pre-requisite in getting an event manager position. This was due to the fact that institutionalized educational programmes specializing in event management subjects did not exist. As described above, prior to the last few years there were no available academic programmes specializing in event management. Therefore employees gained the management and event knowledge through an optional course within a master's in tourism or as part of on-the-job training. It is still the case that the formal regulations are not strictly pre-requisites; the quality of a certification is not centrally controlled, so degrees and certificates are advantages but not necessary to acquire an event manager position. Instead of formal requirements, field-relevant skills and competences are required from the applicants. This could be controlled by the event-related associations, as they could define formal qualification as a pre-requisite to join the association.

Regulative code of ethics

A regulative code of ethics regarding appropriate professional behaviour is another characteristic of professions. As Table 7.1 shows, many associations have developed such a code, which is agreed to by its members. The code of ethics is designed to regulate and define the appropriate behaviour and to ensure honest practice among event professionals. Generally the code of ethics prescribes the ethical market behaviour: it promotes sharing of knowledge and expertise, and excludes economic superiority, any business secret violation, fame spoiling, bungling and the achievement of dishonest competitive advantage. The members of the associations that have ethical codes have accepted these and apply them in practice. The presidency warns the service provider in the case of assessed unethical behaviour, or may exclude it. Interviewed event managers agreed that the code has primarily been drawn up as an instrument for self-regulation. It demonstrates that the event companies are aware of their social responsibility and also provides security for the client that event companies work with needed economic competence.

Professional culture

A professional culture is continuously developing. Norms, symbols, language of events, and media initiatives such as specialized magazines exist in Hungary, which aim to strengthen the identity of event managers and emphasize the importance of event services and the profession. The event management associations issue regular press releases and publish a newsletter for professionals and all interested bodies. Association culture is measured by the existence of the event-related professional associations and the increased participation of event companies in the professional associations. The strength of professional culture has another implication on the commitment to the work. The active professional lives (associations' meetings combined with leisure activities) strengthen the network of professionals and outline a prospering and interesting range of career options.

Conclusion

This research has demonstrated that in the event management sector we are witnessing an entrepreneurial professionalism, with a higher level of occupational control over the work and more flexibility and autonomy. As envisaged, event management work is very innovative, and combines individual decision-making processes and teamwork (by dividing tasks with colleagues and negotiating with service providers, etc.), so a collegial form of authority is witnessed. The nature of the work is based on the trust of the client and the event manager. Event management work requires formal education and/or training. The occupational socialization process develops in the workplace and is strengthened by the membership of event-related associations. This progress has been undertaken earlier in other countries and in the case of other professions. In Hungary, we have seen the professional associations continue to promote the field and work out monitoring systems for events and for event businesses. The professional associations are also attempting to create competency standards for event management, highlighting the importance of accredited professional educational programmes. The formal requirements and professional competency standards could be used as a benchmark of excellence.

The importance and advantages of events have been recognized in the context of the commercialization process, with the value and the volume evidence demonstrating the virtue of the economic logic, and event management is now being recognized throughout the country as a professional field. Event managers themselves incorporated the idea of being professionals; however, not all service providers demonstrate a high level of certified knowledge and quality of service provision. Even if it has gained some recognition as a profession (which is only measured by the growing demand for event services and publicity for event management), event management is still in the process of constructing field-specific professionalism, including quality guidelines and competence standards.

The pattern of professionalization is twofold: on the one hand specialization within the profession can be observed (festival manager, PCO, etc.), as event management is more and more divided into sub-professions by fragmenting the market needs; on the other hand the associations and educational institutions, through their efforts at professionalization, have moved the field in the direction of a generic event management profession. This leads towards a less straightforward, more contradictory and complex dynamic of professionalization that will require further study. In this changing environment the professionals try to react to the new nature of the market by dividing professions into sub-professions and providing more specialized services.

In parallel with the strengthening of the profession, the prestige of the field is growing. As events are still expanding, the need for competent employees is obvious, and with a well-defined formal and informal qualification level, the field could be more attractive to potential job candidates, providing challenging job opportunities and a rewarding career path.

References

Auster, C. (1996) *The Sociology of Work*. Pine Forge Press, Thousand Oaks, California.

Boyce, A. (2008) Professionalism meets entrepreneurialism and managerialism. In: Kuhlmann, E. and Saks, M. (eds) *Rethinking Professional Governance: International Directions in Health Care*. Policy Press, Bristol, UK, pp. 77–95.

CEDEFOP (European Centre for the Development of Vocational Training) (1998) *Transparency of Vocational Qualifications*. Luxembourg Publication Office, Luxembourg.

Evetts, J. (2006) Short note: the sociology of professional groups' new directions. *Current Sociology* 54(1), 133–143.

Formádi, K. (2008) From health to tourism: being mobile in the wellness sector. In: Kuhlmann, E. and Saks, M. (eds) *Rethinking Professional Governance: International Directions in Health Care*. Policy Press, Bristol, UK, pp. 187–201.

Greenwood, E. (1957) Attributes of a profession. *Social Work* 2(3), 44–55.

Hall, R. (1994) *Sociology of Work*. Pine Forge Press, London.

Hanlon, G. (1998) Professionalism as enterprise. *Sociology* 32(1), 43–63.

Hungarian Convention Bureau (2006) Budapest helyezése romlott a nemzetközi szervezeti kongresszusok piacán. Available at: http://www.hcb.hu/downloads/study18.doc (accessed 17 November 2008).

Hungarian Convention Bureau (2007) A Magyar Turizmus Zrt. Kongresszusi Irodájának tájékoztatója. Available at: http://www.hcb.hu/downloads/study20.doc (accessed 17 November 2008).

Van der Wagen, L. (2007) *Human Resource Management for Events*. Elsevier, London.

Voß, G. and Pongratz, H. (2001) From employee to entreployee – towards a self-entrepreneurial work force? *Concepts of Transformation* 8(3), 239–254.

III Flexibility in Events Work

The two chapters that comprise this part investigate the flexibility of work in the events sector from the perspective of pulsating major sports event organizations (Hanlon and Jago, Chapter 8) and episodic volunteering (Lockstone and Smith, Chapter 9).

Hanlon and Jago (Chapter 8) highlight the relationship between flexibility and pulsating organizations and explore the human resource challenges associated with organizations that rapidly expand and contract to meet the operational needs of major sporting events. The chapter provides insights into the strategies that the event organizations behind three high-profile Australian major sports events have used to successfully deal with the influx and subsequent withdrawal of large numbers of paid staff and volunteers to ensure the smooth running of these events. Using the case study examples, Hanlon and Jago discuss how the use of technology, the establishment of formal communication and training processes, and proactive measures towards culture building and career path development have been applied by these major sport event organizations to meet the challenges of personnel selection, induction and retention, and team management.

As chapters elsewhere in this book also demonstrate (see Chapters 10, 11, 12, 13 and 14), episodic volunteering is an important response to the personnel demands of pulsating event organizations. In this section, Lockstone and Smith (Chapter 9) explore the flexibility outcomes of event volunteering and discuss the acceptance of temporal, numerical and functional flexibility practices by volunteers. As a point of comparison, volunteers working episodically in an event context are compared with their more traditional, sustained volunteering counterparts working in museums, visitor information centres and visitor attractions. Lockstone and Smith highlight one of the key reasons why event organizations should be concerned with providing flexible outcomes for their episodic volunteers. Findings indicate that volunteers who were more satisfied with the flexibility of their event roles were also more likely to continue to commit to their host organization, suggesting that enhanced flexibility outcomes can potentially lead to improved retention of volunteers.

8 Managing Pulsating Major Sporting Event Organizations

CLARE HANLON AND LEO JAGO

Victoria University, Australia

Introduction

Major sports events are big business. In Australia, events such as the Melbourne Cup and the Australian Tennis Open have become cultural fixtures (Green, 2001), and on an international scale play a significant role in generating economic and tourism revenue (Hanlon and Jago, 2000). Worldwide, companies spend over US$240 billion each year on sports sponsorship (Amis and Cornwell, 2005). Despite the growing economic and cultural importance of major sports events, the ramifications of growth for management practices in this thriving industry are not well understood.

The sports industry differs from the mainstream business world in a number of key dimensions. Sport is a 'people business', driven by the passion and loyalty of its fans, participants and personnel (Cuskelly *et al.*, 2004; Hoye *et al.*, 2006; Monga, 2006). Indeed, it has been observed that within the sports industry, a traditional business focus on shareholder interests is replaced by recognition of the many contributors to the industry as key stakeholders (Mullins, 2007).

Major sporting event organizations (MSEOs) are heavily reliant on vast and complex workforces that grow and diminish around the life cycle of their event (Hanlon, 2003). These dynamic or 'pulsating' workforces (Toffler, 1990) are not easily managed, and the needs of personnel can easily be eclipsed by the many operational pressures to stage a successful event on generally tight timelines and budgets and often subject to international media scrutiny (Hanlon and Jago, 2004; Monga, 2006). Effective management of 'pulsating' workforces has been found to be key to the success of major sports events (Taylor *et al.*, 2008), and it is critical that the human resource management (HRM) challenges that they present should not be underestimated.

Whilst research associated with management practices in pulsating organizations is still relatively new, the few studies that have been undertaken have indicated that generic HRM practices do not always address the specific needs of MSEOs and their workforces (Hanlon and Stewart, 2006). Rather, evidence suggests that managers need to adjust or augment mainstream human resource (HR) strategies with practices that specifically accommodate the characteristics of MSEOs, in order to achieve outcomes that align with good practice.

This chapter considers some of the unique challenges that MSEOs pose for management. In particular, it investigates the impact that significant fluctuations in personnel numbers have on an organization's structure and culture, as the organization moves through a typical 'event cycle' (Hanlon, 2003), and the implications of this dynamic for human resource management. The chapter draws upon primary data that were collected by the authors in previous studies (Hanlon and Jago, 2000, 2004; Hanlon, 2003; Hanlon and Stewart, 2006), supplemented with secondary data from relevant MSEO web sites.

Pulsating Organizations

The concept of pulsating organizations originated in the early 1990s to describe bodies that expand and contract over their life cycle (Toffler, 1990; Crawford, 1991). This pulsating dynamic is typically seen in MSEOs, where the workforce fluctuates in size according to a three-stage event cycle: namely, pre-event, during the event and after the event (Hanlon, 2003). MSEOs operate with a small core of personnel for much of the year, expanding rapidly with an influx of temporary personnel in the lead-up to an event, then returning to the core number of personnel as the event winds up. This pulsating workforce dynamic can present a daunting landscape for HR managers, as one MSEO manager explained in Hanlon and Stewart (2006:83):

> You've lost control. It explodes. We do literally go from 20 to about 30 from October to December and then over a 3 or 4 day period it goes to at least 3000 staff on the site and that's of course not including any of the players or the media. It really is an explosion.

Regular rhythm and single pulse organizations

Toffler distinguished between two types of pulsating organizations: 'regular rhythm' organizations, which manage recurring events such as the Australian Tennis Open and the Melbourne Cup, and 'single pulse' organizations, which manage one-off events such as the Olympic or Commonwealth Games (Toffler, 1990). Although the Olympic and Commonwealth Games are staged every 4 years, they are held in a different location each time and thus they are considered as 'single pulse' by the specific host destinations. Regular rhythm organizations expand and contract around a periodic cycle, while single pulse bodies expand in the lead-up to an event, then decline and are dismantled at their conclusion. Each type of pulsating organization presents different HR challenges to management.

Regular rhythm organizations must continually shift focus and strategy across the event cycle, in accordance with different personnel dynamics. One of the greatest HRM challenges in regular rhythm organizations is retaining seasonal staff from one event to the next. Managers must attempt to influence the behaviour of staff beyond their employment contract, maintaining contact, interest and sufficient motivation for them to return for the following season (Hanlon and Jago, 2004). In contrast, management in single pulse organizations must contend with an environment that presents no organizational history or established relationships to assist the development of its workforce, such as the establishment of staff compatibility. Managers in single pulse environments are not able to draw upon the corporate knowledge of an organization in the development and management of their personnel, despite the complex profiles of their workforces (Hanlon, 2003). They do, however, have the opportunity to draw upon staff who have worked in this type of environment for other organizations.

How pulsating organizations differ from generic business organizations

While management practices in mainstream or generic business organizations are based on the concept of a relatively stable workforce, in terms of numbers, and clearly defined and recognized power and communication channels, managers in pulsating organizations must accommodate a rapid and far-reaching process of change, as their organization grows in size and diversity in the lead-up to an event (Hanlon and Jago, 2000). This requires an organizational model that is flexible and innovative enough to allow positive communication and coordination to continue amidst significant structural and cultural change (Hall, 1995; Ancona *et al.*, 1996; Slack, 1997). Management supports this change process through the adoption of complex information and personnel management strategies.

Major sporting event organizations

Typically, the structure of a pulsating MSEO is centralized for major decision making throughout the year and in the period after an event but decentralized leading up to and during the event (Hanlon, 2003). A high degree of formalization of processes facilitates this decentralization, as the high number and variety of personnel arriving and departing from the organization at different times requires immediate guidance and access to clear information on a range of issues (Hanlon and Jago, 2000). The development of a central information and knowledge-sharing system (Halbwirth and Toohey, 2001) can assist management in maintaining control and order in this highly volatile environment. However, this requires management to employ innovative strategies such as the codification and classification of information and use of tools such as databases and manuals to establish and maintain an effective information system. Formalization of process is less important in generic business organizations owing to the level of corporate knowledge and opportunities for personnel to learn from each other in a more stable environment (Hanlon, 2003).

A distinctive cultural environment also builds up around MSEO workforces, where permanent, seasonal, outsourced and volunteer workers form temporary work teams whose cohesion is based more upon high levels of adrenalin, passion and commitment than on the process of establishing long-term working relationships (Hanlon and Jago, 2004). While there are benefits for management as a result of operating in a high-energy environment, these teams and relationships are inherently volatile and require significant management for them to remain stable and effective.

The structural and cultural characteristics of MSEOs add great complexity to the task of HRM. Managers must understand how their organizational structure influences staff and organizational efficiency (Taylor *et al.*, 2008), ensuring, for example, that rapid change does not add to the already demanding staff workloads. Managers need to employ a range of communication tools and technologies (Torkildsen, 1992; Robbins and Barnwell, 1998) to maintain team cohesion and motivation, while tailoring strategies to both accommodate the communication priorities of various event stages (Hanlon, 2003) and align with the needs of different categories of personnel (Saul, 1996; Challadurai, 1999). Managers must also be innovative in their response to the unscoped needs of their workforce (Halbwirth and Toohey, 2001). All this occurs in a highly pressurized environment (Hanlon, 2003).

Human Resource Management

An Australian study of pulsating MSEOs found that standard HR practices, such as staff selection and induction, managing teams and retaining talent, are less effective in MSEO environments (Hanlon and Stewart, 2006). Characteristics unique to MSEOs, such as the complex structure and multi-skill requirements of staff (Challadurai, 1999), the broad range of personnel categories (Crawford, 1991; Graham *et al.*, 1995), the high proportion of staff on short-term contracts (Compton and Nankervis, 1998) and the pulsating effect of personnel movements (Toffler, 1990; Crawford, 1991), can adversely affect personnel management (Hanlon, 2003). For example, the Sydney Organizing Committee for the Olympic Games (SOCOG) in 2000 grew from a core staff of 16 to a workforce of over 47,000 across a 7-year period (Halbwirth and Toohey, 2001).

Research findings suggest that HR managers must alter or augment mainstream practices to accommodate these organizational elements of MSEOs. In particular, HRM can benefit from the adoption of different retention, motivation and team performance strategies, greater formalization of processes to manage the large and varied influx of seasonal staff, and tailoring strategies to accommodate different stages of an event cycle (Hanlon and Stewart, 2006).

The following sections explore four key HRM functions to show in more detail the types of strategies that need to be used in pulsating MSEOs. The functions include selecting and inducting personnel, managing teams and retaining talent. Data from three Australian MSEO case studies undertaken by the authors will be used to highlight the tailored strategies required within each of the four HRM functions identified above.

The case studies comprise the Australian Open Tennis Championships (AOTC), the Confederation of Australian Motor Sports (CAMS), which organizes the officials for the Australian Formula One Grand Prix (AFOGP), and the SOCOG. These cases relate to major sporting events that are or were held in Australia, are international in scale, and vary in event length from 4 days (AFOGP) to 2 weeks (AOTC) and 16 days (Sydney Olympic Games). Each organization conducting these events expands and contracts in personnel numbers and comprises a mass of employees in varied employment groups (full time, outsource, seasonal and volunteers); the majority of personnel have a limited contract time and are located in temporary work groups. The discussion of these cases will have broad application to pulsating events in general.

Qualitative data in the form of interviews with key personnel were collected by the authors in previous studies (Hanlon and Jago, 2000, 2004; Hanlon, 2003; Hanlon and Stewart, 2006). These data were coded and indexed for both theme and content. A second researcher also coded the data incorporating Babbie's (1998) approach, wherein the lead researcher explained the code category meaning and then distributed the first transcript. Coding comparisons were then made, discrepancies were discussed and coding was modified accordingly. A check-coding procedure was performed to ensure coding schemes were similar. The qualitative data were supplemented with secondary data from AOTC and CAMS web sites and literature that concentrated on the SOCOG.

Selecting personnel

Specialized recruitment and induction strategies are required to identify, communicate with and manage large numbers of permanent, returning and new personnel. Increasingly, MSEOs are adopting technology solutions and innovations to streamline the recruitment process.

Australian Open Tennis Championships (AOTC)

The AOTC embarks on an enormous recruitment drive each year. Ten months before the tennis tournament, which is held annually in January, applications are opened for a wide range of positions, including court services staff, ball kids, courtesy car drivers, corporate hospitality assistants and media workroom staff. Over the year, the AOTC grows from a core permanent staff of 108 to a workforce of over 1500, comprising the core staff plus temporary full-time and part-time staff, and then shrinks back to its core number in the space of a year (Tennis Australia, 2007). In addition, an international visitors' programme for ball kids requires the recruitment of over 300 children from across Australia and internationally (Tennis Australia, 2007). By its scale alone, this is an ambitious recruitment process.

The AOTC has streamlined its recruitment approach with the use of techno-logical innovations such as e-recruitment. An online applicant assessment process has been devised that requires prospective employees to successfully answer module review questions until they progress through the 'draw' to reach the 'final' and 'win' their Australian Open accreditation. Transferring the process to an online format has enabled centralized applicant information, enhanced management reporting, improved communication with applicants, and reduced manual labour in relation to advertising and the short-listing process (Tennis Australia, 2007).

In this case, the AOTC developed technological tools to reduce the burden surrounding the recruitment process, given the size of the recruitment task and the tight timeframe involved. The centralization of information for recruiters and, in the AOTC's case, for applicants as well, improved accessibility of key informa-tion and simplified the process, freeing management to focus on issues such as the appropriateness and compatibility of staff (Hanlon, 2003).

Inducting personnel

One of the biggest differences between the induction of new staff into MSEOs compared with conventional organizations relates to the relative numbers of new staff. In conventional organizations, the number of new staff who would be inducted at any given time is generally low in comparison to the number of staff already employed by the organization. For MSEOs, however, the number of staff being inducted at certain times can be far in excess of the number of existing staff. Whilst this situation provides 'economies of scale' for MSEOs in terms of the induction process, the drawback is that there are often not sufficient staff within the organization who can provide guidance or a reference point for new staff after completion of the induction process.

The induction of staff in MSEOs has also benefitted from a range of techno-logical innovations that ensure the comprehensive introduction of a wide variety of personnel categories to an organization. MSEOs have found that it is impor-tant to induct each personnel category separately and to incorporate active group information sessions in the process. Without this level of attention, sea-sonal staff in particular can find they are left to fend for themselves, learning informally on the job, which can be problematic for both the staff and the orga-nization. Making key information about organizational structure and processes centrally available to all staff can significantly reduce feelings of neglect and frus-tration amongst personnel (Hanlon and Stewart, 2006) as well as greatly enhance the speed at which new staff make substantive contributions to the organization. The three case studies identified for the purpose of this chapter are examples of MSEOs that have taken advantage of technological innovations in order to assist the induction and communication process with a large number of personnel for the purpose of a major sporting event.

Confederation of Australian Motor Sports (CAMS)
CAMS organizes the officials for the AFOGP. Beyond its core workforce, CAMS annually inducts 1000 volunteers to officiate at the AFOGP (CAMS, 2007a). A

coordinated strategy employing formal communication and training processes has been devised to assist CAMS in managing this influx of staff in the lead-up to the AFOGP. The organization's web site provides a dedicated staff area, with online features such as a regular newsletter, to assist induction and improve communication with event officials (CAMS, 2007a). CAMS has also simplified its official career path structure, reducing and renaming category levels for easier recognition. The new system, which replaces the extensive list of categories titled according to numbered levels with the universally recognized categories of bronze, silver and gold, creates a more user-friendly structure that clearly delineates roles and responsibilities for officials who enter the organization's workforce. The categories are divided into subcategories to represent the leadership and specialized knowledge required as an official (CAMS, 2007b). Non-permanent staff can immediately place themselves within the organizational structure and obtain a sense of place and clarity of purpose.

Australian Open Tennis Championships (AOTC)

The AOTC uses an intranet site to introduce new staff to the organization. Employee profiles are placed on the intranet on their first day. Staff are then inducted with the assistance of a self-paced e-learning system, containing modules of content relating to a range of induction areas, such as occupational health and safety and emergency procedures. All casual tournament staff and contractors must complete a combination of short-answer and multiple-choice questions, with 80% accuracy required in order to complete their induction. They have a month to complete the process and, once successful, HR is notified and the successful employee or contractor is able to download a certificate confirming their accreditation (Tennis Australia, 2007).

Sydney Organizing Committee for the Olympic Games (SOCOG)

SOCOG devised a Games Code System of 'mission critical terminology' that was made centrally available to all staff. This codification of key information and terminology proved vital in the establishment phase of the event, when over 90 different professional areas, ranging from publicity to catering, were beginning to coordinate their activities. In developing its information system, SOCOG drew on the experiences of the Atlanta Games Organizing Committee, which found a loss of productivity and cohesive planning occurred when staff felt the need to continually double-check information with colleagues (Halbwirth and Toohey, 2001).

Successful induction strategies for MSEOs are not necessarily limited to technology tools and innovations demonstrated in the preceding case studies. When inducting personnel for the Melbourne Cup, the Victorian Racing Club provides comprehensive staff manuals that cover issues such as race times, personnel rights and obligations, and detailed maps of the venue. The Australian 500CC Motorcycle Grand Prix has used lead-up events at the racing circuit, or 'test events', to familiarize staff with surroundings, resources and processes (Hanlon and Stewart, 2006).

Managing teams

As MSEOs expand their ranks and pressure begins to build in the lead-up to an event, the organizational culture also begins to change (Halbwirth and Toohey, 2001). Work teams fluctuate in size as staff enter and exit the organization at different stages. Relationships are required to develop in a rapid fashion in a quite intense environment, and teams strive to achieve a state of self-management (Saul, 1996). The inherent instability and intensity of this environment can impact on team performance and significantly complicate the management process (Marquis and Huston, 1992; Stoner *et al.*, 1994; Hanlon and Stewart, 2006).

Research has revealed that rivalry and conflict can occur between different categories of staff, involving both permanent and non-permanent personnel (Auld, 1994; Hanlon and Stewart, 2006). The large and vitally important volunteer workforces that major events generally rely upon present particular challenges for management in this regard. Volunteer motivation to participate in major sports events has been found to be heavily influenced by intangible or intrinsic rewards, such as the enjoyment of participation (Pearce, 1993). Studies have found that a considerable proportion of volunteers (up to 25% at the Atlanta Olympic Games) will not maintain their participation throughout an event if they are poorly managed (Howden, 2003). Understanding what motivates commitment and loyalty amongst the range of personnel, from full-time staff to volunteers, is a complex but key consideration for management (Cuskelly *et al.*, 2004; Monga, 2006).

Successful team management in a pulsating MSEO requires the establishment and maintenance of an environment that supports relationship building, commitment and motivation within potentially tense and fractured work situations (Halbwirth and Toohey, 2001). Managers must demonstrate flexibility and sensitivity to a range of work experiences and occupational backgrounds of personnel. Successful team building requires the development of a cohesive environment where there is a strong sense of belonging to the group, which in turn will enhance the morale of the organization (Hanlon and Stewart, 2006).

Whilst some mainstream organizations have adopted a 'team approach' to staffing and management, the approach is still not common, unlike in MSEOs, where it tends to be the modus operandi, due largely to the massive swings in personnel numbers across the cycle of the organization.

Australian Open Tennis Championships (AOTC)
The AOTC has recognized the importance of developing a 'one team' culture. Internally, initiatives such as employee communication sessions, monthly morning teas, quarterly major events, the TA Fun Club or 'Tennis Angels', and 'Getting to know...' e-mail bulletins are used to increase communication between the teams and provide socializing opportunities for personnel (Tennis Australia, 2007). These strategies enable positive work relationships to develop in a temporary environment that would not normally be conducive to strong team development.

Sydney Organizing Committee for the Olympic Games (SOCOG)
The Sydney 2000 Olympic Games utilized its formal information system to inculcate a culture of shared learning throughout its vast workforce. The creation

of a virtual shared workspace and knowledge portal helped to create a sense of community amongst workers, who were encouraged to share rather than 'hoard' knowledge. This, in turn, broke down a 'silo' mentality that had permeated the organization's culture in its early phases (Ruggles, 1998; Halbwirth and Toohey, 2001). This approach also improved relationship building amongst staff over the long term.

Retaining talent

As most organizations are only as good as their key staff, the retention of key staff is an important objective. As there is a specific focus in time for the activities of MSEOs, loss of key staff in the lead-up to the actual staging of the event can have very serious consequences. The fact that most staff employed by MSEOs are on contracts that terminate shortly after the conclusion of the event means that there is a real temptation for staff to start exploring other employment options prior to the event being staged so that they have continuing employment options after the event. On occasions, a position may become available with another employer prior to the event being staged and a key employee may have to resign from the MSEO prematurely in order to obtain that position. Clearly, this can have serious consequences for the MSEO in successfully staging the event.

The need for successful retention strategies presents pulsating MSEOs with perhaps their greatest HR challenge. Managers must devise a range of strategies to motivate and retain the various personnel 'types' in their workforce at different stages of the event cycle (Hanlon and Jago, 2004).

Australian research has found the ability of management to attract, motivate and retain personnel is heavily influenced by the stage at which the organization is placed in an event cycle (Hanlon and Jago, 2004). The lead-up to an event is an exciting time for staff as anticipation grows around the ensuing sports spectacle. Staff passion and commitment are also relatively easy to maintain during the event itself, although teams require careful management to preserve positive working relationships and cohesion. As events wind up, however, HR management needs to employ motivational strategies to stop staff 'going flat' or losing a sense of connection with the event and the organization. It is at this point, and over the following year, that major retention challenges specific to the various personnel categories emerge.

As indicated earlier, non-permanent staff often seek and accept new employment opportunities during the final days of an event (Catherwood and Van Kirk, 1992; Graham *et al.*, 1995). A range of retention strategies can be employed at this point to reduce the incidence of this occurring, including staggering pay over the event cycle (Graham *et al.*, 1995) or using performance-based remuneration around agreed targets (Jordan and Morris, 1997). Full-time staff have proven difficult to retain immediately after an event, or in the 'trough' stage when personnel numbers drop, teams disperse and a sense of urgency is replaced by complacency and boredom (Hanlon and Jago, 2004). At this point in the event cycle, management needs to re-establish team environments for full-time personnel and initiate opportunities for career growth within the organization.

As many of the staff that are attracted to work with MSEOs thrive on the 'adren-alin rush' of the event, they very easily get bored after the event and can be quite difficult staff to hold during the quieter parts of the event cycle.

Another enormous challenge faced by regular rhythm MSEOs, which is quite different from conventional organizations, relates to the fact that they need to entice seasonal staff back in the lead-up to the event in the following year. Short-term or seasonal staff who have been successful in their roles with a regular rhythm event become extremely valuable to a MSEO and well worth attracting back the following year. Such staff are familiar with both the MSEO and the event itself and thus do not require substantial induction and can often play a mentoring role with new staff. Although it is often not possible to hold such staff on a continuing basis, there is a substantial incentive for the MSEO to encourage such staff to return. As these staff are not ongoing employees of the MSEO, attracting them back year after year for the event is not 'retention' under the strict definition of the term, but it has some similarities and is therefore discussed in this section. For management of MSEOs, it is quite a challenge to attract seasonal personnel back for the next event (Hanlon and Jago, 2004) as management needs to influence personnel beyond their employment with the organization.

MSEOs have been shown to exercise limited influence over seasonal staff in an external environment, where a person's primary form of employment places competing demands on their time (Warn, 1994). Some simple retention strate-gies at this point may include timing an event so it is unlikely to interfere with conventional working commitments. The Australian Grand Prix, for example, is always held over a 4-day period, which often coincides with a holiday weekend. Beyond practical strategies, however, managers must embark on a complex culture-building process, where a sense of belonging or ownership is created amongst personnel around an MSEO and its associated events.

During an event, managers must establish strong communication channels that help strengthen the relationship between staff and the organization (Halbwirth and Toohey, 2001). Providing feedback to individuals in the form of evaluations and debriefs during and immediately after an event can create a sense of place in the organizational community (Hall, 1995; Hanlon and Jago, 2004) and enhance feelings of contribution, responsibility and ownership (Hall, 1995; Turbidy, 1997). For seasonal staff, the opportunity to progress through different roles over time also encourages positive connection with an organization and retention over the long term (Hanlon and Jago, 2004).

Indeed, some MSEOs have introduced what is akin to career structures within their different categories of personnel so that there is a sense of achieve-ment derived by staff within these different categories as they move up the structure in terms of positions occupied over the years. Such structures need to be well publicized amongst staff so that they understand the significance of these different positions and have goals for which they can aim.

Recognition and reward systems are also effective strategies, such as 'thanks' parties immediately after an event, sending birthday and Christmas cards to staff over the non-event period and providing opportunities to be involved in associ-ated events throughout the year. Exit interviews are also useful for informing management about what motivates different staff to participate in the following season. University students, for example, have been found to prize the money and contacts they obtain through participation in major events (Donohoe and Southey, 1996; Freedman, 1997; Grote, 1999), while many volunteers have been found to be motivated by the opportunity to contribute to a local community event (Pearce, 1993).

Confederation of Australian Motor Sports (CAMS)
In recognition of its vital resource of non-permanent staff, CAMS National Officiating Program (CAMS, 2005) has established a career path that officials can pursue over the long term. Maintenance of official accreditation and licensing has also been streamlined in line with the new career structure, and more formalized training processes have been introduced. CAMS found that under their previous system, where officials were simply able to tick which classification they wished to attain, people developed unrealistic expectations. This led to accreditation downgrades and disillusionment amongst staff (CAMS, 2007b). The more formalized approach to training and accreditation has improved accessibility to, and maintenance of, the licensing of CAMS officials. The new system also provides suitably qualified officials who operate in related areas such as rally and off-road with easier entry into the AFOGP workforce.

Australian Open Tennis Championships (AOTC)
The AOTC has devised a professional development programme that provides the range of staff members with the opportunity to develop leadership and management skills. The AOTC's stated aim in this regard is to build a leadership team that can facilitate the improved engagement of its full complement of staff through the establishment of shared visions and goals (Tennis Australia, 2007). The AOTC has been very successful at attracting volunteers to return over many years to work at the Australian Open. Although the 'celebrity attraction' of the event is a key attractor for volunteers, the fact that the AOTC provides a career structure for these volunteers has been an important factor. For example, volunteers have often commenced their involvement with the event as drivers of players and have had the opportunity to move to coordinator of drivers, then on to rostering practice tennis courts and then to supervisor of practice courts. This is but one example of a career structure that has been put in place for a category of personnel.

Management Challenges and Responses in Major Sporting Event Organizations

The growing economic and cultural significance of major sports events has created the need for a new form of HRM. The ever-changing nature of the organizations that run major sporting events presents managers with significantly more complex environments than their 'normal' or 'generic' business counterparts. The highly dynamic nature of MSEO workforces requires managers to adopt different strategies to induct, support and retain vital 'talent' while accommodating the needs of a rapidly changing organizational environment.

The broad range of personnel categories used by MSEOs, and the large numbers of staff in most of these categories, demands a highly structured selection process to be adopted, which allows for the rapid establishment of a complex workforce without compromising the quality of the staff employed. Managers must then ensure that the volatile working environment faced by most major sporting events does not diminish staff efficiency. The creation of a 'learning' environment by management is vital so as to allow different functional areas to receive timely and accurate information, which facilitates smooth coordination of multiple functions.

Management must maintain staff passion, interest, motivation and a sense of connection with the organization. Maintaining contact and commitment across a large, diverse staff network throughout the various stages of the event cycle is a unique challenge. The establishment and maintenance of a 'one team'-oriented culture can assist positive relationship building and the establishment and retention of a vital pool of 'talent' from one season to the next. Finally, MSEO managers must show great flexibility, foresight and innovation as they align their HR strategies with different event stages (before, during and after an event) and a range of personnel categories (full time, part time, contract, volunteer, outsourced) (Saul, 1996).

Conclusion

It is clear that the pulsating characteristics of MSEOs pose a range of unique challenges for management of these organizations, which are not faced by managers of more conventional organizations. These pulsating characteristics have substantial consequences for the manner in which personnel are recruited, selected and managed in MSEOs, and failure to adequately address these issues can have disastrous consequences for the successful operation of major sporting events.

The HR tasks presented by MSEOs require Herculean efforts by management. Embarking on such a complex and challenging journey is not for the faint hearted. Australian research has revealed, however, that in the past MSEO managers have had little guidance or formalization of learning around these unique HRM challenges. Instead, many have relied on an ad hoc approach to their multiple tasks (Hanlon, 2003). This has resulted in management practices that are inconsistent and haphazard, leading to frustration and disenchantment amongst personnel, who ultimately seek employment elsewhere (Hanlon and Stewart, 2006).

In this increasingly vibrant and dominant sector of the sports industry, there is a growing need for clear, formalized guidance around best practice HR management. The economic and cultural costs of failure in this area are potentially considerable. MSEOs can move towards best practice through the creation of detailed operational and policy documentation, which guides both management and personnel successfully through this highly challenging but rewarding work experience.

As major sporting events have become such an important component of the tourism industry in so many developed economies, many more events are now on offer and there is an expectation that these events will be run in a manner that meets the increasing expectations of consumers. Whilst the practices identified in earlier sections of this chapter will enhance the professionalism of the staffing dimension of MSEOs, the fact that there are now more MSEOs and organizations that manage a wide range of different events has the potential to enhance further the performance of staff in this sector. There is now more opportunity for staff to be employed on a continuing basis by some of these bigger event organizations and then have their individual time allocated to different events across the year. This reduces the need to have to continually recruit new staff and it provides an increased opportunity for staff to have ongoing employment in the sector. It will be a few years before the outcomes of this change can be fully assessed. Clearly, determining the strategies to incorporate in the HRM functions of selecting personnel, inducting personnel, managing teams and retaining personnel within all MSEOs cannot be identified in this study of just three organizations. However, future studies can build upon the knowledge gained in this chapter to examine other MSEOs or pulsating events in general.

References

Amis, J. and Cornwell, T.B. (2005) (eds) *Global Sport Sponsorship*. Berg Publishers, Oxford.

Ancona, D., Kochan, T., Scully, M., Van Maanen, J. and Westney, D.E. (1996) *Managing for the Future: Organizational Behaviour and Processes*. South-Western College, Cincinnati, Ohio.

Auld, C. (1994) Changes in professional and volunteer administrator relationships: implications for managers in the leisure industry. *Australian Journal of Leisure and Recreation* 4(2), 14–22.

Babbie, E. (1998) *The Practice of Social Research*, 8th edn. Wadsworth, Belmont, California.

CAMS (2005) *New initiatives to strengthen CAMS national officiating program*. Available at: http://www.cams.com.au/content.asp?PageID=Officials&ObjectID=5 (accessed 21 February 2008).

CAMS (2007a) *CAMS manual*. Available at: http://www.camsmanual.com.au (accessed 21 February 2008).

CAMS (2007b) *New licensing structure for CAMS accredited officials*. Available at: http://www.cams.com.au/downloads/officials/NOP_Review_Spring06_article.pdf (accessed 21 February 2008).

Catherwood, D.W. and Van Kirk, R.L. (1992) *The Complete Guide to Special Event Management: Business Insights, Financial Advice, and Successful Strategies from Ernst and Young*. Wiley, New York.

Challadurai, N. (1999) *Human Resource Management in Sport and Recreation*. Human Kinetics, Champaign, Illinois.

Compton, R.L. and Nankervis, A.R. (1998) *Effective Recruitment and Selection Practices*, 2nd edn. CCH Australia, Sydney.

Crawford, R. (1991) *In the Era of Human Capital: the Emergence of Talent, Intelligence, and Knowledge and the World-wide Economic Force and What it Means to Managers and Investors*. Harper Business, New York.

Cuskelly, G., Auld, C., Harrington, M. and Coleman, D. (2004) Predicting the behavioural dependability of sport event volunteers. *Event Management* 9, 73–89.

Donohoe, F. and Southey, G. (1996) Design strategy for a manager's performance management process in QIDC. *Asia Pacific Journal of Human Resources* 34(2), 99–109.

Freedman, H.A. (1997) Event critiques…making your event better the next time!! *Fund Raising Management* July, 30–31.

Graham, S., Goldblatt, J.L. and Delph, L. (1995) *The Ultimate Guide to Sport Event Management and Marketing*. Richard Irwin, Homewood, Illinois.

Green, B.C. (2001) Event management: lessons for design and implementation. In: Kluka, D. and Schilling, G. (eds) *The Business of Sport*. Meyer & Meyer, Oxford, pp. 91–103.

Grote, K. (1999) Staff performance advice for CPAs. *Journal of Accountancy* July, 12–18.

Halbwirth, S. and Toohey, K. (2001) The Olympic Games and knowledge management: a case study of the Sydney Organizing Committee of the Olympic Games. *European Sport Management Quarterly* 1(2), 91–111.

Hall, C.M. (1995) *Introduction to Tourism in Australia: Impacts, Planning and Development*, 2nd edn. Longman, Sydney.

Hanlon, C.M. (2003) Managing the pulsating effect in major sport event organizations. PhD thesis, The University of Victoria, Australia.

Hanlon, C.M. and Jago, L.K. (2000) Pulsating sporting events: an organizational structure to optimize performance. In: Allen, J., Harris, R., Jago, L.K. and Veal, A.J. (eds) *Events Beyond 2000: Setting the Agenda – Proceedings of Conference on Event Evaluation, Research and Education*. Australian Centre for Event Management, Sydney, pp. 93–104.

Hanlon, C.M. and Jago, L.K. (2004) The challenge of retaining personnel in major sports events organizations. *Event Management* 9, 39–49.

Hanlon, C. and Stewart, B. (2006) Managing personnel in major sport event organizations: what strategies are required? *Event Management* 10, 77–88.

Howden, D. (2003) Countdown to calamity. *South China Morning Post*, 17 August.

Hoye, R., Smith, A., Westerbeek, H., Stewart, B. and Nicholson, M. (2006) *Sport Management Principles and Applications*. Butterworth-Heinemann, Oxford.

Jordan, L. and Morris, C. (1997) Developing your managers. *Human Resource Monthly* August, 12–16.

Marquis, B.L. and Huston, C.J. (1992) *Leadership Roles and Management Functions in Nursing: Theory and Application*. Lippincott, Philadelphia, Pennsylvania.

Monga, M. (2006) Measuring motivation to volunteer for special events. *Event Management* 10, 47–61.

Mullins, J. (2007) Why is everyone in sports administration so tense? *Mullins Sport* 25, 1.

Pearce, J.L. (1993) *Volunteers: the Organizational Behaviour of Unpaid Workers*. Routledge, London.

Robbins, S.P. and Barnwell, N.S. (1998) *Organization Theory: Concepts and Cases*, 3rd edn. Prentice-Hall, Sydney.

Ruggles, R. (1998) The state of the notion: knowledge management in practice. *California Management Review* 40(3), 80–89.

Saul, P. (1996) Managing the organization as a community of contributors. *Asia Pacific Journal of Human Resources* 34(3), 19–36.

Slack, T. (1997) *Understanding Sport Organizations: the Application of Organization Theory*. Human Kinetics, Champaign, Illinois.

Stoner, J.A.F., Yetton, P.W., Craig, J.F. and Johnston, K.D. (1994) *Management*, 2nd edn. Prentice Hall, Sydney.

Taylor, T., Doherty, A. and McGraw, P. (2008) *Managing People in Sport Organizations: a Strategic Human Resource Management Perspective*. Butterworth-Heinemann, Oxford.

Tennis Australia (2007) *Tennis Australia 2006/07 Annual Report.* Tennis Australia, Melbourne, Australia.

Toffler, A. (1990) *Power Shift.* Bantam Books, New York.

Torkildsen, G. (1992) *Leisure and Recreation Management,* 3rd edn. Spon Press, London.

Turbidy, D. (1997) Surveys bring precision to organizational effectiveness. *Human Resource Monthly* August, 18.

Warn, J.R. (1994) Factors influencing the turnover of skilled personnel: a case study. *Asia Pacific Journal of Human Resources* 32(1), 29–40.

9　Episodic Experiences: Volunteering Flexibility in the Events Sector

Leonie Lockstone[1] and Karen A. Smith[2]

[1]Victoria University, Australia; [2]Victoria University of Wellington, New Zealand

Introduction

The profile of event volunteering has increased in recent years due to the prominence afforded to volunteers at mega-events such as the Olympics and Commonwealth Games. Given the importance of this activity, it is vital that organizations recruit and retain volunteers to undertake a myriad of unpaid roles. Volunteers in general are increasingly attracted to volunteering opportunities that provide them with a degree of flexibility in choosing how often and in what way they contribute to organizations (Volunteering Australia, 2006). Currently, research is lagging behind practice, as the concept of flexibility has overwhelmingly been studied in the context of paid working environments, first in manufacturing and more recently in relation to service sectors. Little work has investigated the application of flexible work practices to volunteering (Lockstone, 2005). From the organizational perspective, there may be some instances where organizations are unwilling or unable to bend to the flexibility needs of volunteers. For example, Lockstone and Baum (2006) and Downward *et al.* (2005), respectively, reported that due to the operational complexities of the 2006 Melbourne and 2002 Manchester Commonwealth Games a 'take it or leave it' attitude was evident on the part of organizers to rostering volunteers. At the same time, however, a high degree of flexibility was asked of volunteers, with regard to both their time commitment to the Games and their willingness to fill certain roles.

Through survey data, this chapter investigates the experiences of volunteers working in the events sector in Australia with regard to the flexibility of their roles and rosters. To contextualize this investigation, comparisons are made between these episodic volunteers and volunteers working in a sustained or ongoing capacity within Australian tourism organizations (museums, visitor attractions and visitor information centres) to ascertain whether and, if so, how the flexibility outcomes made available to volunteers are affected by organization type. The main focus of the chapter, however, relates these findings to episodic volunteers,

© CAB International 2009. *People and Work in Events and Conventions: a Research Perspective* (eds T. Baum *et al.*)

and as such it will draw upon relevant areas of literature on episodic volunteering, event volunteering and flexibility theory. This review highlights the need for greater research attention in order to provide a better understanding of how and when event organizations are required to meet the flexibility needs of their volunteers to ensure positive recruitment and retention outcomes for all parties involved.

Episodic Volunteering in the Event Sector

The traditional view of volunteering is that of the volunteer making a commitment to service an organization(s) on an ongoing and regular basis. Current trends overwhelmingly suggest that work–life balance issues and the demand they place on people's time (from employment, family, leisure) are increasingly affecting the time both current and potential volunteers can commit to volunteering (Gaskin, 2003; Merrill, 2006). Lack of extra time is a key barrier to increased voluntary activity (McClintock, 2004; Kitchen *et al.*, 2006). Australian data suggest that while more people are volunteering, the median weekly hours of voluntary work have decreased (ABS, 2007). Bryen and Madden (2006) suggest that this trend supports the growth of short-term volunteering assignments. Similarly, trend data from the USA dating back to 1989 confirm the growth of episodic volunteering (Grimm *et al.*, 2006). In light of these trends, episodic volunteering has attracted increased research attention over recent years; however, it is hardly a new phenomenon (Handy *et al.*, 2006).

Macduff (1991) first coined the term 'episodic volunteering' to refer to one-off volunteering assignments that offer a flexible relationship with an organization. This is consistent with Harrison's (1995:372) contention that volunteer participation can be 'discrete or episodic, rather than continuous or successive'. Subsequently, Macduff (2005) has classified these episodic opportunities along a time continuum, all of which have relevance for the events sector. This continuum ranges from the most distant and flexible form of episodic volunteering, temporary volunteering, through to interim and then occasional volunteering. Applying these concepts to the event context, temporary volunteers provide service only for a relatively short period of time (e.g. on the day of the event); interim volunteers may work on a regular basis for a defined period (e.g. volunteering on a project basis in the lead-up to a large-scale, one-off event) and occasional volunteers give short periods of service at regular intervals (e.g. a volunteer who makes an annual commitment to an event). Akin to the latter category, Bryen and Madden (2006) use the term 'bounce-back' to describe volunteers who return or re-engage with a single organization in a series of episodic relationships.

Hustinx and Lammertyn (2004) offer another theoretical perspective with which to conceptualize traditional and newer styles of volunteering. Collective volunteering is aligned to the traditional perspective of volunteering. Volunteers of this type make an ongoing commitment to their organization of choice. In contrast, reflexive volunteering represents newer styles of volunteering, people who 'demand a high level of mobility and flexibility in their involvement, and they are primarily functionally orientated' (Hustinx and Lammertyn, 2004:552). In testing the theory on a sample of Red Cross volunteers, Hustinx and Lammertyn reported that a cluster of volunteers fitted the pattern of reflexive volunteering. This volunteer type is labelled as 'distant', to describe their loose, infrequent, short-term and activities-based involvement in the organization (Hustinx and Lammertyn, 2004:568).

There is a growing body of research examining volunteering in the events sector (Williams *et al.*, 1995; Elstad, 1996; Kemp, 2002; Downward and Ralston, 2006; Monga, 2006). Most of the volunteering in this sector, by its very nature, short-term and infrequent, is episodic. Some volunteers, particularly those in leadership roles, may undertake ongoing positions in event organizations akin to traditional volunteering. Investigation of these roles is beyond the scope of the current chapter. In reviewing this body of event research, little mention is made of the phenomenon of episodic volunteering (exceptions include Ralston *et al.*, 2004, 2005), with more attention being focused on the related issues of commitment (Green and Chalip, 2004) and retention (Coyne and Coyne, 2001). One study (Handy *et al.*, 2006) has specifically developed a categorization for episodic volunteering, which has clear parallels with the work of Macduff (2005), and tested it in an event setting. This categorization includes long-term committed volunteers (LTVs), who not only volunteer episodically when required but also make a regular, ongoing commitment to their event organization or in another formalized setting. Handy *et al.* (2006) contend that habitual episodic volunteers (HEVs) undertake at least three volunteering episodes throughout the course of a year for one or more organizations, whilst genuine episodic volunteers (GEVs) 'contribute their time sporadically, only during special times of the year, or consider volunteering as a one-off event' (Handy *et al.*, 2006:33). Testing in a festival setting showed mixed support for this classification.

The remainder of this chapter adopts the overarching term episodic volunteer to encapsulate all these variations, in order to contrast this form of volunteering with sustained or ongoing activities. Nevertheless, the specific nature of the episodic volunteering relationships of those involved in the study will be briefly discussed.

Flexibility and volunteering

Having reviewed the limited research relating to episodic volunteering in the events sector, attention is now turned to the scant literature highlighting the nexus between flexibility and volunteering, in particular focusing on how the flexibility of the volunteer work can influence recruitment and retention outcomes.

It has been suggested that the organization of formal volunteering often requires a high degree of operational flexibility (Geber, 1991), and that for volunteers and paid staff, working in the voluntary sector generally demands a flexible approach (Gann, 1996). There is some evidence that volunteers are increasingly taking up flexible volunteering opportunities. Analysis of UK data found that whilst regular volunteering has remained relatively static, overall people are giving more time, but volunteering in more transient and flexible ways (nfpSynergy, 2005). Fourth-fifths of current volunteers surveyed by Volunteering Australia (2006) identified that flexible volunteering hours are important to them.

Flexible options are seen as particularly important for increasing activity in segments of the population that traditionally have a low propensity to volunteer. Flexible scheduling is regarded as crucial for encouraging more young people to volunteer (Gaskin, 1998, 2003) and can reduce the barriers to volunteering for culturally diverse youths (Calgary Immigrant Aid Society, 2005). Similarly, time flexibility is a desire for older volunteers (Gaskin, 2003; Warburton and Cordingley, 2004), particularly baby boomers (nfpSynergy, 2005), who often feel they do not have enough time to volunteer and do not want to commit to volunteering long term (Esmond, 2001).

In response to changing demands and needs of volunteers, organizations are developing a range of flexible volunteering opportunities (Gaskin, 2003) that are 'short term, time specific and flexible' (Esmond, 2001). Borgiattino (2005) identifies flexibility as one of six success factors necessary to increase participation in volunteering. Australian organizations involving volunteers seem to have recognized this demand for flexibility, variously offering flexible hours, and short-term and one-off opportunities (Volunteering Australia, 2006). Virtual volunteering options are proposed as a way of introducing flexibility in both temporal and geographical terms (McClintock, 2004; Merrill, 2006).

At present the opportunity exists to understand and evaluate the roles, functions and structure of volunteering in terms of the recognized forms of flexibility: namely functional, temporal and numerical. Functional flexibility involves workers utilizing multiple skills, working jobs at different skill levels or shifting between functions. In contrast, numerical flexibility involves adapting the size of the workforce readily and at short notice in response to the prevailing level of economic activity. Temporal flexibility adjusts the quantity and timing of existing staff resources (Rimmer and Zappala, 1988). It is closely associated with numerical flexibility but does not utilize additional workers to meet workload fluctuations. Fryar (2007) has suggested that a more pragmatic approach is needed to understand flexibility in volunteering, related to activity choice, the organizational processes supporting volunteering and volunteer assignments.

The types of strategies recommended to increase volunteering predominantly relate to temporal flexibility, suggesting one-off, short-term or drop-in volunteering (Gaskin, 2003), or volunteering at times outside traditional (paid) working hours (The Urban Institute, 2004). In addition to the temporal flexibility offered by episodic volunteering opportunities, Gaskin (2003) also suggests having a flexible rota system that recognizes that volunteers can often make only a limited commitment. Numerical flexibility can be achieved through a pool of volunteers (Gaskin, 2003), so demands are not unrelenting, and Borgiattino's (2005) recommendation for flexibility in terms of work content could be interpreted as functional.

Developed in the context of paid working environments, one flexibility theory that encapsulates the various forms of flexibility and delineates them based on worker type is Atkinson's (1984) Flexible Firm Model. According to this theory, core workers undertake the most important functions within the organization and as such are partially rewarded through the provision of functional flexibility practices. Peripheral workers are less secure in their positions and are subject to temporal and numerical flexibility practices. At face value, parallels can be drawn between episodic volunteering and Atkinson's use of 'distancing' as the third level of his workforce model. Atkinson (1987) maintains that distance workers conduct activities from which the organization has chosen to distance itself, tasks that can be either highly specialist or very mundane, performed on a planned basis or only when the need arises. This description could apply equally well to the use of episodic volunteers.

Despite recognition of the importance of flexibility to recruiting and retaining volunteers (Gaskin, 2003), very few studies have linked the underlying tenets of specific flexibility theories to volunteering. An exception is Lockstone (2005), who, after due consideration of the seminal works of Atkinson (1984) and Piore and Sabel's (1984) Flexible Specialization Model, developed and tested a model of convergent flexibility specifically with volunteer settings in mind. Convergence, in this instance, was the degree of alignment between flexibility practices in terms of their assessed availability and value. The study highlighted a positive link between functional flexibility practices and the job satisfaction outcomes of volunteers and paid workers in the museums sector. Given these preliminary findings and the different research setting, there is ample scope to revisit and examine the application of all these theories and various components of them to episodic volunteering.

Research Aims

The research aims to provide an exploratory insight into the flexibility options made available and preferred by episodic volunteers working within the events sector. The limited state of current research means that the areas of episodic volunteering and flexible work options are ripe for combined study. In particular, the extent of flexibility available to volunteers will be assessed from the volunteers' own perspective, as will the contention that volunteers perceive that certain organizational characteristics (e.g. number of volunteers, number of paid staff, operating budgets) affect the ability of their host organizations to negotiate with them regarding flexibility outcomes. The research also investigates how best to position flexibility in order to enhance volunteers' satisfaction with the flexibility of their assignments and rosters, which ultimately may enhance recruitment and retention outcomes.

Methodology

A survey-based quantitative methodology was selected as the appropriate data collection medium for enabling adequate access to volunteers in episodic settings. Two highly similar questionnaires were designed to assess the extent of volunteering flexibility: one from the volunteer perspective and one from the organization perspective.

This chapter reports on the findings of the volunteer survey only; however, it is important to briefly mention the organizational survey, as responding organizations provided the access to volunteers for the second stage of the research. First, convenience sampling was used to distribute the organization questionnaire to volunteer coordinators/managers representing events of varying scale and appeal. To enable comparative analysis around traditional and newer styles of volunteering, the questionnaire was also distributed to related tourism organizations (museums, visitor attractions and visitor information centres), whose operations generally require more of an ongoing commitment from their volunteers. Distribution of the paper-based questionnaire to a database of 303 organizations in the Australian state of Victoria yielded 44 responses (response rate of 14.5%).

Secondly, in order to distribute the volunteer questionnaires with the participating organization's permission, their volunteers were indirectly approached and asked to complete the survey either online or in paper-based format. Ethical considerations prevented the direct distribution of the survey to volunteers; this mirrors the authors' previous experiences (Smith, 1999; Lockstone, 2005) of the difficulties in accessing volunteer populations, especially on a probability basis. Without knowing the size of the sample population, 238 usable responses were received from volunteers, sufficient to undertake the planned data analysis. One hundred and fifty-three respondents volunteered at an event, and 83 at a museum/gallery, visitor/tourism attraction or visitor information centre. Of the event volunteers, 76% of respondents volunteered at the same event organization. This large proportion of the sample significantly impacts upon the representativeness of the findings. Furthermore, while 68% of the online responses to the questionnaire were completed by event volunteers, responses from the ongoing volunteers were overwhelmingly received via the paper-based version. It appears older respondents, typically in regional areas, had difficulty accessing the questionnaire in its online form.

A variety of analytical techniques were used to examine the exploratory data. Descriptive analysis was used for data screening purposes, as well as providing an initial snapshot of the volunteers, their host organizations and to what extent flexibility affected their volunteer assignments. Significance testing using *t*-tests was used to analyse group differences in the interval-scaled data (adopting a five-point Likert scale). This analysis was based around certain variables that were considered to best reflect the organizational dynamics and working relationships of the volunteers surveyed. Pearson's product–moment correlations were also conducted to determine the extent of association between the interval-scaled flexibility variables. Given the methodological limitations discussed above, it might be questioned whether the application of inferential statistics to the collected data is entirely appropriate. This treatment adopts Coyne and Coyne's (2001) approach in applying parametric statistics to non-parametric data in their study of volunteers working at a golf event. De Vaus (2002) also notes the increasing acceptance of such testing in social science journals.

Results and Discussion

To provide a point of comparison in presenting the research findings, the type of organization the respondent volunteered for was recoded into one of two categories: volunteering for an event was recoded as episodic volunteering (n = 153 respondents) and volunteering for a museum/gallery, visitor/tourism attraction or visitor information centre was recoded as sustained or ongoing volunteering (n = 83 respondents). The results in Table 9.1 provide a summative profile of episodic and ongoing volunteers, based on common responses (excluding missing data), according to this recoding.

Despite the different organization types, leading responses to both volunteering scenarios indicated that volunteer respondents were most likely to be retired (episodic, 29%, n = 43; ongoing, 77%, n = 61), aged 60+ years (episodic, 34%, n = 40; ongoing, 78%, n = 58) and female (episodic, 66%, n = 94; ongoing, 73%, n = 56). That said, however, there was a broader range of responses recorded to the first two questions in the case of episodic volunteers. The major demographic difference, apart from organization type, was location. Nearly the entire episodic cohort volunteered in a metropolitan location (99%, n = 149), whereas the overwhelming majority of ongoing volunteers worked in regional settings (92%, n = 162). This finding may point to sampling error.

Table 9.1. Volunteer profile.

Volunteer relationship with event/organization	Episodic volunteers (n = 153)		Ongoing volunteers (n = 83)	
	%	n	%	n
Regular/ongoing basis	12	18	96	74
Ongoing basis, irregularly	9	13	4	3
Once-only basis	79	115	0	0

Extent of relationship	Once-only basis (n = 115)			Regular/ongoing basis (n = 74)		
	Largest category	%	n	Largest category	%	n
Tenure	2 weeks–1 month	70	76	6+ years	36	26
How regularly they volunteer	Daily	74	81	Weekly	65	46
How many hours in that period	6–10 hours	50	56	2–5 hours	73	51
Other volunteering activity	Yes, volunteer for one other event/ organization	41	46	Yes, volunteer for one other event/ organization	31	22

Further analysis of the episodic cohort (n = 153), based on the nature of their volunteering relationship, found that in terms of sheer numbers they can be categorized as occasional and temporal volunteers (according to Macduff, 2005), and habitual and genuine episodic volunteers (according to Handy *et al.*, 2006). Table 9.2 highlights the common responses to the variables indicating the extent of these episodic volunteers' relationship with their host organizations.

Examining the above findings more closely, further comparative insights can be drawn between these volunteering patterns and Handy *et al.*'s (2006) categorization of episodic activity. In their study, Handy *et al.* predicted their category of LTVs would have longer tenure and contribute more hours to their event organizations; however, these findings were only partially supported. Handy *et al.*'s second and more episodically prone category of HEVs were actually found to have volunteered for longer than the other two groups (LTVs and GEVs), and indeed the findings in Table 9.2 indicate that, in the current context, event volunteers who volunteered on a regular and ongoing basis (most closely aligned to LTVs) and those who volunteered on an ongoing but irregular basis (most closely aligned to HEVs) both experienced similar levels of tenure (less than 1 month).

Handy *et al.* (2006) did find, however, that LTVs contributed more hours to their volunteer assignments than HEVs and GEVs but that the expected difference in time expended by the latter two groups did not eventuate (this is in light of the prediction that GEVs were the most episodic of the categories under study). The findings in Table 9.2 indicate that, across the board, episodic volunteers

Table 9.2. Extent of episodic volunteering.

Volunteering relationship	Volunteer with this event on a regular/ongoing basis (12%, n = 18)			Volunteer with this event on an ongoing basis but irregularly/infrequently (9%, n = 13)			Volunteer with this event on a once-only basis (79%, n = 115)		
	Largest category	%	n	Largest category	%	n	Largest category	%	n
Tenure	Less than 1 month	44	9	Less than 1 month	64	8	2 weeks–1 month	70	76
How regularly do they volunteer	Daily	50	8	Daily	39	5	Daily	74	81
				Yearly	39	5			
How many hours in that period	6–10 hours	53	9	6–10 hours	50	6	6–10 hours	50	46
Other volunteering activity	No	44	8	Yes, one other organization/event	39	5	Yes, one other organization/event	41	46

were uniform in contributing 6–10 hours on a daily basis, despite differences in the exact nature of their volunteering relationship with their host organization. This uniformity of response may be partially a product of poor questionnaire design, given that those respondents who indicated that they volunteered on an ongoing basis but infrequently (e.g. for an annual event) were only able to select one option to describe their frequency of volunteering on the questionnaire when in fact, for these respondents, two selections may have been more appropriate (e.g. volunteer yearly on a daily basis). This flaw may explain the equal split in findings depicted in Table 9.2.

As would be reasonable to expect, event volunteers making an irregular, ongoing commitment to one organization indicated that they did not participate in any other volunteer activity (see Table 9.2). What is interesting, however, is that, as indicated in Table 9.1, 31% of ongoing volunteers working in sustained settings such as museums, visitor information centres and visitor attractions found the time to formally volunteer for at least one other organization or event. In this instance, this finding is likely to be partially or fully explained as a result of the lesser time commitment generally associated with the respondents' ongoing volunteering (Table 9.1 indicates the majority of ongoing volunteers work on a weekly basis, contributing between 2 and 5 hours) as opposed to that of event volunteers, as mentioned above. Unfortunately, the scope of the current questionnaire did not collect data in relation to in what setting the additional commitment of these ongoing volunteers was taking place, e.g. if ongoing volunteers were picking up opportunities to volunteer on an episodic basis or if this effort was directed towards another sustained volunteering position. This is a worthwhile topic for future research.

Applying the concepts and terminology borne of flexibility theory in paid working environments (Friedrich et al., 1998; Hall et al., 1998; Kramar, 1998; Volberda, 1998; Reilly, 2001), Table 9.3 provides a descriptive profile of what types of flexibility are most common to episodic volunteers in the events sector. To contextualize this examination, comparisons are made between these event volunteers and volunteers working in an ongoing capacity within related tourism organizations (museums, visitor attractions and visitor information centres), to determine whether the flexibility practices applied to volunteers are affected by organization type.

In general, the mean results indicate that episodic volunteers perceive that demand-driven temporal and numerical flexibility practices are more applicable to their work in the events sector. Independent t-tests found significant differences in the flexibility practices applied to episodic and ongoing volunteers in relation to flexitime ($t[234] = 2.34$, $P > 0.05$) and job sharing ($t[234] = 2.31$, $P > 0.05$). As it might be reasonable to expect, these respective temporal and numerical practices were rated more highly by episodic volunteers, reflecting their greater relevance to the short-term nature of event volunteering. No other significant differences were found between the two groups. In contrast, volunteers involved in ongoing roles indicated that functional flexibility practices, with the underlying aims of up-skilling and multi-skilling workers, were slightly more prevalent in their sectors, probably given the greater commitment over time these volunteers make to their host organizations.

Table 9.3.   Descriptive profile – types of flexibility.

	Volunteer type	n	Mean	SD
Functional flexibility				
Job enlargement				
Volunteers are provided with tasks that extend	Ongoing	83	3.67	0.89
the content or quantity of their work	Episodic	153	3.51	0.99
Job enrichment				
Volunteers are provided with tasks that add	Ongoing	83	3.64	0.86
to the quality of their volunteer work	Episodic	153	3.49	1.04
Job rotation				
Volunteers are able to shift between various	Ongoing	83	3.34	0.79
jobs or departments to improve their work	Episodic	153	3.30	1.11
versatility				
Temporal flexibility				
Flexitime				
Volunteer hours may vary, usually in terms	Ongoing	83	2.96	1.20
of start/finish times; however, a set number	Episodic	153	3.33	1.16
of hours must be worked within a specified				
time period				
Zero-hour contracts				
Volunteers do not have regular hours. They	Ongoing	83	2.07	0.94
only volunteer when specifically requested	Episodic	153	3.14	1.24
to do so by the organization				
Shift working				
Volunteer hours are assigned on a shift basis	Ongoing	83	3.37	1.27
	Episodic	153	3.94#	0.92
Voluntary reduced hours				
Volunteers are able to reduce their volunteer	Ongoing	83	3.40	1.16
hours to assist with domestic duties or	Episodic	153	3.62	0.98
pursue another interest				
Numerical flexibility				
Job sharing				
The tasks of one full-time position are shared	Ongoing	83	2.63	1.11
between two or more volunteers	Episodic	153	2.99	1.20
Fixed-term contracts				
Volunteering for a limited period of time with	Ongoing	83	2.20	1.16
a finish date specified	Episodic	153	4.13#	0.96

#, Skewed result.

The temporal or time component of operations is only one characteristic that distinguishes volunteering opportunities available in museums, visitor information centres and visitor attractions, as opposed to events. The research set out to assess other differences that may impinge upon the ability of organizations to cater to the flexibility needs of volunteers. Volunteers assessed on a five-point scale the degree to which they agreed with certain operational descriptions of their host organization. Table 9.4 provides the results of this descriptive analysis (significant findings from *t*-test analysis are also reported where appropriate).

Table 9.4. Descriptive profile – organizational characteristics.

	Volunteer type	n	Mean	SD	df	t
Size of volunteer workforce						
Too few volunteers to cover	Ongoing	74	3.20	1.30	212	3.31*
shifts	Episodic	140	2.56	1.39		
Sufficient volunteers to cover	Ongoing	72	2.96	1.20	214	−2.76*
shifts	Episodic	144	3.45	1.26		
Too many volunteers	Ongoing	69	1.71	0.75		
	Episodic	140	2.69	1.36		
Size of paid workforce						
Small number of paid staff	Ongoing	71	2.89	1.60	206	−2.74*
	Episodic	137	3.50#	1.48		
Moderate number of paid staff	Ongoing	67	1.97	1.33	202	−2.83*
	Episodic	137	2.51	1.26		
Large number of paid staff	Ongoing	66	1.50	1.03	202	−3.46*
	Episodic	138	2.14	1.32		
Size of operating budget						
Small operating budget	Ongoing	69	3.17	1.58	203	2.91*
	Episodic	136	2.52	1.49		
Moderate operating budget	Ongoing	61	2.33	1.52		
	Episodic	135	2.44	1.41		
Large operating budget	Ongoing	64	1.72	1.21		
	Episodic	136	2.54	1.59		
Volunteer turnover						
Organization seems to	Ongoing	75	2.99	1.26	210	1.98*
experience difficulties	Episodic	137	2.59	1.46		
recruiting new volunteers						
Organization seems to	Ongoing	70	2.41	1.03		
experience difficulties	Episodic	137	2.58	1.45		
keeping volunteers						

#, Skewed result; *$P < 0.05$.

The descriptive data generally show that tourism organizations that need volunteers in order to operate on an ongoing basis appear to struggle in terms of having access to less resources (volunteers, paid staff, smaller budgets). Episodic volunteers working in the events sector generally perceived their host organizations to have sufficient volunteer numbers to cover shifts and to experience fewer challenges in recruiting new volunteers to make up shortfalls. These differences were significant when compared with the responses of their ongoing counterparts. Further frequency analysis lends weight to these findings. Specifically, 59% of the ongoing volunteers surveyed estimated that the total volunteer workforce of their host organization was less than 50 people. In comparison, 79% of episodic volunteers estimated this figure to be between 1000 and 4999 people for their respective event organizations. Once again, such extreme findings probably point to sampling error.

The results of descriptive and correlation analysis show poor support for the contention that volunteers perceived these organizational characteristics to affect the ability of their host organizations to negotiate with them regarding flexibility outcomes. All of the variables listed in Table 9.4 were separately assessed by the volunteer respondents using a five-point scale to see what influence (very little through to very great) they had on these outcomes (e.g. the volunteer assignments and rosters). In the case of the episodic volunteers, the mean results indicate that, for all but one variable, respondents considered that these characteristics had very little or little influence on the ability of their event organizations to provide them with flexibility outcomes. Sufficient volunteer numbers (mean = 2.75) was the single variable that was found to have 'some influence' on these assessments. The average scores of the ongoing volunteers provides even less support for this line of thinking. Separate bivariate analyses on the combined data set (ongoing and episodic volunteers), using the characteristic variables listed in Table 9.4 and the corresponding variables assessing their influence, all resulted in Pearson correlation coefficients that showed positive linear relationships at a significant level ($P < 0.05$). However, the absolute values of these coefficients (ranging from $r = 0.346$ to $r = 0.585$) indicated that the strength of these relationships was generally poor. This contention might be better evaluated from an organizational perspective, given that volunteer coordinators and managers need to take a broader, less personalized view when considering factors that influence their operations (this represents the next stage of the research, to be reported in subsequent publications).

It would be remiss, however, to diminish these findings off hand. They may be indicative of the very nature of volunteering itself, the exercise of free will. Volunteers who consider that their role places too many demands on their time or is rigid and inflexible have the relative freedom to leave their host organization, having experienced few repercussions personally as a result of doing so. Likewise, such inflexibility may act as a deterrent in the first place for potential volunteers considering taking up roles. This effectively means that volunteers who persist in their roles may seemingly be happy with their lot and this assumption can be applied to the ratings of questionnaire respondents. These findings may also relate to the temporal nature of event volunteering. That is, episodic volunteers may be more willing than their ongoing counterparts to accept that flexibility is tied to the time constraints of running events (potentially longer shifts over a relatively short period of time) rather than the operational requirements of specific event organizations. Supportive of this contention, Downward *et al.*'s (2005) study of volunteer expectations relating to the 2002 Manchester Commonwealth Games found that female respondents were more accepting than their male counterparts that the experience of volunteering at this mega-event would probably leave them feeling tired and overwhelmed. Further research is required to shed light on when and why volunteers choose to accept or reject the flexibility options on offer in event organizations.

The current research does provide insight as to how best to position flexibility in order to enhance volunteer satisfaction with assignments and rosters. Specifically, Table 9.5 details findings relating to episodic volunteers and their assessments of overall satisfaction with particular drivers determining the extent of flexibility associated with their roles. For the purpose of this analysis the interval-scaled satisfaction variable was collapsed into categorical form based on

Table 9.5. Flexibility options available to episodic volunteers.

Flexibility to make changes to:	Satisfaction with level of flexibility	n	Mean	SD	df	t
Days when volunteering	Below median	29	2.89	1.25	134	−3.84***
occurs	Above median	109	3.75	0.99		
Number of hours	Below median	25	2.80	1.38	131	−3.66***
volunteered	Above median	108	3.70	1.04		
Start/finish times of shifts	Below median	25	2.68	1.41	132	−3.01*
	Above median	109	3.49	1.16		
Types of jobs/tasks	Below median	25	2.28	1.28	133	−3.47*
performed	Above median	110	3.23	1.22		

*$P < 0.05$; ***$P < 0.001$.

its median score (4.00 on a five-point scale ranging from very dissatisfied through to very satisfied).

The results confirm that those episodic volunteers who felt they had more freedom to alter their volunteering commitment in terms of when they were rostered to work (days, number of hours and start and finish times) and the form that the work took (types of jobs/tasks performed) were more satisfied with the level of overall flexibility associated with their roles. This outcome is hardly surprising. It is interesting to note, however, that related analysis applied to the ongoing respondents found that for all but one of the variables listed in Table 9.5 (flexibility of start and finish times), volunteers working on a continuous basis in museums, visitor information centres and visitor attractions assessed themselves as having greater flexibility over the days they volunteered (ongoing, mean = 3.87; episodic, mean = 3.57), the number of hours they volunteered for (ongoing, mean = 3.53; episodic, mean = 3.48) and the types of jobs/tasks they performed (ongoing, mean = 3.58; episodic, mean = 3.03). Once again, these findings may be indicative of the immediate and short-term commitment necessitated by volunteering at events in contrast to the often longer-term relationship ongoing volunteers have with their host organizations.

Further analysis utilizing the flexibility satisfaction variable highlighted one of the key reasons why tourism organizations of all types, whether they offer episodic or ongoing volunteering opportunities, should be concerned with flexibility. Namely, volunteers were asked to indicate whether or not they would be likely to leave their host organization if their flexibility needs were not effectively met. Intention to leave was assessed on a five-point scale using the descriptors 'definitely leave' through to 'definitely stay'. Significance testing indicated that episodic volunteers who rated above the median in terms of the level of satisfaction they experienced with the flexibility of their event roles were more likely to persist with volunteering for their host organization (mean = 3.89 probably stay, $t[119] = −2.61, P < 0.05$). Analysis of the combined data set (including ongoing volunteers) yielded a similar finding. This finding lends support to the contention that enhanced flexibility outcomes for volunteers can potentially lead to improved retention outcomes for event and tourism organizations, whether they be ongoing operations that require volunteers on a regular basis or more episodic in nature, needing volunteers to bounce back (Bryen and Madden, 2006) to service an infrequent and irregular event. Regardless of organizational type, the savings in terms of reduced training times and having a pool of job-ready volunteers to provide high-quality service to visitors and guests are just some of the reasons why these organizations can directly and indirectly benefit from addressing the flexibility needs of their volunteers.

Conclusions and Implications

In addressing the stated aims of the research, the chapter has provided an insight into the flexibility options made available to and preferred by episodic volunteers working within the events sector. Namely, these volunteers, the majority of whom can be classified as occasional and temporal volunteers (according to Macduff, 2005) and habitual and genuine episodic volunteers (according to Handy *et al.*, 2006), indicated that demand-driven temporal and numerical forms of flexibility were more applicable to their event sector roles, in point of comparison with ongoing volunteers working in museums, visitor information centres and visitor attractions, for whom functional flexibility was more prevalent.

The contention that episodic volunteers perceive certain organizational characteristics (e.g. number of volunteers, number of paid staff, operating budgets) as affecting the ability of their host organizations to negotiate with them regarding flexibility outcomes was not supported by the research findings. This lack of support may be an indication that episodic volunteers are generally accepting of the operational pressures necessitated by the event context itself, as opposed to particular characteristics associated with an individual event organization that might act to diminish flexibility for volunteers. Further research is needed to examine the questions of when and why volunteers choose to accept or reject the flexibility options offered by organizations and, from an organizational perspective, particular facilitators and inhibitors to delivering these options.

The findings of the current research provide insight into a key motivation for organizations in adopting a more flexible approach to dealing with their episodic volunteers: namely, the positive link between a volunteer's level of satisfaction with their flexibility options and intention to stay with their host organization. Replication of this study, preferably using a longitudinal methodology, would enable further testing of this link and the inclusion of associated constructs such as commitment and performance, in order to provide for a fuller picture of how the application of flexibility practices to volunteers can maximize their organizational contribution whilst making allowance for their lives outside of volunteering.

Event organizations have long depended on volunteers but only more recently have researchers begun to acknowledge and explore the complexities of episodic volunteering at events. This research demonstrates the potential for applying theories developed in the context of the paid workforce to a volunteering context. The difficulties involved in accessing volunteer populations and the associated degree of error arising from the sampling technique used and potentially the administration of the questionnaire have been noted. Despite these limitations, this research provides empirical support to the intuitive reasoning that events are in a strong position to capitalize on the growing demand from volunteers for flexibility. It is important to recognize that while those volunteering at events do seek flexible work practices they are also conscious of the demands that working at a short-term event places on them. By understanding the flexibility preferences of volunteers, organizations are better positioned to recruit and retain volunteers, and offer them a rewarding and satisfying volunteering experience.

References

ABS (2007) *Voluntary Work, Australia*. Australian Bureau of Statistics, Canberra.

Atkinson, J. (1984) Manpower strategies for flexible organizations. *Personnel Management* August, 28–31.

Atkinson, J. (1987) Flexibility or fragmentation? The United Kingdom labour market in the eighties. *Labour and Society* 12(1), 87–105.

Borgiattino, S. (2005) *Promoting + Developing Volunteering*. EFIL (European Federation for Intercultural Learning), Brussels.

Bryen, L. and Madden, K. (2006) *Bounce-back of Episodic Volunteers: What Makes Episodic Volunteers Return?* Working Paper No. CPNS 32. Queensland University of Technology, Brisbane, Australia.

Calgary Immigrant Aid Society (2005) *Culturally Diverse Youth and Volunteerism: How to Recruit, Train, and Retain Culturally Diverse Youth Volunteers*. Volunteer Canada, Ottawa, Canada.

Coyne, B.S. and Coyne, E.J. Sr (2001) Getting, keeping and caring for unpaid volunteers for professional golf tournament events. *Human Resource Development International* 4(2), 199–214.

de Vaus, D.A. (2002) *Analyzing Social Science Data*. Sage Publications, London.

Downward, P. and Ralston, R. (2006) The sports development potential of sport event volunteering: insights from the XVII Manchester Commonwealth Games. *European Sport Management Quarterly* 6(4), 333–351.

Downward, P., Lumsdon, L. and Ralston, R. (2005) Gender differences in sports event volunteering: insights from Crew 2002 at the XVII Commonwealth Games. *Managing Leisure* 10, 219–236.

Elstad, B. (1996) Volunteer perception of learning and satisfaction in a mega-event: the case of the XVII Olympic Winter Games in Lillehammer. *Festival Management and Event Tourism* 4, 75–86.

Esmond, J. (2001) *'BOOMNET': Capturing the Baby Boomer Volunteers: a 2001 Research Project into Baby Boomers and Volunteering*. Department for Community Development, Government of Western Australia, Perth, Australia.

Friedrich, A., Kabst, R., Weber, W. and Rodehuth, M. (1998) Functional flexibility: merely reacting or acting strategically? *Employee Relations* 20(5), 504–523.

Fryar, A. (2007) Yoga for the volunteer management practitioner: the practicalities of remaining flexible. *Australian Journal of Volunteering* 12(2), 89–93.

Gann, N. (1996) *Managing Change in Voluntary Organizations: a Guide to Practice*. Open University Press, Buckingham, UK.

Gaskin, K. (1998) *What Young People Want from Volunteering*. Institute for Volunteering Research, London.

Gaskin, K. (2003) *A Choice Blend: What Volunteers Want from Organization and Management*. Institute for Volunteering Research, London.

Geber, B. (1991) Managing volunteers. *Training* June, 21–25.

Green, B.C. and Chalip, L. (2004) Paths to volunteer commitment: lessons from the Sydney Olympic Games. In: Stebbins, R.A. and Graham, M. (eds) *Volunteering as Leisure/Leisure as Volunteering: an International Assessment*. CAB International, Wallingford, UK, pp. 49–67.

Grimm, R., Dietz, N., Foster-Bey, J., Reingold, D. and Nesbit, R. (2006) *Volunteer Growth in America: a Review of Trends Since 1974*. Corporation for National and Community Service, Washington, DC.

Hall, R., Harley, B. and Whitehouse, G. (1998) Contingent work and gender in Australia: evidence from the 1995 Australian Workplace Industrial Relations Survey. *The Economic and Labour Relations Review* 9(1), 55–81.

Handy, F., Brodeur, N. and Cnaan, R.A. (2006) Summer on the island: episodic volunteering. *Voluntary Action* 7(3), 31–46.

Harrison, D.A. (1995) Volunteer motivation and attendance decisions: competitive theory testing in multiple samples from a homeless shelter. *Journal of Applied Psychology* 80(3), 371–385.

Hustinx, L. and Lammertyn, F. (2004) The cultural bases of volunteering: understanding and predicting attitudinal differences between Flemish Red Cross volunteers. *Nonprofit and Voluntary Sector Quarterly* 33(4), 548–584.

Kemp, S. (2002) The hidden workforce: volunteers' learning in the Olympics. *Journal of European Industrial Training* 26(2/4), 109–117.

Kitchen, S., Michaelson, J., Wood, N. and John, P. (2006) *2005 Citizenship Survey: Active Communities Topic Report*. Department for Communities and Local Government, London.

Kramar, R. (1998) Flexibility in Australia: implications for employees and managers. *Employee Relations* 20(5), 453–460.

Lockstone, L. (2005) Managing the volunteer workforce: flexible structures and strategies to integrate volunteers and paid workers. PhD thesis, Victoria University, Melbourne, Australia.

Lockstone, L. and Baum, T. (2006) Volunteers and the 2006 Commonwealth Games in Melbourne: an inlooker perspective. In: Chen, C. (ed.) *Hospitality and Tourism Education: Trends and Strategies*. Proceedings of the 2006 joint conference of APTA and APacCHRIE, Hualien, Taiwan. Taiwan Hospitality and Tourism College and National Taiwan Normal University.

Macduff, N. (1991) *Episodic Volunteering: Building the Short-term Volunteer Program*. MBA Publishing, Walla Walla, Washington.

Macduff, N. (2005) Societal changes and the rise of the episodic volunteer. In: Brudney, J.L. (ed.) *Emerging Areas of Volunteering*. ARNOVA Occasional Paper Series 1(2), pp. 49–61.

McClintock, N. (2004) *Understanding Canadian Volunteers: Using the National Survey of Giving, Volunteering and Participating to Build your Volunteer Program*. Canadian Centre for Philanthropy, Toronto, Canada.

Merrill, M.V. (2006) Global trends and the challenges for volunteering. *The International Journal of Volunteer Administration* XXIV(1), 9–14.

Monga, M. (2006) Measuring motivation to volunteer for special events. *Event Management* 10, 47–61.

nfpSynergy (2005) *The 21st Century Volunteer: a Report on the Changing Face of Volunteering in the 21st Century*. nfpSynergy, London.

Piore, M.J. and Sabel, C.F. (1984) *The Second Industrial Divide*. Basic Books, New York.

Ralston, R., Downward, P. and Lumsdon, L. (2004) The expectations of volunteers prior to the XVII Commonwealth Games, 2002: a qualitative study. *Event Management* 9, 13–26.

Ralston, R., Lumsden, L. and Downward, P. (2005) The third force in events tourism: volunteers at the XVII Commonwealth Games. *Journal of Sustainable Tourism* 13(5), 504–519.

Reilly, P. (2001) *Flexibility at Work: Balancing the Interests of Employer and Employee.* Gower, Hampshire, UK.

Rimmer, M. and Zappala, J. (1988) Labour market flexibility and the second tier. *Australian Bulletin of Labour* 14(4), 564–591.

Smith, K.A. (1999) The management of volunteers at heritage attractions: literary heritage properties in the UK. PhD thesis, Nottingham Trent University, UK.

The Urban Institute (2004) *Volunteer Management Capacity in America's Charities and Congregations: a Briefing Report.* The Urban Institute, Washington, DC.

Volberda, H.W. (1998) *Building the Flexible Firm: How to Remain Competitive.* Oxford University Press, Oxford.

Volunteering Australia (2006) *National Survey of Volunteering Issues 06.* Volunteering Australia, Melbourne, Australia.

Warburton, J. and Cordingley, S. (2004) The contemporary challenges of volunteering in an aging Australia. *Australian Journal on Volunteering* 9(2), 67–74.

Williams, P.W., Dossa, K.B. and Tompkins, L. (1995) Volunteerism and special event management: a case study of Whistler's Men's World Cup of Skiing. *Festival Management and Event Tourism* 3(2), 83–95.

IV Recruitment and Retention in Events and Conventions

This part deals with the recruitment, selection and retention of staff, both paid and volunteer, within the events industry and highlights areas for future research, development and professional practice. Whilst the following chapters concentrate mainly on perspectives from Australia and the USA, conclusions and recommendations are equally applicable to the international events industry.

Although each of the contributing authors recognizes the wealth of research already devoted to the topic of human resource management within organizations in general, they also recognize that there is a need to concentrate more specifically on recruitment and retention practices within the events sector (as distinct from the wider hospitality and tourism sector), as the needs of this rapidly expanding industry are quite different from those of the 'normal' organization. Chapters are enhanced by the use of case studies, research findings and recommendations by event specialists as to the types of skills and people required by the profession and how these might best be applied to different sectors of the industry – including the leisure and sporting events sectors, the business events sector, the volunteer sector and the cultural festival sector. All of the contributors mention the unique nature of many events and highlight the challenges and opportunities this 'uniqueness' poses to event managers and organizers, not least for the recruitment and retention of a suitably qualified, trained and motivated workforce.

The first chapter, by Deery (Chapter 10), reviews literature on recruitment and retention in the hospitality and tourism industry, to offer lessons for the events sector. While job satisfaction is vital to the retention of all staff, she also highlights the difficulties of generalizing about recruitment and retention across the events sector. For those working in pulsating organizations such as leisure events and the facilitation of business events, it is important to offer flexible working arrangements, supportive supervision and peers, and the opportunity to take leave for emotional and physical well-being. For those within more traditional organizations, such as jobs in convention centres or visitors' bureaus, strategies to recruit and retain staff need to focus on providing a good working environment, sound supervision, reasonable pay and reasonable workloads.

Goldblatt and Matheson (Chapter 11) present a comparative analysis of Australian and American event volunteering. Through a survey of the literature and four expert interviews, they discuss the commonalities with regard to the supply and demand, motivations, recruitment and retention of volunteers in both countries. The chapter includes a volunteer motivation typology and presents the volunteering experience as a life cycle, where engaging volunteers through a series of touch points is fundamental to their continued volunteering. Goldblatt and Matheson also note differences; only in the USA are volunteers heavily involved in business events, in addition to the more widely recognized leisure event volunteering.

The final chapter in this part, by Smith and Lockstone (Chapter 12), moves from the macro-level to the micro-level and is a comparative study of volunteering across 12 cultural festivals in Australia. It offers an organizational perspective and presents empirical data to consider three key stages of volunteer management: retention of existing volunteers, recruitment of new volunteers, and the selection and screening process. Smith and Lockstone note that, by relying on a returning cohort of volunteers, for many reoccurring events recruitment is as much about retention and satisfaction. New volunteers can be recruited as individuals or groups, and an informal approach to recruitment and selection dominates. They also present examples of best practice, illustrating how event organizations can work with a range of community and business stakeholders to promote, develop and manage their volunteering workforce effectively.

10 Employee Retention Strategies for Event Management

Victoria University, Australia

Introduction

Employee retention is key to the success of organizations, particularly service organizations, where employee knowledge and service quality are priorities. Managing and retaining staff and volunteers in the events industry, in both leisure and business events, is extremely important, as the success of the industry depends on a high-quality experience. A definition of events, as presented by Getz (2008:404), states that 'planned events are spatial–temporal phenomenon, and each is unique because of interactions among the setting, people, and management systems – including design elements and the program'. Events other than leisure events are discussed in this chapter, and while the term 'convention' is used frequently in relation to the meetings industry, this chapter will use the phrase 'business events' as it is more embracing of activities such as exhibitions and incentives. According to the Business Events Council of Australia (BECA), the definition of a business event is:

> any public or private activity consisting of a minimum of 15 persons with a common interest or vocation, held in a specific venue or venues, and hosted by an organization (or organizations). This may include (but not be limited to): conferences, conventions, symposia, congresses, incentive meetings, marketing events, special celebrations, seminars, courses, public or trade shows, exhibitions, company general meetings, corporate retreats, training programs.
> (cited in Deery *et al.*, 2005:109)

This chapter examines the research findings on staff recruitment and retention in the leisure and business events sectors. Although both areas deal with events, the two are quite different, with the business event environment being very similar to that of 'normal' organizations in structure, while leisure events tend to be what Hanlon and Jago (2000) call 'pulsating events', applying

Toffler's 1990 concept. The chapter will begin with an overview of the generic literature on recruitment and retention and then use this literature to inform the discussion of recruitment and retention in leisure and business events.

Recruitment and Retention

There is a substantial amount of literature in the area of recruitment and retention in organizations and it is tempting to examine this literature to set the scene for a general discussion of retention and recruitment. However, it can be argued that events are part of the tourism industry and so the discussion that follows will examine these issues in the context of the hospitality and tourism industry.

Recruitment: Lessons from the Hospitality and Tourism Industry

The issue of recruitment within any industry, particularly labour-intensive areas such as hospitality and tourism, is strongly linked to the ability to retain staff. The key difficulty facing these industries in recruiting staff is the image of a low-paying, low-status and casualized industry with few or no career opportunities (see, for example, Jolliffe and Farnsworth, 2003). These authors, like many others, argue that both recruitment and retention are made more difficult because of its image and, in many cases, the reality of working in the hospitality and tourism industry. Martin *et al.* (2006) test this assessment, with particular attention to managerial and supervisory staff. Their findings confirm that the image of low pay and lack of career potential and development opportunities is still the greatest challenge to recruitment in the hospitality and tourism industries. They also argue that a respected profession is often linked with a well-established system of training and staff development, and they recommend that hospitality and tourism should be encouraged to have more university courses to enhance the image of the professionalism of the industry.

One of the issues relating to recruitment in the hospitality and tourism industry is the way that recruitment occurs. Very often, particularly for the lower-skilled areas, recruitment is done in an ad hoc way through brief and informal interviews and little reference checking. Dermody *et al.* (2004) argue that employers in the industry do not understand the motivations of employees to join the industry and, consequently, why they would leave the industry. These authors suggest that employers think they know what hospitality and tourism employees want but this is incorrect. Dermody *et al.* (2004) argue that employees are motivated, among other elements, by the organization they work for, the supervisor, money, the work itself, the work environment, recognition, peers and status, but employers do not understand which of these is the most important. These authors found that although hospitality and tourism employees are initially motivated by money to join the industry, they remain in their jobs because of the work environment.

Recruitment strategies

Rowley and Purcell (2001) provide some measures to assist recruitment levels through the targeting of particular segments of the workforce. Specifically, they argue that parents and full-time students can be offered flexible hours to suit both the organization and the employees and that these staffing arrangements are offered on a long-term basis (e.g. 3 years). Such arrangements provide an opportunity to engender loyalty on both sides. These authors also suggest, as do other researchers, that older workers should be employed to provide good customer care. It is argued that this cohort is less concerned about the lack of career development opportunities than younger workers and may be motivated more by the social environment in which they work. Finally, Rowley and Purcell (2001) acknowledge the benefits of employing staff based on personality and attitude and suggest that if the employer is able to be successful in achieving a strong fit between the organization and the employee there is greater potential for stability.

A solution to the recruitment of staff into the hospitality and tourism industry, used in a number of countries, has been the use of migrant labour. Choi *et al.* (2000) argue that, with the continued growth of the industry, some countries, such as the USA, the UK and Australia, do not have sufficient populations to staff the growing industry. They suggest that there are 'push and pull' factors (p. 63) that encourage the use of migrant labour. The pull factors include the flexible hours, opportunities for females and minorities, and opportunities to learn a skill. In Australia, similar discussions have occurred in order to increase the availability of labour. The Australian government now offers specific visa arrangements, and tourists, as well as migrants, are able to take advantage of these. The main difficulty with the Working Holiday Visa, as it is known, is that the skills learnt do not stay within the country.

Baum (2007) discusses the use of various labour markets to fill the ever-increasing demand for hospitality and tourism employees, with a particular focus on the changing skill requirements for the industry. He suggests that not only do service industry staff need to be technically skilled but also need to have the ability to cope with the emotional and aesthetic labour required. It is because of the need to possess such skills that he recommends that the industry go 'beyond the traditional recruitment pools for tourism jobs' (p. 1393).

Recruitment in the Events Industry

Recruitment practices in the events industry vary according to whether they are being employed in the leisure or business events sectors, and the skills required in each of these areas differ also. Leisure events may require staff to have a certain level of creativity, while business events staff may need to have some search skills, to be able to provide the appropriate speakers and ambience for specific industry conferences.

As stated previously, the structure of leisure events resembles a 'pulsating organization', with peaks and troughs of employment. Allen *et al.* (2008) suggest that there are a number of ways to assist in the recruiting process. These include using stakeholders such as councils or suppliers to communicate the event needs in terms of staff. They also suggest that there could be a clause included in the sponsorship agreement, specifying the supply of temporary staff. In addition, they suggest targeting specific people in the community with the specific skills required. Recruitment in business events, on the other hand, reflects far more traditional practices, with the organizational structure resembling more normal recruitment methods.

Recruitment in leisure events: lessons from the Australian Tennis Open

The concept of the pulsating organization, developed by Hanlon and Jago (2000), provides a clear framework for the discussion of recruitment practices in the events sector. As an illustration of the concept of the pulsating organization, Deery (2001) provides a case study of recruitment practices for the Australian Open Tennis championships and this case study underpins the following discussion. The 2008 event, for example, employed in excess of 4500 members of staff, including 319 ball kids, 365 umpires, 195 courtesy car drivers and 45 statisticians. These staff, however, are only needed at the time of the event, which takes place over a 2-week period. In order to have the required number of staff in place for a successful event, Tennis Australia and Melbourne Park (the venue) manage a well-tried and -timed recruiting process, which begins almost immediately after the previous event has concluded. Rewards for these staff include pay as well as access to available seats at the various courts, free meals, uniforms and some free transport.

Unlike most other events, the Australian Open does not need to advertise its positions, and each year there are thousands of applications for the main jobs. Applications are made for ball kid positions on the web site www.ausopen.org. In the case of the ball kids, applications are taken immediately following the Championship in January each year, with the selection of the successful candidates occurring in May. Training sessions for these ball kids begin in May of each year for the event that is held 9 months later.

Hiring other staff for the Australian Open begins in the September of the previous year, although many of the staff are retained from year to year. In order to hire such large numbers of appropriate staff, the recruiting company runs group interviews that explore the candidates' previous work experience, their customer service skills and attitudes, and why the candidates would wish to work at the Australian Open. These interviews run for approximately 2 hours and also include briefings on the company, the Australian Open, and standards required for uniforms and grooming, as well as the expectations of training and induction sessions.

Following the recruitment process, induction sessions are held and are compulsory for each member of staff. These induction sessions are vital for understanding the culture of the event and the organization for which the staff are working.

Recruitment in the business events sector

Rogers (2008:229) argues that the business events sector is 'a people industry' and that there are unique skills required to undertake positions within the industry successfully. In summarizing the various positions, Rogers states that each one has specific needs; take, for example, the conference administrator, who needs to be a 'computer literate, well organized, meticulously accurate team player' (p. 230). Other positions he discusses are those of the conference and publicity coordinator; the event coordinator, who liaises between the conference centre and the client; and the conference organizer, as well as various roles in the convention bureau. Weber (2001) provides some idea of the skills required for the tasks that convention bureau staff need. These tasks include destination information, referral services, lead services, facilitating familiarization trips and housing assistance, as well as attention promotion and registration services. In addition, Bauer *et al.* (2001) narrow the skills needed to providing services quality, and management and language skills.

Rogers points out that the business events sector, at this stage, does not have a clearly identified career path and so recruiting into such a sector is difficult because of the uncertainty of where such positions lead. McCabe's (2001) research confirms this lack of career paths, both into and within the sector.

One of the key issues perceived as a problem in the business events area, therefore, is in human resources and, in particular, the issues of recruitment and retention (Weber and Ladkin, 2004). Using a panel of experts as part of a Delphi study, these authors found that high levels of professionalism and service quality were important in maintaining both the British and the Australian business events sectors as competitive and attractive to external clients. Research by Leask and Spiller (2002) on issues facing conference venues confirms that these attributes for conference staff are important but are difficult to supply to the industry. One of their findings was that venue sales staff, for example, were not sufficiently trained in all aspects of conference running. As the supply of conference facilities increases, so too does the need for trained and skilled staff, and recruiting these staff may prove difficult. McCabe's (2001) work provides some insights into the ways in which recruitment occurs in the business events area in order to achieve sound-quality personnel. She found that many of her respondents, who were currently working as conference organizers and in other roles within the business events area, had worked previously in the hotel industry.

An example of recruitment issues within the business events area comes from research undertaken by Jago and Deery (2007) for Tourism Australia, examining the changes that were occurring in business events. One of the findings, through FutureWatch (2007), suggested many meeting planners outsource much of the logistics of facilitating conferences and meetings but retain the strategic and consulting part of their jobs. This suggests that there is increasing opportunity for actually producing the conferences and meetings.

The study also found that there is a growth in the number and role of association management companies (AMC). An AMC is described as:

> a firm of skilled professionals whose goal is to provide management expertise and specialized administrative services to organizations in an efficient, cost-effective manner, based on the concept of shared resources, for example:
>
> - Monthly newsletters
> - Membership programmes
> - Annual meeting/trade show management
>
> AMCs provide a centralized office that serves as headquarters for the Association. Like the other Central Key Contacts, the AMCs can be the decision-maker, but may also be assigned by decision-makers within the Association to recommend destinations and venues.
>
> (Jago and Deery, 2007:25)

Changes such as the growth of AMCs and the outsourcing of the logistics of meetings and conferences impact greatly on the type of skills that are required in the business events area and it is possible that educational institutions have not kept pace with such changes. Recruitment for these positions, therefore, is becoming increasingly more difficult.

It is not possible to make a general statement with regard to recruitment in the events industry as the skills required for business and leisure events are quite different in some ways, but suffice to say that it is important that people entering the industry have a number of skills, which range from being creative to being strategic and possessing strong management skills.

Retention: Lessons from the Hospitality and Tourism Industry

The hospitality and tourism industry has a reputation for high turnover rates and many of the attributes associated with that industry also exist in the events industry. These attributes include working unsociable hours, low pay and high levels of casualization. The hospitality and tourism industry has introduced a number of strategies in an attempt to combat these high turnover rates, including providing greater flexibility in working hours and better job security.

In examining the key causes for the high turnover rates in the hospitality and tourism industry, a number of areas arise. Research into the antecedents of labour turnover has traditionally focused on the role that job attitudes, such as job satisfaction and organizational commitment, have on an employee's intention to leave (Deery, 2002, 2008). Equally, the role that personal attributes, such as positive and negative affectivity (Griffeth and Hom, 1995), play in employee turnover decision making has been examined substantially. Key turnover researchers, such as Iverson and Currivan (2003), have found that other variables, such as job opportunities, distributive justice, routinization of job tasks and kinship responsibilities, impact on the turnover decision-making process, and they examine the consequences of these variables within the company context.

Hjalager *et al.*'s (2001:127) work on tourism employment, among others, confirms the declining level of staff retention in the tourism sector, stating that the desire to have a 'pleasant lifestyle' is important for employees in tourism. Their work also argues, however, that the temporary nature of tourism work suits the younger generations, and they conclude that 'tourism.... more than any other industry in the economy attracts the ultramobile, the virtual and the boundaryless' (p. 128).

The following sections examine the causes that have been found to have an impact on an employee's decision to leave an organization. While much of the discussion here uses the findings from the hospitality and tourism literature, it is argued that the problems and issues are similar in the events sector.

The role of job satisfaction and organizational commitment in turnover decisions

Job satisfaction and organizational commitment have been consistently found to influence employee turnover and have underpinned studies by hospitality and tourism researchers such as Robinson and Barron (2007), and Tutuncu and Kozak (2007). Other work, such as that by Carbery *et al.* (2003), investigates the role that the psychological contract, career expectations and managerial competencies have in the decision to leave an organization. Important research by Robinson and Barron (2007) focuses on the issues of deskilling and standardization, and it is argued that this leads to a lack of job satisfaction and organizational commitment and ultimately to the decision to leave the organization. Many of these studies use the job descriptive index (JDI) by Smith *et al.* (1969), in which the key components of job satisfaction are the work itself, pay, co-workers, supervision and an overall job satisfaction variable. In relating the use of the JDI to the events industry, it is clear that each of the elements of the scale could impact greatly on employee satisfaction but in a very condensed and intense way. In research by Gustafson (2002) on employees in private clubs in the USA, the findings confirm the role that low pay, and the opportunity for better pay, plays in the decision to leave an organization.

The role of personal attributes in turnover decisions

Another area for examination in determining the causes of employee turnover focuses on attitudes that the employees have that contribute to their desire to leave an organization. These attributes are important in an industry where emotional labour is such a key component of the work. Research by Lee and Shin (2005) examines the role that psychological dimensions such as job burnout and exhaustion play in an employee's decision to leave an organization. These authors use a job burnout construct with three components, namely emotional exhaustion, depersonalization and diminished personal accomplishment. Emotional exhaustion is a particularly relevant construct in the hospitality, tourism and events industries, where long hours and back-to-back rosters are the norm. Their study used a number of other dimensions, including examining the role of positive and negative affectivity on an employee's intention to leave. As has been the case in other studies, the authors found that turnover intention was positively correlated with negative affectivity, workload, exhaustion and cynicism. In particular, the items of cynicism and workload were found to be significant predictors of turnover intentions. People working in these industries are often more exposed to being exhausted, which may then change their attitude to the work environment. Such findings are consistent with recent research into the causes of work–life conflict.

The research by Karatepe and Uludag (2007) also tests, among others, the relationship between exhaustion and employees' intention to leave the organization. Their study found that frontline employees who had difficulty in spending time with their family or in keeping social commitments were likely to be emotionally exhausted. This, in turn, impacted negatively on their job satisfaction and ultimately influenced their intention to leave the organization. Karatepe and Uludag (2007) discuss the relationship between these personal employee dimensions and work–life balance, and the implications of these findings are discussed in the next section.

The final article discussed in this section is that by Rowley and Purcell (2001). While this paper examines a number of causes and strategies relating to employee turnover, it does elaborate on the impact that stress and job burnout have on the employees' intentions to leave an organization. The authors note, in particular, the role that understaffing and unrealistic job expectations have on the retention rates in hotels.

Retention in the Events Industry

Retaining staff in the events industry can be even more difficult than achieving this in the hospitality and tourism industry, due to the 'stop/start' nature of running events. Again, it is important to make the distinction between leisure and business events. Another distinction to be made is between paid staff and volunteers, and it is interesting to note that the small amount of research undertaken examining retention in the events industry has mainly looked at volunteers. Elstad (2003), for example, examined volunteers' reasons for quitting as a volunteer. Her findings suggest that too great a workload will encourage volunteers to leave, as will the fact that the volunteers do not feel appreciated. Appropriate rewards for volunteers have been found to be extremely important in retaining volunteers (Deery and Jago, 2001).

Other research, by Coyne and Coyne (2001), on retention within the events industry also focuses on volunteers, at golfing tournaments. Coyne and Coyne (2001:212) suggest that:

> Retention is the result of sound volunteer management (especially at the first level of volunteer interface – the 'good volunteer supervisor' so highly prized by the veteran volunteers). Open and frequent recognition of the work of others is the hallmark of a good supervisor. The sponsoring organization itself also has an obligation in this regard.

It is interesting to note that research by Ralston *et al.* (2004:16), again examining volunteer motivations and causes of turnover, found that there were a number of stressors for event volunteers that could cause potential burnout. These factors included aspects such as:

> an intense time and energy commitment; overdemanding workloads; insufficient numbers of volunteers; tensions between volunteers, staff, and others; open public scrutiny; lack of effective leadership; absence of tangible rewards; insecurity over one's appointment or volunteer role; and boring or unfulfilling labor.

Retaining paid staff in the events industry requires careful management of both their physical and their emotional well-being. This is particularly important in the leisure events industry. Because there are significant periods of high and low activity in the 'pulsating event', the need for sound and caring supervision is extremely important. It is important for event organizations to recognize the exhaustion and burnout that can occur as a consequence of running events. Retaining staff in such an environment may call for flexible working arrangements, particularly with regard to working hours and leave.

Strategies to retain business event staff are similar to those required by 'normal' organizations to a certain extent. Such a statement applies to staff employed in, for example, a convention and exhibition centre or a visitors' bureau. However, for those who actually organize conferences and exhibitions, the issues facing leisure events organizers and employees are relevant here. Again, the long hours and stress during the build up to the event, as well as during the event, require sensitive and professional supervision. The ability to allow for flexible hours and working arrangements around the facilitation of an event is extremely important in retaining staff.

Conclusion

As stated earlier, it is difficult to generalize about recruitment and retention in the events industry, as the issues relate to whether it is a business or leisure event. For those parts of the events industry that are similar to 'normal' organizations, such as jobs in convention centres or visitors' bureaus, strategies to recruit and retain staff focus on providing a good working environment, sound supervision, reasonable pay and reasonable workloads. For those working in leisure events and the facilitation of business events, however, it is important to offer flexible working arrangements, supportive supervision and peers, and the opportunity to take leave for emotional and physical well-being. Finally, it is important that, in any of these positions, staff enjoy their jobs, as the role that job satisfaction has in retaining staff cannot be overestimated.

References

Allen, J., O'Toole, W., Harris, R. and McDonnell, I. (2008) *Festival & Special Event Management*. Wiley, Milton, Australia.

Bauer, T., Lambert, J. and Hutchison, J. (2001) Government intervention in the Australasian Meetings, Incentives, Conventions and Exhibitions Industry (MICE). *Journal of Convention & Exhibition* 3(1), 65–87.

Baum, T. (2007) Human resources in tourism: still waiting for change. *Tourism Management* 28, 1383–1399.

Carbery, R., Garavan, T., O'Brien, F. and McDonnell, J. (2003) Predicting hotel managers' turnover cognitions. *Journal of Managerial Psychology* 18(7), 649–679.

Choi, J., Woods, R. and Murrman, S. (2000) International labor markets and the migration of labor forces as an alternative solution for labor shortages in the hospitality industry. *International Journal of Contemporary Hospitality Management* 12(1), 61–66.

Coyne, B.S. and Coyne, E.J. (2001) Getting, keeping and caring for unpaid volunteers for professional golf tournament events. *Human Resource Development International* 4(2), 199–214.

Deery, M. (2001) Managing staff at the Australian Open. In: McDonnell, I., Allen, J. and O'Toole, W. (eds) *Festival and Special Event Management*, 2nd edn. Wiley, Sydney, pp. 157–159.

Deery, M. (2002) Labour turnover in international hospitality and tourism. In: Watson, S., D'Annunzio-Green, N. and Maxwell, G. (eds) *Human Resource Management: International Perspectives in Hospitality and Tourism*. Continuum, London, pp. 51–63.

Deery, M. (2008) Talent management, work–life balance and retention strategies. *International Journal of Contemporary Hospitality Management* 20(7), 23–28.

Deery, M. and Jago, L. (2001) Managing human resources. In: Drummond, S. and Yeoman, I. (eds) *Quality Issues in Heritage Visitor Attractions*. Butterworth-Heinemann, Oxford, pp. 175–193.

Deery, M., Jago, L., Fredline, L. and Dwyer, L. (2005) *National Business Events Study*. Common Ground, Altona, Australia.

Dermody, M., Taylor, M. and Young, S. (2004) Identifying job motivation factors of restaurant servers: insight for the development of effective recruitment and retention strategies. *International Journal of Hospitality & Tourism Administration* 5(3), 1–13.

Elstad, B. (2003) Continuance commitment and reasons to quit: a study of volunteers at a jazz festival. *Event Management* 8, 99–108.

FutureWatch (2007) *A Comparative Outlook on the Global Business of Meetings*. MPI, Dallas, Texas.

Getz, D. (2008) Event tourism: definition, evolution, and research. *Tourism Management* 29, 403–428

Griffeth, R.W. and Hom, P.W. (1995) The employee turnover process. *Research in Personnel and Human Resources Management* 13, 245–293.

Gustafson, C. (2002) Employee turnover: a study of private clubs in the USA. *International Journal of Contemporary Hospitality Management* 4(3), 106–113.

Hanlon, C.M. and Jago, L.K. (2000) Pulsating sporting events: an organizational structure to optimize performance. In: Allen, J., Harris, R., Jago, L.K. and Veal, A.J. (eds) *Events Beyond 2000: Setting the Agenda – Proceedings of Conference on Event Evaluation, Research and Education*. Australian Centre for Event Management, Sydney, pp. 93–104.

Hjalager, A.-M., Andersen, S. and Denmark, A. (2001) Tourism employment: contingent work or professional career? *Employee Relations* 23(2), 115–129.

Iverson, R. and Currivan, D. (2003) Union participation, job satisfaction, and employee turnover: an event-history analysis of the exit-voice hypothesis. *Industrial Relations: a Journal of Economy and Society* 42(1), 101–105.

Jago, L. and Deery, M. (2007) The International Association Market in Australia: perceptions of trends and future directions, international and national perspectives. Confidential report for Tourism Australia.

Jolliffe, L. and Farnsworth, R. (2003) Seasonality in tourism employment: human resources challenges. *International Journal of Contemporary Hospitality Management* 15(6), 312–316.

Karatepe, O. and Uludag, O. (2007) Conflict, exhaustion and motivation: a study of frontline employees in northern Cyprus hotels. *International Journal of Hospitality Management* 26, 645–665.

Leask, A. and Spiller, J. (2002) UK conference venues: past, present, and future. *Journal of Convention & Exhibition Management* 4(1), 29–54.

Lee, K.-E. and Shin, K.-H. (2005) Job burnout, engagement and turnover intention of dieticians and chefs at a contract foodservice management company. *Journal of Community Nutrition* 7(2), 100–106.

Martin, A., Mactaggart, D. and Bowden, J. (2006) The barriers to the recruitment and retention of supervisors/managers in the Scottish tourism industry. *International Journal of Contemporary Hospitality Management* 18(5), 380–397.

McCabe, V. (2001) Career paths and labour mobility in the conventions and exhibitions industries in eastern Australia: results from a preliminary study. *International Journal of Tourism Research* 3, 493–499.

Ralston, R., Downward, P. and Lumsdon, L. (2004) The expectations of volunteers prior to the XVII Commonwealth Games, 2002: a qualitative study. *Event Management* 9, 13–26.

Robinson, R. and Barron, P. (2007) Developing a framework for understanding the impact of deskilling and standardization on the turnover and attrition of chefs. *International Journal of Hospitality Management* 26, 913–926.

Rogers, T. (2008) *Conferences and Conventions: a Global Industry*, 2nd edn. Butterworth-Heinemann, Amsterdam.

Rowley, G. and Purcell, K. (2001) 'As cooks go, she went': is labour churn inevitable? *International Journal of Hospitality Management* 20, 163–185.

Smith, M., Kendall, L. and Hulin, C. (1969) *The Measurement of Satisfaction in Work and in Retirement: a Strategy for the Study of Attitudes*. Rand McNally, Chicago, Illinois.

Toffler, A. (1990) *Power Shift*. Bantam Books, New York.

Tutuncu, O. and Kozak, M. (2007) An investigation of factors affecting job satisfaction. *International Journal of Hospitality & Tourism Administration* 8(1), 1–19.

Weber, K. (2001) Meeting planners' use and evaluation of convention and visitor bureaus. *Tourism Management* 22, 599–606.

Weber, K. and Ladkin, A. (2004) Trends affecting the convention industry in the 21st century. *Journal of Convention & Event Tourism* 6(4), 47–63.

11 Volunteer Recruitment and Retention: an Australia–USA Comparison

JOE GOLDBLATT AND CATHERINE M. MATHESON

Queen Margaret University, UK

Introduction

According to Getz (2007), the field of events management rapidly expanded from the publication of the first textbook by Goldblatt (1989). A study by the Association of Event Management Educators (AEME, 2007, cited in The Higher Education Academy, 2008:43) determined that there was a 400% increase in the number of event management students in the UK in the past 10 years. In a study conducted by Goldblatt (2010), 200 event management modules, courses and curricular programmes were identified throughout the world. The concentration of programmes was primarily in the USA and Australia. The expansion of the modern events industry has resulted in increasing the challenges, including the development and sustainability of a qualified workforce to contend with this development.

Owing to the high degree of concentration of event programmes in Australia and the USA, a qualitative research study was conducted to examine the following questions, which may impact the future volunteer human resources that are available to populate the modern events industry in these two countries.

This chapter compares and contrasts the event volunteer recruitment and retention issues that impact both Australia and the USA. Furthermore, the chapter provides a forecast of potential challenges and opportunities for event organizers that require support from the voluntary sector. Finally, best practices identified in the literature and from expert interviews are provided to improve the practice of event organizers when recruiting and retaining volunteers.

Following a review of the events management literature directly related to human resource issues, three questions were identified with regards to developing a sustainable workforce for this industry in Australia, the USA and perhaps other countries throughout the world. First, what are the current and future supply and demand factors for human resources for events such as meetings, incentives, conventions and exhibitions (MICE), festivals, sports and other sectors within the event industry in Australia and the USA? Secondly, what are the best practices for identifying, recruiting, hiring and retaining the best human resources for event organizations in Australia and the USA? Thirdly and finally, what are the key motivations and goals of event workers (compensated and volunteer) and how may event organizations in Australia and the USA continually improve productivity and quality through better understanding and satisfying these needs?

Methodology

A focused review of human resource literature related to events studies literature was conducted and four key informants were identified through the use of an expert referral system. The expert referents selected were Lynn Van Der Wagen of Australia and Steven Wood Schmader of the USA. Van Der Wagen is an international authority in the field of human resource development in the events industry. Among other accomplishments, Ms Van Der Wagen was part of the team that designed the training programmes for the 50,000 volunteers that were engaged in the 2000 International Olympic Games in Sydney, Australia.

Schmader is the President and Chief Executive Officer of the International Festivals and Events Association, which is based in the USA, and the former Executive Director of the Boise River Festival, and supervised 3000 volunteers for this event. He is also the co-author of one of the early books in the field, *Special Events: Inside and Out* (Schmader and Jackson, 1997). Schmader leads one of the pre-eminent event industry organizations, with over 3500 members, the majority of which are located in the USA.

Schmader and Van Der Wagen, based upon their professional experience and expert knowledge, referred the researchers to additional experts in both Australia and the USA. Structured written interviews were conducted with four experts with extensive experience in event volunteer recruitment and retention. The experts agreed in advance to be identified in the study. The results of these interviews were reviewed using a traditional content analysis to determine areas of consensus and discord.

The unstructured interviews with the key informants (experts) included posing broad questions and then probing to gain greater insights regarding their expert views. The interviews were transcribed and then analysed for concurrence and dissonance.

Issues and Trends in Events Volunteering

Volunteering means any activity in which time is given freely to benefit another person, group, or organization. This definition does not preclude volunteers from benefiting from their work.

(Wilson, 2000:215)

Volunteering activities take place against a backdrop where time has become a scarce commodity within parts of the industrialized world. Consequently, motivations to volunteer are particularly significant. Clary *et al.* (1998) argue that there is a set of motivational functions utilized within volunteering, which comprise values, understanding, social, careers, protective and enhancement. Van der Wagen (2007) argues that a volunteer's motivation is closely related and linked to social interest, and this, in turn, leads to satisfaction with the volunteering experience. A 2003 United Nations report stresses the value of sports volunteering to the community by observing that 'once involved through sport, volunteers can be mobilized to donate their time to other activities' (cited in Van der Wagen, 2007:63). Schondel and Boehm (2000) observed that adolescents, college students and adults shared common motivations, including helping others, social interactions and recognition of their contributions. It has been argued that engaging in volunteering activities can have a positive impact upon the individual. Wilson (2000) suggests that the following consequences may be identified: first, there are citizenship impacts, as volunteers are more politically engaged; secondly, engaging in volunteering activities can act as a mechanism to control antisocial behaviour among youth groups; thirdly, volunteer engagement can contribute to physical and mental health well-being; and, finally, volunteering can be utilized as a pathway in socio-economic development and achievement. Engaging in volunteering activities can proffer a multitude of benefits to the individual and, moreover, to the human resources of the recipient organization. From a human resources perspective, volunteering trends have critical implications for the stability of the future volunteering supply base. In 2002, more than one-third of all adult Australians had completed some form of volunteering activity over the year (Volunteering Australia, 2004). In the USA, 26.2% of the population volunteered (2006–2007) (Bureau of Labour Statistics, 2008).

These trends have strategic planning implications across various industry sectors. However, there can be little doubt about the impact and significance of volunteering trends upon the events sector. It has been argued that, in some cases, events are dependent upon volunteers (Elstad, 2003). Monga (2006) suggests that volunteers have become a key resource in events as a means to reduce the cost of event production, and there is certainly an economic value to volunteers' contribution to events (Solberg, 2003). Indeed, there are events that have become so reliant upon volunteer services they would not function in the same way otherwise. This is illustrated in Kemp's (2002) study of the Lillehammer Winter Olympic Games (1994) and the Sydney Summer Olympic Games (2000). Kemp (2002:110) argues that 'volunteers were critical to the successful staging of both the Lillehammer and Sydney Olympic Games events because they provided the substantial amount of unpaid additional labour that was needed'. Moreover, 'without the personal investment of the volunteers, these mega-events could simply not have been arranged'. The events industry dependence upon volunteers is demonstrated by a growth in volunteer numbers. The Los Angeles Summer Olympics (1984) had 28,700 volunteers (Solberg, 2003); the Nagano Winter Olympic Games (1998) had 32,579 volunteers (Green and Chalip, 2004); and the Sydney Summer Olympic Games (2000) required 40,000 volunteers (Kemp, 2002).

It seems probable that the deployment of event volunteers will continue and possibly increase as a result of wider forces and trends in the events environment, most notably the events industry growth. At the Turin Winter Olympic Games in 2006 there were 25,000 volunteers. By contrast, 47% of the human resources for the Sydney Summer Olympic Games in 2000 were volunteers, and in Athens just 4 years later, 42% of the human resources were from the volunteer sector (Van der Wagen, 2007). Goldblatt (2000) argues that the growth in the events sector is attributable to a set of key shifts, both within the USA and elsewhere. First, a global demographic change of an ageing population has implications for the demand for celebratory events and experience-rich events. Secondly, technological developments are an integral element of work and leisure, which contributes to the potential development of event audiences. Thirdly, an increase in disposable income has accelerated the demand for events. Finally, a decline in unrestricted leisure time and the blurring of work/leisure time impacts upon the demand for events. However, an element of caution is required in interpreting this growth. Such a development lies against a backdrop of significant and omnipresent major forces and trends, which will have significant implications for the supply of and demand for events. Getz (2000) identifies a set of major forces which relate to the macro-environment and key trends in the production of events. With regard to the former, key themes are demographic, economic, technological and cultural changes. With regard to the latter, the continued growth of events, strategic event development, special-purpose event venues, sponsorship, accountability, protest, legal issues, events professionalism and private sector initiatives do, and will continue to, have a substantial impact upon strategic planning within the events sector. A growth in the events sector, and the attendant challenges of future trends, brings to the fore a set of human resource issues. In essence, it contributes to an increased demand for personnel that can contend with the requirements of events production and strategic planning, and, similarly, there will be an increased demand for event volunteers. However, given the aforesaid trends and challenges, recruitment and retention strategies become increasingly significant.

Volunteer Recruitment and Retention Issues

Given the strategic planning issues and the continued reliance on volunteers, there is a need for sophisticated, focused recruitment and retention strategies which take into account volunteer motivation and satisfaction. Although it has been suggested that volunteer recruitment and retention strategies are essentially a marketing issue (Green and Chalip, 1998), the onus for developing such strategies lies within the realms of human resource management. Van der Wagen (2007:124) argues that 'recruitment is the process of attracting potential candidates to the organization'. A key theme underpinning the recruitment process is volunteer motivations. If volunteers are providing discretionary unpaid labour to events production, then an understanding of motivation dimensions is pivotal to the recruitment strategy. A limited appreciation of volunteering trends or a failure to grasp the meaning and significance of volunteering motivations has the potential to have dire consequences for organizational morale, the development of volunteer human resources and the event production (Strigas and Jackson, 2003). Furthermore, there is a correlation between both motivation and recruitment and satisfaction and retention. 'It is vital that organizers understand volunteer motivation and their satisfaction with the volunteering experience in order to respond effectively to management needs in the areas of recruitment, retention, and daily operations' (Farrell *et al.*, 1998:288–289).

A plethora of work has developed pertaining to event volunteer motivations, and a number of dimensions can be delineated. Motivational factors are purposive (Farrell *et al.*, 1998; Strigas and Jackson, 2003), solidary (Farrell *et al.*, 1998; Monga, 2006), external traditions (Farrell *et al.*, 1998), commitment (Farrell *et al.*, 1998), material (Strigas and Jackson, 2003), leisure (Strigas and Jackson, 2003), egoistic (Strigas and Jackson, 2003) and external (Strigas and Jackson, 2003). Such motivational factors can also be focused upon affiliatory, fulfilling experiences, career development and personal rewards (Monga, 2006). These dimensions highlight the complexity of volunteer motivations and require consideration within recruitment strategies. Clary *et al.* (1998) argue that continued volunteerism is dependent upon whether there is a fit between the volunteer role and their personal motivations. They suggest that volunteers who engage in roles related to their own motivations will attain more satisfaction from their activities and are more likely to continue volunteering than those volunteers whose motivations are not linked to their activities. Thus, if event managers possess an understanding of their volunteers' motivations then this can be harnessed in the development of training activities. Training that takes account of volunteer motivations is likely to have a positive impact upon the volunteer experience, which then links to volunteer retention. Ralston *et al.*'s (2004) study of volunteer expectations at the XVII Commonwealth Games in Manchester (2002) highlights the relationship between motivations and training needs. The volunteer experience was limited by the skills assessment undertaken, as volunteers argued '…that previous experience and particular skills were rarely taken into account during the recruitment process' (Ralston *et al.*, 2004:21). Nevertheless, an underpinning volunteer motivation was to be involved in the Games, which meant that they had no specific preference for the roles they would undertake. In essence, this meant that the roles allocated to volunteers met and, in some cases, exceeded volunteer motivations and expectations. Volunteers also gave a mixed response to the training provided as, while the training was of a high quality, there were issues regarding timing and a lack of organization of the training processes. A wider issue is that the induction and training process within events is somewhat different as a consequence of their pulsating nature, whereby organizations expand and contract over their life cycle (Hanlon and Cuskelly, 2002).

However, one issue that arises is the generalizability of event volunteer motivations. Volunteering motives can be linked to the cultural and social mores of a nation; for instance, as to whether volunteering is embedded within social practices. For example, in high-context cultures (North America and Western Europe), the engagement of volunteers appears to be higher, whereas in lower-context cultures (Asia, South and Central America) there is less engagement.

This has potential repercussions regarding the utilization and transferability of existing work and how volunteer motivations and decision-making processes are understood. Commentators have largely focused upon sporting events (Farrell *et al.*, 1998; Coyne and Coyne, 2001; Strigas and Jackson, 2003; Green and Chalip, 2004; Ralston *et al.*, 2005), which opens the possibility of variability in volunteer motivations among other events. In addition, motivation dimensions also illustrate a commitment to the individual event. There is evidence to suggest that the uniqueness of the event and the sporting form can be a motivating factor for volunteers (Coyne and Coyne, 2001; Ralston *et al.*, 2004, 2005). Consequently, it has been suggested that event volunteer motivations may be different from other voluntary activities because of the commitment and nature of the event (Farrell *et al.*, 1998). Commitment to the event is also reflected in volunteer retention.

Volunteer Retention Issues

Furthermore, although there have been significant studies in North America regarding volunteers that are linked to professional associations (American Society of Association Executives, 2008), these types of studies are rare in other parts of the world. The culture of volunteerism in North America is primarily through professional association and not-for-profit organizations, including faith-based programmes. However, the literature regarding volunteer engagement within the convention sector – one of the most visible activities of a professional association – is also sparse. However, Susan Sarfati, President and founding Chief Executive Officer of the Center for Association Leadership in Washington, DC, recognizes both challenges and opportunities in connecting association members to voluntary participation. According to Sarfati:

> The Internet has changed the equation in terms of the array of volunteer and networking opportunities our members expect from us. We have every evidence that our members want to engage with us and each other face-to-face. We also know our members are pressed for time and that there are other ways we can and should connect with them. Someone's geographic location shouldn't prevent them from deriving equal benefit of membership. Basically, technology lets us reach more of our members, and in the manner of their choosing. I think the challenge always lies in keeping members engaged, even if they're primarily accessing benefits online. There needs to be engagement, whether that's through volunteering in person or agreeing to write for blogs or other available social media technology.
>
> (S. Sarfati, personal communication, 2008)

Elstad's (2003) study of a Norwegian jazz festival ascertained that volunteers' continuance commitment at the festival was linked to how long they had worked at the event. This has implications for retention strategies, given the significance of event commitment within motivation and retention strategies. Conventional retention strategies focus upon, for example, pay and reward schemes, performance appraisal and promotion. In contrast, Hanlon and Jago (2004) argue that there is a need for different retention strategies for personnel within major sporting event organizations due to the pulsating nature of the organization and the distinct stages within the event cycle: leading up to, during and after an event, and throughout the year. They suggest that sporting event organizations are transitory, have different operating stages and their employee numbers expand for a short period of time, for example in the duration of the event. In their study of the Australian Open Tennis Championships and the Australian Formula One Grand Prix, they suggest that retention strategies should instead be focused upon the stages of an event cycle. They concluded that retention was not problematic leading up to and during an event. However, there were difficulties in retaining staff immediately after the event. While this study was focused upon personnel in general, there are key lessons which are applicable to volunteerism and retention, which comprise the refinement of retention strategies according to the event cycle and the identification of key stages when personnel leave an organization.

Commentators have explored the rationale for volunteers leaving events organizations. In Elstad's (2003) study, 30% of volunteers had considered leaving and the most important factor in this decision-making process was the workload.

Issues of workload are also highlighted in Getz's 'Why festivals fail' (2002). He notes that one of the human resource problems within festivals relates to volunteer burnout. These issues may also be generalized to other types of event experiences, including convention management. According to McCabe et al. (2000), in the Australian, and indeed global, meetings, incentives, conventions and exhibitions (MICE) sector, there are four stages to ensure labour is being properly utilized. First, labour demand must be forecast properly. Secondly, labour supply must be carefully analysed. Thirdly, there must be a strong balance between supply and demand considerations. Finally, staffing strategies for paid workers as well as volunteers must be carefully formulated to meet organizational needs.

Assessing workload allocation is clearly an issue to be worked into retention strategies if volunteers' commitment to events is to be maintained. It is often argued that commitment and satisfaction are linked. In a study of the Sydney Olympic Games, Green and Chalip (2004:62) argue that 'satisfaction with their event experience is an important driver of volunteers' eventual commitment, and satisfaction is itself driven by benefits and the sense of community that volunteers obtain at the event'. Green and Chalip's (2004) study is valuable in that, while identifying a link between commitment and satisfaction, they also explore the drivers to volunteer satisfaction, which comprise the sense of community, learning obtained, excitement obtained and helping obtained.

Therefore, it may be surmised from a review of the literature ___ whilst there is sufficient evidence to draw general conclusions about supply ___ nd and motivations of volunteers for sports, festivals, music and o___ of events, the convention or MICE sector lacks empirical evidence th___ perhaps inform a more effective comparison between these types of e___ their volunteer resources. As a result, there is a need, as evidenced fro___ ature, to conduct empirical studies in the MICE sector regarding volu___ nd to compare and contrast these motivations and issues with other t___ ents to determine if there are, as the United Nations (2006) report sugg___ tunities to engage a volunteer from one sector in multiple sectors as a result of their positive experiences.

Findings

Key informants in both Australia and the USA confirmed that the desire to volunteer is especially strong among young as well as older members of society. However, the discretionary time that is available for volunteer activities is declining. As a result of this dichotomy, convention and event organizations must carefully determine the demand factors for their programmes to best utilize the limited time that volunteers may be able to provide for their events. Furthermore, as Susan Sarfati suggests, event organizers must find alternative opportunities for volunteers to be engaged, other than the in-person experience (S. Sarfati, personal communication, 2008). These alternative means of voluntary engagement may increasingly be linked to technological advancements through Web 2.0 and other interactive virtual communities.

Through a comprehensive survey of the literature, as well as structured interviews with four key informants, it may be concluded that both Australia and the USA share several common issues with regard to supply and demand, motivations and other issues concerning volunteers in the conventions and events sectors. The literature reveals that similar motivational requirements and satisfaction levels are required for many different types of events in different destinations (Farrell *et al.*, 1998:288–289). Table 11.1 depicts the similarities and differences found within the two nations.

Although both countries have many similarities with regard to volunteer engagement across all event sectors, in the specific sector of conventions, the US volunteer appears to have many more complex motivations and issues concerning

Table 11.1. Australia and the USA: volunteer similarities and differences.

Australia	USA
Ageing population interested in volunteering	Ageing population somewhat interested in volunteering
Strong volunteer culture	Strong volunteer culture
Motivated by intangible rewards	Motivated by intangible rewards, such as networking and status, and tangible rewards, such as networking
Supervision of volunteers is often poor	Supervision of volunteers is not standardized
Recruitment through print and Internet consumer media in key publications (i.e. GLBT for the Gay Games)	Recruitment by referral, word of mouth and motivation
Volunteer motivation directly linked to social needs and type of event offering	Volunteer motivation linked to social and professional needs
Very little anecdotal information about volunteers in the convention sector	Convention volunteers versus other event volunteers are motivated by professional networking, advancement and status

their engagement, as shown in Table 11.2. This is supported by the literature, which identified that motivations for different sets of volunteers, as well as individual volunteers, may indeed be highly complex (Clary *et al.*, 1998). Table 11.2 demonstrates the variance in motivational complexity between the USA and Australia.

When analysing volunteer motivations as well as likes and dislikes, however, there are extensive studies in the festival and non-convention event sector, such as that shown from the BorderFest celebration in Hidalgo, Texas. According to the comments from the BorderFest volunteers, as shown in Table 11.3, a

Table 11.2. Australia and the USA: volunteer motivations.

Australia	USA
Leisure	Recognition
Fun	Contributing to progress
Being part of a cause	New experiences
Socialization	Connections
	Future career advancement
	Training
	Organization responds to and listens to their needs
	Various channels availabe for volunteer engagement including technology platforms such as blogs or chatrooms

Table 11.3. Volunteer preferences from a major festival in the USA.

20 Reasons why volunteers liked working at BorderFest

1. Serving the public and showing off BorderFest
2. They work well together
3. My own parking space
4. Meeting and working with people
5. Being busy and the people were great
6. Service to all and seeing all the happy faces
7. Seeing the smiles
8. Providing assistance and enjoying the participation.
9. I enjoy working with interesting people
10. Late nights and interaction with people
11. I like to show off the efforts of the place I work for and the people there
12. The little time that I got out, just the smiles in the faces
13. Sense of accomplishment – people (lots of them) enjoying what I helped create. Best feeling in the world!
14. Just being part of BorderFest is an honour
15. Met interesting people – some were a challenge
16. See the fun and excitement of the people who attend, especially the kids
17. Meeting with new people, especially from different parts of the country
18. The work, the people and the experience!
19. Getting to meet new people and seeing them come back
20. The camaraderie, spending time with colleagues and discussing topics other than work

significant number of individuals state that meeting people for a variety of reasons is a key motivation for their participation. The literature provides numerous examples of the importance of satisfying the expectations of volunteers with the event volunteer experience. The gaps between volunteer expectations and final perceptions, as related to the training they received for the Manchester Commonwealth Games, demonstrate the importance of goodness of fit regarding the pre-assessment of volunteer abilities (Ralston *et al.*, 2004:21).

Joe Vela, the managing director of this event, states that the loyalty of the volunteers for BorderFest is directly linked to the perception of value that they receive from the overall volunteer experience (J. Vela, personal communication, 2008). Therefore, annually, his organization surveys volunteer perceptions to better align their recruitment, orientation, training recognition and reward methodology with the changing expectations of their volunteers.

As a result of contrasting and comparing the volunteer motivations of both Australia and the USA, as described by the key informants and the literature, a typology has been established, listing the roles that volunteers may seek to perform. The *taker* is primarily motivated by recognition and reward and may represent the top tier of the volunteer hierarchy but is also the smallest percentage of volunteers typically engaged in the organization. Whereas, the *experiencer* appears to be a growth area for volunteers; they are primarily motivated by the opportunity to explore new experiences for personal and professional growth. The final role is that of the *giver*. The giver is the volunteer that is primarily motivated by their altruistic ideals, their belief in and devotion to the cause, and therefore will, in the future, represent one of the largest potential sectors for cause-related event organizations. Figure 11.1 depicts the hierarchy of this typology.

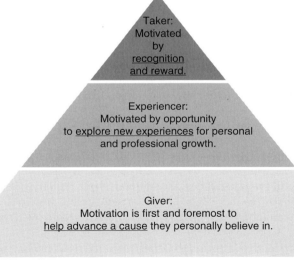

Fig. 11.1. Conceptual volunteer motivation typology.

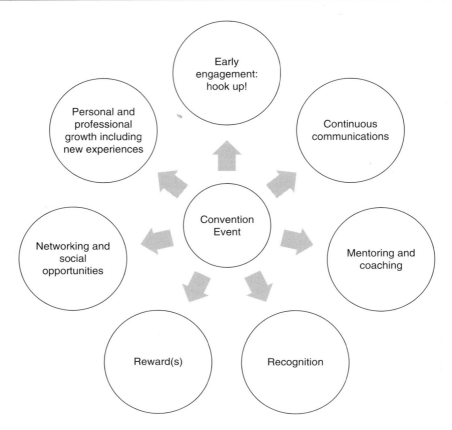

Fig. 11.2. Conceptual volunteer points of engagement model: key touch points of the volunteer experience.

According to the literature from the MICE industry in Australia and the key informant interviews with convention planners in the USA, convention volunteers experience significant touch points when providing services for a convention. Figure 11.2 depicts these various touch points and when carefully aligned and used in concert together they may provide a strong positive connection for those volunteers in the role of experiencers.

Sarfati and others in the USA have identified a wide variety of methods for engaging volunteers in the convention experience. The literature describes, as in the example of the Norwegian jazz festival, that the more touch points a volunteer experiences the greater their continuance as a volunteer with the event (Elstad, 2003). The touch point model in Fig. 11.2 may be further strengthened through direct involvement of volunteers, as shown in Fig. 11.3.

The literature strongly suggests that most events have a general life cycle for volunteer engagement (Elstad, 2003). The longer this life cycle, in many cases, the more cohesive and sustainable the event will become in the future. However,

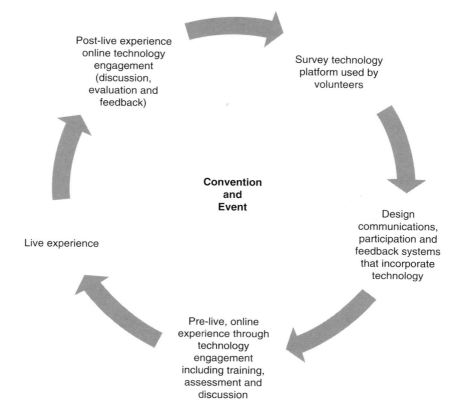

Fig. 11.3. Technology engagement model for convention and event volunteers.

when there is high turnover of experienced volunteers, the event organization may also suffer and face implosion. Therefore, Fig. 11.4 provides several best practices for extending the volunteer life cycle.

Experienced and successful volunteer coordinators and leaders have identified a series of dos and don'ts when working with volunteers. These principles, as shown in Table 11.4, may be applied to conventions as well as sports, festivals, music and other types of events.

Goldblatt states that 'People generally only do what they are rewarded for' (J. Goldblatt, personal communication, 2006). The reward system for volunteers, as confirmed by the key informant interviews and the literature, is highly complex. However, failure to recognize individual volunteers is similar to the story of the starfish on the sea shore: one day a young boy was walking with his grandfather and found a starfish on the sea shore. The old man picked up the starfish and hurled it back into the sea. The young boy asked, 'Grandfather why do you bother to do that; there are millions of starfish that land on the shore. It doesn't really matter at all that you throw it back in the sea.' The grandfather kneeled down beside the boy and said, 'It mattered to that one'. And indeed, every volunteer, at some level, seeks recognition for his or her efforts on behalf of the event organization.

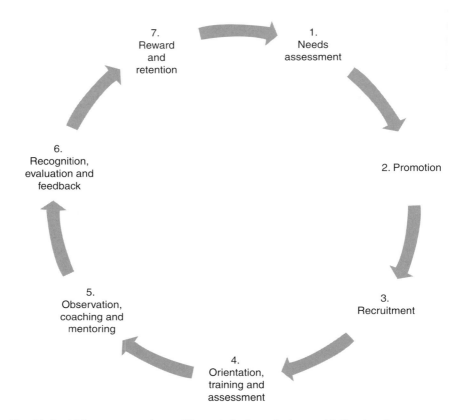

Fig. 11.4. Volunteer experience life cycle before, during and following the event.

Table 11.4. Key strategies for retaining convention and event volunteers.

Do	Don't
Appoint the right volunteer to perform the right task	Appoint volunteers without thorough screenings and assessment to ensure goodness of fit
Provide orientation and training	Underutilize a volunteer's skill, talent and experience
Assign a mentor and/or coach	
Provide feedback	
Promote continuous communications	Promote miscommunication through delays, barriers, cumbersome filters
Reward, recognize and promote retention	Provide the wrong rewards
	Fail to recognize early and often the contribution of volunteers

Table 11.5.   Five ways to effectively recognize and reward convention and event volunteers.

1. Thank them in person, early and often
2. Thank them publicly, early and often, through group meetings and publications (online and in print)
3. Provide amenities such as complimentary food, drink and parking
4. Provide recognition clothing, such as official T-shirt or other clothing with the term 'Official' and event title/logo on front and back
5. Provide rewards such as a certificate of achievement, emblematic jewellery such as a lapel pin, a thank you letter to the volunteer's employer or family, and a social event to honour them

Conclusions and Recommendations

A comparative analysis of Australian and US volunteer culture for conventions and other events demonstrates that, whilst there are many common supply, demand and motivational factors, the gap in the literature regarding volunteers specifically for conventions in Australia demonstrates perhaps the subtle but important differences in organizational culture. In both countries, volunteers are highly prized and heavily recruited for sports, festivals, music and other types of events. However, in Australia, conventions are primarily staffed by professional congress organizers or other skilled and compensated professionals.

As the USA experiences the demographic shift to older volunteers, who may have fewer hours available to contribute to volunteering at conventions, convention organizers may observe and learn from the Australian model that automation through technology and other efficiency mechanisms may have to support the supply and demand gap for volunteers in the future. Conversely, Australian event organizers may begin to experience the complexity of volunteer motivations in the future, and therefore they will need to adjust their reward and recognition schemes to satisfy these motivations.

Finally, there is a significant need for a comprehensive quantitative study of volunteer supply and demand across all event sectors, including conventions, festivals, music, sports and others, to determine how best to allocate what appears to be scarcer human resources in the future to ensure high-quality and sustainable events in both countries. Steven Wood Schmader, President and Chief Executive Officer of the International Festivals and Events Association, reminds event organizers to always remember: 'We are in the people business. Events may be automated by computers, but they are run by people' (S.W. Schmader, personal communication, 2007). Therefore, it is critically important that an event's most precious resource, the volunteer workforce, be continually examined to ensure that sufficient quantity and quality of human resources are available throughout the future to meet the growing demand and expansion of the global events industry.

References

American Society of Association Executives (2008) *Volunteer Engagement and Motivation Survey 2008*. ASAE, Washington, DC.

Bureau of Labour Statistics (2008) *Volunteering in 2007*. Bureau of Labour Statistics, Washington, DC.

Clary, E.G., Synder, M., Ridge, R.D., Copeland, J., Stukas, A.A., Haugen, J. and Miene, P. (1998) Understanding and assessing the motivations of volunteers: a functional approach. *Journal of Personality and Social Psychology* 74(6), 1516–1530.

Coyne, B.S. and Coyne, E.J. (2001) Getting, keeping and caring for unpaid volunteers for professional golf tournament events: a study of the recruitment/retention of unpaid volunteers for staging large, mass-attended, high-profile Professional Golf Association (PGA) golf tournaments. *Human Resource Development International* 4(2), 199–214.

Elstad, B. (2003) Continuance commitment and reasons to quit: a study of volunteers at a jazz festival. *Event Management* 8, 99–108.

Farrell, J.M., Johnston, M.E. and Twynam, G.D. (1998) Volunteer motivation, satisfaction, and management at an elite sporting competition. *Journal of Sport Management* 12, 288–300.

Getz, D. (2000) Developing a research agenda for the event management field. In: Allen, J., Harris, R., Jago, L.K. and Veal, A.J. (eds) *Events Beyond 2000: Setting the Agenda – Proceedings of Conference on Event Evaluation, Research and Education*. Australian Centre for Event Management, Sydney, pp. 10–21.

Getz, D. (2002) Why festivals fail. *Event Management* 7, 209–219.

Getz, D. (2007) *Event Studies*. Butterworth-Heinneman, Oxford.

Goldblatt, J. (1989) *Special Events*. Van Nostrand Reinhold, New York.

Goldblatt, J. (2000) A future for event management: the analysis of major trends impacting the emerging profession. In: Allen, J., Harris, R., Jago, L.K. and Veal, A.J. (eds) *Events Beyond 2000: Setting the Agenda – Proceedings of Conference on Event Evaluation, Research and Education*. Australian Centre for Event Management, Sydney, pp. 2–9.

Goldblatt, J. (2010) *Special Events: the New Frontier and Next Generation*. John Wiley and Sons, New York (in press).

Green, B.C. and Chalip, L. (1998) Sport volunteers: research agenda and application. *Sport Marketing Quarterly* 7(2), 14–23.

Green, B.C. and Chalip, L. (2004) Paths to volunteer commitment: lessons from the Sydney Olympic Games. In: Stebbins, R.A. and Graham, M. (eds) *Volunteering as Leisure/Leisure as Volunteering: an International Assessment*. CAB International, Wallingford, UK, pp. 49–67.

Hanlon, C. and Cuskelly, G. (2002) Pulsating major sport event organizations: a framework for inducting managerial personnel. *Event Management* 7, 231–243.

Hanlon, C. and Jago, L. (2004) The challenge of retaining personnel in major sport event organizations. *Event Management* 9, 39–49.

The Higher Education Academy (2008) *Link 20*. Hospitality, Leisure, Sport, and Tourism Network, Oxford.

Kemp, S. (2002) The hidden workforce: volunteers' learning in the Olympics. *Journal of European Industrial Training* 26, 109–116.

McCabe, V., Poole, B., Weeks, P. and Leiper, N. (2000) *The Business and Management of Conventions*. Wiley, Milton, Australia.

Monga, M. (2006) Measuring motivation to volunteer for special events. *Event Management* 10, 47–61.

Ralston, R., Downward, P. and Lumsdon, L. (2004) The expectation of volunteers prior to the XVII Commonwealth Games, 2002: a qualitative study. *Event Management* 9, 13–26.

Ralston, R., Lumsdon, L. and Downward, P. (2005) The third force in events tourism: volunteers at the XVII Commonwealth Games. *Journal of Sustainable Tourism* 13(5), 504–519.

Schmader, S.W. and Jackson, R. (1997) *Special Events Inside and Out*. Sagamore Publishing, Springfield, Illinois.

Schondel, C. and Boehm, K. (2000) Motivational needs of adolescent volunteers. *Adolescence* 25(138), 335–344.

Solberg, H.A. (2003) Major sporting events: assessing the value of volunteers' work. *Managing Leisure* 8, 17–27.

Strigas, A.D. and Jackson, E.N. (2003) Motivating volunteers to serve and succeed: design and results of a pilot study that explores demographics and motivational factors in sport volunteerism. *International Sports Journal* 7(1), 111–123.

United Nations (2006) Sport for development and peace. Available at: www.un.org/themes/sporty/index.htm (accessed 17 May 2006).

Van der Wagen, L. (2007) *Human Resource Management for Events: Managing the Event Workforce*. Butterworth-Heinemann, Oxford.

Volunteering Australia (2004) *Snapshot 2004: Volunteering Report Card*. Volunteering Australia, Melbourne, Australia.

Wilson, J. (2000) Volunteering. *Annual Review of Sociology* 26, 215–240.

12 Involving and Keeping Event Volunteers: Management Insights from Cultural Festivals

KAREN A. SMITH[1] AND LEONIE LOCKSTONE[2]

[1]Victoria University of Wellington, New Zealand; [2]Victoria University, Australia

Introduction

Recruitment and retention are crucial to the success of volunteer programmes; however, involving and keeping volunteers is often a significant challenge for those managing volunteers (Hager and Brudney, 2004; Zarinpoush et al., 2004; Volunteering Australia, 2006). Hall et al. (2001) suggest that people are becoming more selective in their choice of volunteering activities and are looking for new ways of volunteering. In response to changing demands and needs of volunteers, there is an acknowledged trend towards more flexible volunteering commitments (Gaskin, 2003; Brudney, 2005; Merrill, 2006), including one-off and short-term volunteering. Event volunteering typifies these 'episodic' volunteer opportunities, although volunteers can also be involved in event organizations in an ongoing capacity in organizational, managerial or governance roles within the event organization (Saleh and Wood, 1998; Handy et al., 2006). Increasingly, more complex typologies or continua of event volunteering are being proposed, recognizing that while the volunteering activities may be short term, the volunteers may return or re-engage with a single organization in a series of episodic relationships (Macduff, 2005; Bryen and Madden, 2006; Handy et al., 2006).

This chapter focuses on the recruitment and retention of episodic event volunteers and offers management insights from a comparative research study of 12 festival organizations in the state of Victoria, Australia. It considers three key management issues. First, how can event organizers encourage past volunteers to return? Secondly, in order to understand recruitment strategies, how are new volunteers involved and what factors influence event organizers' choice of recruitment methods? Thirdly, how, if at all, does the screening and selection of potential volunteers occur and what is the perceived value of the different methods?

Previous Research

Notwithstanding an increased desire for episodic volunteering opportunities, recruitment is a particular challenge for events (Saleh and Wood, 1998). The recruitment process is important for inspiring volunteers whilst creating realistic expectations regarding workload commitments, responsibilities, organizational support, and the overall volunteer event experience (Williams *et al.*, 1995; Ralston *et al.*, 2004). During recruitment, the core values of the organization (Karkatsoulis *et al.*, 2005) and the benefits of volunteering can be communicated (Downward *et al.*, 2005). The recruitment process can also be a source of dissatisfaction, which can influence other expectations of the event volunteering experience (Ralston *et al.*, 2004).

For those recruiting episodic volunteers, it also has to be considered that the retention or re-enlistment rate of 'veteran', or repeat, volunteers will partly determine how many new volunteers need to be recruited (Coyne and Coyne, 2001). Bryen and Madden (2006) conceptualize this as 'bounce-back', the re-engagement or return of episodic volunteers, although the extent to which this is incorporated into recruitment policies is not clear. Event organizations can use a range of methods to recruit volunteers, and previous research indicates the importance of informal word-of-mouth recruitment (Williams *et al.*, 1995; Coyne and Coyne, 2001; Monga and Treuren, 2001). While case studies and post-event evaluation reports detail the recruitment methods events have used to attract volunteers, there is little work exploring the range of options available to the event organizer, or how organizers perceived the value of different recruitment methods.

Once attracted to volunteer at an event, how are individuals then selected to fill the available volunteering roles? Selection and screening for the most suitable, competent and motivated candidates is important for the success of the event and the quality of service delivery (Reeser *et al.*, 2004) and also contributes to a volunteer's evaluation of their experience (Ralston *et al.*, 2004). Data suggest that sporting mega-events receive many more applications than there are volunteer positions, and post-event reports (Baum and Lockstone, 2007; also see, for example, Manchester 2002, 2002; SOCOG, 2002; Walker, 2002; Karkatsoulis *et al.*, 2005) contain descriptive details of the selection process and sometimes the selection criteria. Many events have application forms, variously submitted by post or online, and even at large-scale events interviews are a commonly used selection tool. However, the event organizer's rationale for adopting particular selection procedures (for example, interviews), and the perceived value and usefulness of these strategies, has not been explicitly considered in previous research.

At recurring events, retaining volunteers reduces the requirement for future recruitment and builds a core of experienced and competent volunteers (Saleh and Wood, 1998; Coyne and Coyne, 2001; Downward *et al.*, 2005). While the desirability of retaining past volunteers is widespread, it is not clear in studies (for example, Coyne and Coyne, 2001) whether previous volunteers who are interested in returning are automatically taken on, undergo any additional screening or assessment of their past performance, or perhaps have to reapply with other new applicants.

Management Insights from Cultural Festivals

The majority of this previous research on recruitment and retention focuses on collecting data from the volunteers themselves, rather than an organizational perspective. Case studies of single events dominate, with a few exceptions where multiple events are compared (for example, Monga and Treuren, 2001; Cuskelly *et al.*, 2004; Handy *et al.*, 2006). This chapter also takes a multi-event approach and attempts to contribute to the understanding of the organizational approaches to volunteer management. By focusing on recurring events and specifically cultural festivals, this study offers a counterbalance to the dominance of research on volunteering at sporting and mega-events. The chapter discusses the ways in which event organizers can encourage volunteers to return, or bounce back, and then considers the dominant approaches to the recruitment, selection and screening of new volunteers. By drawing on the experiences and opinions of event organizers responsible for volunteer management, the chapter offers three examples of best practice in finding and keeping event volunteers.

Interviews were carried out in late 2006 with volunteer managers representing 12 annual cultural festivals in Victoria, Australia. Each interview lasted between 1 and 1.5 hours and was conducted *in situ*. The profile of represented events, which spanned the arts, music, food and wine, and annual celebrations (Christmas, Easter, etc.), is provided in Table 12.1. Events were selected purposely to obtain a mix of locations (metropolitan, regional centres, rural) and a spread of ownership models. Five events were managed by local councils; the remainder were voluntary organizations governed by a volunteer committee or trustees. Of these, in four cases the event was managed by these volunteer committee members; two events employed paid management staff year round; and one event was managed as a short-term paid consultancy. The

Table 12.1. Profile of festivals.

Festival	Governance	Management[a]	Location	Approx no. of volunteers (2006)	Event duration
Arts I	Voluntary	Paid staff	Metropolitan	30	17 days
Arts II	Voluntary	Paid staff	Regional centre	220	3 months
Children's	Council	Paid staff	Regional centre	1100	8 days
Community I	Council	Paid staff	Metropolitan	100	1 day
Community II	Council	Paid staff	Regional centre	400	4 days
Community III	Voluntary	Volunteer	Rural	67	5 weeks
Community arts	Council	Paid staff	Metropolitan	1000+	4 days
Floral	Council	Paid staff	Regional centre	100	3 days
Music I	Voluntary	Paid staff	Regional centre	33	3 days
Music II	Voluntary	Volunteer	Rural	80	3 days
Music III	Voluntary	Volunteer	Rural	1000	4 days
Wine and food	Voluntary	Volunteer	Rural	30	2 days

[a]Event managed primarily by paid staff or volunteer committee; some volunteer-run events may additionally employ paid staff in support roles or during the delivery of the event.

research focuses on the involvement of rank-and-file volunteers working in operational roles, primarily during the event but also in the immediate build-up and shut-down periods. It excludes core volunteers (Saleh and Wood, 1998; Handy *et al.*, 2006), who work primarily in managerial and governance positions. It is important to acknowledge, however, that this latter group of volunteers may additionally give their time in operational roles during the event.

Interviews were transcribed and analysis supported through NVivo. Key themes in the data were identified; these were developed from the research questions, with additional themes emerging from the data. This chapter focuses on three key stages of volunteer management: retention of existing volunteers, recruitment of new volunteers, and the selection and screening process. For each stage, trends in the approaches to volunteer management are analysed and selected quotes from the interviews are used to illustrate points. Three examples of best practice are highlighted; these are events that have taken creative approaches to managing their volunteer programmes. They offer more detailed illustrations of how event organizations can work with a range of stakeholders to promote, develop and manage their volunteering workforce effectively.

Retention: Encouraging Volunteers to Bounce Back

All but one of the events studied rely heavily on returning, or bounce-back, volunteers: having three-quarters of volunteers returning each year is not unusual. The main advantage to the event of bounce-back volunteers is that they bring their past experience and knowledge of the event and tasks. Often volunteers return to the same role, and over time build up confidence, expertise and ownership. Repeat volunteers often require less training and involvement from management. There are also suggestions that experienced volunteers can be more reliable, flexible and open to last-minute requests.

In general, past volunteers are contacted first by the event organizers to ascertain how many want to return; other recruitment methods will then be considered to fill the gaps. Organizers did reflect on a volunteer's past performance, and if they were judged to have been unsuitable, they may be invited back but in a different role, or simply not contacted again. In general, returning volunteers did not have to formally reapply; an exception was the children's event, which requires an annual police check, so past volunteers have to resubmit an application.

From a management perspective, encouraging volunteers to return, or bounce back, is related to how volunteers are treated and rewarded, summarized by one respondent as: 'Because we look after them during and after the event' (*Floral Festival*). During the event, organizers concentrate on the intangibles: enjoyment, atmosphere, and making the volunteers feel welcome and involved. Following the event, the focus is on thanking the volunteers (in person and by letter), showing appreciation and giving opportunities for socializing, including post-event functions. Acknowledgement can also come from and via other external stakeholders. Those offering free tickets in return for volunteering felt that while this might attract first-time applicants, it was not a significant factor in retaining bounce-back volunteers.

Most event organizers maintain a volunteer database and use this to target previous volunteers. In addition, occasional but ongoing communication with these volunteers has a role in maintaining their involvement with, and commitment to, the event: 'touching base with volunteers, not just disappearing from their lives' (*Floral Festival*). The notion of a being part of the festival 'family' was referred to on a number of occasions.

Encouraging bounce-back is not without its challenges, not least making volunteers feel involved in the event. Other commitments mean volunteers are often not available *every* year. The only event without a strong returning cohort of volunteers observed that they found it 'difficult sometimes to keep up with volunteers because we find sometimes some of the younger ones, they move on, they disappear, [...] we lose contact with them' (*Community Festival II*). Relying on returning volunteers also means they age with the event and it can be a challenge to involve new and younger people.

Recruiting New Volunteers

While relying on bounce-back volunteers can bring benefits, all the events studied require at least some new volunteers each year to replace those who have left or are unavailable, or to increase the volunteer pool. The remainder of this chapter focuses on the ways event organizers attempt to attract new volunteers to their festival. While each of the events studied adopts a different strategy, they all use a combination of multiple recruitment methods. Evidence from these festivals is that event organizers recruit new rank-and-file volunteers from two main sources: individuals from the local community; and groups of volunteers from local clubs and associations, educational institutions and other event stakeholders.

Involving individuals as volunteers

The first source of volunteers is to recruit individuals from within the local community, and occasionally beyond. Confirming the findings of previous studies (Monga and Treuren, 2001), the main way of getting individuals involved is through word of mouth, with potential volunteers suggested by existing volunteers, committee members and the organizers themselves. This has a number of advantages: '...they know the festival and they know someone who works [here], so they know what the work entails' (*Music Festival III*). Consequently, 'because of the way we recruit people, word of mouth, it's very unusual for people come and say "look I don't like this"' (*Arts Festival II*). The willingness to suggest friends as volunteers also indicates that the current volunteers feel satisfied and appreciated. Personal contacts are also often used when there is a last-minute need for additional volunteers, and whilst they may be 'doing it as a personal commitment to you', rather than a commitment to the event, you 'know them and know them to be reliable' (*Music Festival I*). This ability to judge reliability and trust via word of mouth was a recurring theme. The notion of community, and knowing everyone within a community, was strong not just for events held in rural settings but also in the larger regional centres; indeed, this was mentioned everywhere except central Melbourne.

Event organizers place recruitment advertisements for volunteers in a range of outlets, including print media (particularly local newspapers and council newsletters), the event's own publications (programmes and web site), and occasionally on general volunteering web sites (for example, the Australian web site www.govolunteer.com.au). While most event organizers noted a limited response to adverts, one festival had previously been overwhelmed with applicants following an advert in Melbourne's daily newspaper *The Age*. Overall, adverts were mainly seen as a way of raising awareness of the event and its need for volunteers, with other recruitment methods also required.

Most events primarily recruit from their local community; however, there are cases, particularly arts and music festivals, where volunteers are sourced from a special-interest community, which can be spread over a wider geographical area, potentially including overseas. For these festivals, the Internet is a key recruitment tool. In comparison, most of the other festivals use their web sites primarily for information about the events, rather than as an active volunteer recruitment tool. Where events attract non-locals to volunteer, there is scope to recruit individuals from the volunteer pools of other similar events; this cross-fertilization was evident at two of the music festivals.

A perceived disadvantage of some recruitment methods, particularly advertisements and responding to unsolicited applications, was they attract the 'wrong' volunteers. Many respondents found it hard to verbalize what made a person unsuitable, even those who had developed more formalized job descriptions and had written selection criteria. 'Unsuitability' generally focused on behaviour and attitudes during the event and included volunteers not turning up for scheduled sessions, behaving inappropriately, not taking direction or not fitting into the culture of the organization. The motivations of unsolicited applications were sometimes questioned, for example 'every now and then I'll have someone that will just ring up and say "I want to do it because I want a free ticket", and that immediately sets a little alarm bell ringing for me' (*Music Festival II*). Volunteers recruited through advertisements may be more diverse, as opposed to volunteers recruited through word-of-mouth channels, who may be more homogeneous due to shared interests and social networks. Treuren and Monga (2002) suggest the latter scenario may offer a 'niche' approach to recruitment that aids in reducing volunteer turnover and increases the return to event organizations from investing in the development of volunteers. Research is yet to investigate, however, whether such homogeneity in volunteer populations could stifle events over time.

To overcome some of the concerns of organizers regarding recruitment methods, some events outsource elements of their volunteer recruitment and selection. While there were mixed attitudes towards using job or employment networking organizations, there were generally more positive experiences of volunteer resource centres. A city council that had previously relied on a range of recruitment methods (including advertisements and responding to enquiries) had recently begun to source most new volunteers for their community celebrations through their local volunteer resource centre. The event organizers provide the centre with job specifications, and the centre accesses their database of potential volunteers and also advertises the roles in the centre and via their publications and web site. The centre takes on coordination for recruitment and screening, both time-consuming activities; this leaves the event staff able to focus on other responsibilities. As the organizer of Community Festival II notes, the centre 'acts as a filter', and this has enabled the event to formalize its approach to volunteers and feel more confident about the suitability of the individuals recruited to volunteer.

Targeting those who already have links with the event is also an option. For example, previous visitors have both witnessed the roles volunteers undertake and may also see volunteering as a way of giving back to the festival as an acknowledgment of previous enjoyment at the event, often with an element of nostalgia or personal heritage attached to the event. At events with competitors or other participants, their friends and relatives can be recruited as volunteers, particularly when they can benefit from free tickets.

Involving groups as volunteers

The second source of volunteers is through various established groups within a community. This can work in two ways. First, groups are seen as a source of individual volunteers; for example, advertising for volunteers through a group's newsletter, where interested members contact the event direct. Secondly, and more commonly, events work with particular groups, who then access their membership to provide the event with volunteers. The event focuses on recruiting the groups, and the groups then recruit the volunteers and may also manage them during the event. Those interviewed work with a diverse range of community groups and associations, including scouts, sports clubs, churches, Rotary, Lions, Probus clubs, and specialist groups such as a woodwork club. Often the event already has a link to the group, either historically or typically an event committee member will also be involved in the group.

Outsourcing volunteer recruitment, and potentially coordination, to established groups brings a number of benefits to the event organizer. There is one contact point within the group and the event's relationship can focus on that person, which makes communication more effective. The volunteers already know each other and hopefully work well as a team: 'We don't have to worry about breaking down boundaries as far as people not being comfortable around each other' (Community Festival I). The contact person will have a better knowledge of each person and their capabilities and how best to manage them. Normally events will allocate a particular duty or area to each group (for example, car parking, stewarding, or the children's area); importantly, this can give the group and members a sense of ownership.

Successful group arrangements involve building ongoing, long-term and mutually beneficial relationships with a group and their key contact, and having clear lines of communication. This creates a situation of trust and reliability. There are suggestions that, in this model, individuals may feel more commitment towards their club or group rather than the event, and while this is not necessarily a problem, it is an area that warrants further investigation.

Many council-run events tap into other volunteering groups within their council, most notably, visitor information centre or city ambassador programmes. These have a large pool of available volunteers, and their experience and knowledge mean that training often involves only a briefing about the specifics of the event. They often undertake tourist information-based responsibilities at the events, which is 'fantastic as that's their usual volunteering role' (*Community Arts Festival*). These volunteers may be integrated into the general pool of volunteers or, more commonly, coordinated by their usual visitor information centre volunteer manager.

Two events studied looked beyond community groups for their volunteers and worked with local businesses, who provided staff either through an organized employee volunteer programme or as part of a sponsorship arrangement with the event. By considering these examples in more detail, the opportunities for innovation and creativity in volunteer recruitment and selection can be demonstrated.

Best practice 1 – employee volunteering programmes

Organizers of the Floral Festival have been concerned about the ageing profile of their current volunteers, and the organizers have attempted to attract younger volunteers. Most successful has been linking with a local bank's employee volunteering scheme. As part of their commitment to community involvement, the bank provides staff with 2 days of paid volunteer leave each year. The festival participates in the scheme and these bank employees are brought into the main volunteering pool during the event and individuals' details are entered into the volunteer database for future contacts. A relationship is also maintained directly with the bank, and a separate information session is run for these volunteers at the bank's headquarters.

Best practice 2 – working with stakeholders

A council events team run events and celebrations throughout the year (including Community Festival I) and work with a range of community groups who provide their members' services as volunteers. In particular, they have encouraged local businesses sponsoring the events to get their staff involved: 'A lot of organizations are looking for staff to donate their time in a way that's fun', and it also gives them more involvement and ownership over the events. In addition, each year a charity benefits from funds raised at the Christmas event, and as part of this agreement the charity supplies volunteers to work at the festival, either drawn from their existing volunteer supporters or recruited by the charity to volunteer specifically at the event. This festival has successfully tapped into their network of stakeholders to expand their supporters' contributions to the event.

The final established group of volunteers that can be accessed is students, usually on degree or vocational education courses but also at secondary school. Recognizing the need to gain experience for future employment, some events work with institutions offering event management, tourism and hospitality qualifications, and involve students in event planning and behind the scenes: 'We try and make it so as their volunteering can actually complement the study that they're doing' (*Children's Festival*). Organizers stress the need for aspirant event professionals to understand the realities of the industry: 'get out there and see what it's all about because it is an incredibly rewarding experience but it's also a lot of hard work' (*Community Festival I*). Particular courses can be targeted to recruit students with specific skills; for example, those on early education courses to run children's activities. As with community groups, the initial, and often ongoing, contact is with one person, the lecturer or teacher.

A final example of best practice demonstrates how event organizers can work with stakeholder groups to develop a volunteer programme that is attractive to a targeted group of potential volunteers.

Best practice 3 – stakeholder support for volunteers
As part of their wider sponsorship strategy, organizers of the Children's Festival have enlisted a high-profile sponsor for their volunteer programme. As many of their volunteers are teenagers, they have targeted sponsors who have a high brand profile with this group. The image and credibility of the sponsor can potentially attract new volunteers, and the association can bring rewards to the volunteers. The organizers see the benefits for the sponsor of being associated with the volunteering element of the event as: 'They get to brand every single shirt that a volunteer has worn so I think that's very positive, good corporate citizenship'.

A fundamental element of volunteering definitions is a lack of payment (Cnaan *et al.*, 1996); however, two of the voluntary organizations in this study paid their volunteer groups for their services (Music Festival III and the Wine and Food Festival). For these voluntary events, both in rural locations with small resident populations, paying the contributing groups is a means of recognizing the community's commitment and ownership of the event, and a way of investing the proceeds of the event back into the community and local economy. Payments, or fees, are calculated on the number of volunteers' hours required for a particular task. Despite the payment, these workers are still perceived as volunteers, 'because you're not giving each individual person money' (*Wine and Food Festival*).

Selection and Screening

While most event organizers are happy with the current number of volunteers, they would also be willing to take more. Only two events (Arts Festival I and Music Festival II) had to turn excess volunteers away, and in one case this was people approaching them just before the event. Others expressed a desire for additional volunteers in particular roles or to be able to get volunteers to commit earlier. Only one event felt it had a serious recruitment problem, largely due to the late organization of volunteering at the festival. However, few were in the position to turn down prospective volunteers due to an oversupply of applicants. Given this situation, organizers take a relatively open approach to selection, wanting to encourage participation, and are willing to give people a chance. For example: 'The Festival really does embrace the volunteers. We're very open to whoever wants to come along and if there are issues with volunteers we try and manage those issues rather than turn them away from the event and put them in positions that would be suitable' (*Children's Festival*).

Although selection, or choosing between candidates, was not a requirement for the majority of these events, there was a general recognition of the need to screen applicants. This was seen as a duty of care: 'to the audience as well as to ourselves and the volunteers themselves, that it has to be done in a formal way' (*Community Festival II*); screening can also be a 'safeguard' for the event organizers (*Arts Festival II*). Nevertheless, overall, screening of volunteers is kept relatively informal. More formalization is avoided for a range of reasons: it would put people off applying, particularly some younger and older applicants; screening 'is not that big a deal for people, because they are recruited through word of mouth' (*Music Festival I*); and the volunteer-run nature of an event, and its small scale, does not fit with a highly formalized approach. Even those adopting more formalized screening methods, typically council-managed events, mentioned 'people often judge their own suitability for a role' (*Floral Festival*).

Broadly, the research indicated that there can be five stages in the screening of event volunteers: the initial contact, written application, interview, references, and police check (Fig. 12.1). In practice, screening may be confined to a single conversation with a prospective volunteer, particularly when recruited through word-of-mouth channels.

Screening begins at the first contact point, and organizers use this to get an initial impression of the applicant. Less than half of events in this study had a formal application form; those that did generally used it to collect contact information, availability and an indication of the role or area applicants wanted to volunteer in. Subsequently, an interview of some kind may take place, although organizers stress that this is very informal and may be face to face or by telephone or e-mail. This interview is usually focused around finding out more about the applicant and their motivations or interest in volunteering, and matching them to a suitable role. This informal nature suited many of the organizations studied, because of their small size, their informal working culture and the nature of the volunteering relationship. References may be asked for on an application form; however, these are often not taken up unless doubts are raised during other parts of the screening process. Recruiting via word of mouth often means that organizers feel additional, more-formalized screening methods are not required. Organizers usually ask the person who recommended the prospective volunteer or 'we know them and what they are able to do, and in [this city] everyone knows everyone, especially within communities such as the music community, or if we don't know someone, we know someone who does' (*Music Festival I*).

It is acknowledged that some volunteers may find overt checking a sensitive topic and it can go against a desire to 'embrace community spirit' (*Floral Festival*), and some volunteers, particularly those previously involved, may feel insulted. Nevertheless, 'people are mostly okay with police checks as they understand they are required' (*Floral Festival*). In Victoria, state legislation requires those in

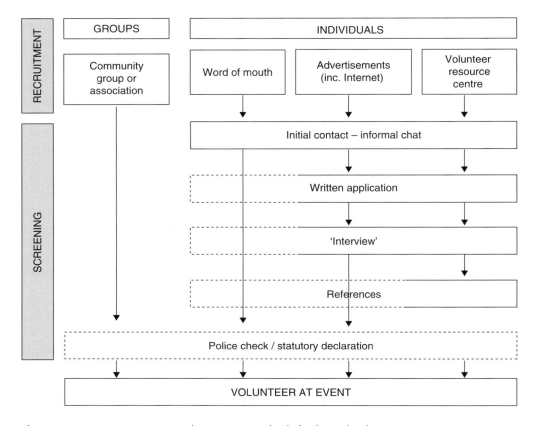

Fig. 12.1. Main recruitment and screening methods for festival volunteers.

roles working directly with children to undertake a police check or make a statutory declaration that they have no police record. None of the events reported
having to reject anyone on the basis of a police check, but two noted that if volunteers are not happy with being asked they are likely to place themselves in
other roles not with children or 'if they know that they've got history then you
just don't hear from them again' (*Children's Festival*). When volunteer recruitment is outsourced to either a volunteer resource centre or other groups the
responsibility for screening individuals is also passed on, with the exception of
the Children's Festival, which, given the focus of the event, processes all police
checks itself.

Conclusions and Implications

This research gives weight to the observation that event volunteering is not just
one-off, rather episodic volunteering can incorporate bounce-back. The reality
for recurring events is they come to rely on a returning cohort of volunteers, so

recruitment is as much about retention: satisfying volunteers by offering them a rewarding experience and acknowledging their input, in an effort to encourage their return. Future research should explore, from the volunteers' perspective, what encourages them to bounce back, and include a more overt consideration of repeat volunteering in the areas of volunteer motivation, satisfaction, commitment and turnover. This is particularly so as there is a long history of research to draw upon from the broader management and volunteer literature and several established, replicable research instruments that could be used to quantitatively investigate these concepts.

For new volunteers, there are two main sources of operational volunteers: individuals and groups. Choice of recruitment methods is linked to whether organizers believe they are able to attract reliable and trustworthy volunteers. An informal approach to recruitment relies on a sense and knowledge of community and, as suggested in previous research (Williams *et al.*, 1995; Coyne and Coyne, 2001; Monga and Treuren, 2001), for individuals, word-of-mouth recruitment dominates. Advertisements also play a role in raising awareness of event volunteering opportunities, and festivals that can tap into an established special-interest community are also using the Internet for recruitment. Outsourcing recruitment and coordination to a trusted third party, such as a volunteer resource centre, can increase the formalization and rigour of an event's recruitment processes and free event staff from this time-consuming role. The benefits of outsourcing also lie behind the recruitment of groups of volunteers, where the event organizer can focus on building relationships with the key contact, and the group can take ownership of the event, or an element of it. While the focus is on local community groups, the best practice case studies in this chapter demonstrate the scope to use volunteering to strengthen relationships and the involvement of the local business community through employee volunteering schemes and sponsorship arrangements.

Unlike one-off mega-events, whose volunteer programmes are typically hugely oversubscribed (Baum and Lockstone, 2007), recurring events are rarely in a position to choose between various applicants to fill a limited number of roles. Rather, selection focuses on screening volunteers to assess their individual suitability. An informal approach to selection and screening, along with a focus on word-of-mouth recruitment, fits with the organizational cultures of these festivals. Screening may be confined to an informal discussion with a potential volunteer, although some events, particularly those run by councils, have procedures for more-structured written applications, interviews and reference checks. The only standardized step is for volunteer roles that involve working directly with children, when legislation requires that police checks or statutory declarations are sought. Future research should contrast this organizational perspective with the opinions of newly recruited and veteran volunteers and their subsequent volunteering experiences. This could explore the relationship between the means of recruitment and retention rates, or the extent of selection and screening and the subsequent performance of volunteers.

By taking a comparative methodology, it is evident that while each festival has its own approach to recruitment and selection, there are commonalities in the event sectors' involvement of volunteers, but also innovation and examples of events working with a range of stakeholders and thinking creatively about ways of diversifying their volunteer base.

References

Baum, T. and Lockstone, L. (2007) Volunteers and mega sporting events: developing a research framework. *International Journal of Event Management Research* 3(1), 29–41.

Brudney, J. (ed.) (2005) *Emerging Areas of Volunteering*. ARNOVA Occasional Paper Series 1(2).

Bryen, L. and Madden, K. (2006) *Bounce-back of Episodic Volunteers: What Makes Episodic Volunteers Return?* Working Paper No. CPNS 32. Queensland University of Technology, Brisbane, Australia.

Cnaan, R.A., Handy, F. and Wadsworth, M. (1996) Defining who is a volunteer: conceptual and empirical considerations. *Nonprofit and Voluntary Sector Quarterly* 25, 364–383.

Coyne, B.S. and Coyne, E.J. Sr (2001) Getting, keeping and caring for unpaid volunteers for professional golf tournament events. *Human Resource Development International* 4(2), 199–214.

Cuskelly, G., Auld, C., Harrington, M. and Coleman, D. (2004) Predicting the behavioural dependability of sport event volunteers. *Event Management* 9, 73–89.

Downward, P., Lumsdon, L. and Ralston, R. (2005) Gender differences in sports event volunteering: insights from crew 2002 at the XVII Commonwealth Games. *Managing Leisure* 10, 219–236.

Gaskin, K. (2003) *A Choice Blend: What Volunteers Want from Organization and Management*. Institute for Volunteer Research, London.

Hager, M. and Brudney, J. (2004) *Balancing Act: the Challenges and Benefits of Volunteers*. The Urban Institute, Washington, DC.

Hall, M., McKechnie, A.-J., Davidman, K. and Leslie, F. (2001) *An Environmental Scan on Volunteering and Improving Volunteering*. Canadian Centre for Philanthropy, Toronto, Canada.

Handy, F., Brodeur, N. and Cnann, R.A. (2006) Summer on the island: episodic volunteering. *Voluntary Action* 7(3), 31–46.

Karkatsoulis, P., Michalopoulos, N. and Moustakatou, V. (2005) The national identity as a motivational factor for better performance in the public sector: the case of the volunteers of the Athens 2004 Olympic Games. *International Journal of Productivity and Performance Management* 54(7), 579–594.

Macduff, N. (2005) Societal changes and the rise of the episodic volunteer. In: Brudney, J.L. (ed.) *Emerging Areas of Volunteering*. ARNOVA Occasional Paper Series 1(2), pp. 49–61.

Manchester 2002 (2002) *Post Games Report*. Manchester 2002, The XVII Commonwealth Games, Manchester, UK.

Merrill, M.V. (2006) Global trends and the challenges for volunteering. *The International Journal of Volunteer Administration* XXIV(1), 9–14.

Monga, M. and Treuren, G. (2001) Human resource management practices in several South Australian event organizations. In: Spooner, K. and Innes, C. (eds) *Employment Relations in the New Economy: Proceedings of the Ninth Annual Conference of the International Employment Relations Association*. IERA, Sydney, pp. 459–474.

Ralston, R., Downward, P. and Lumsdon, L. (2004) The expectations of volunteers prior to the XVII Commonwealth Games, 2002: a qualitative study. *Event Management* 9(1/2), 13–26.

Reeser, J.C., Berg, R.L., Rhea, D. and Willick, S. (2004) Motivation and satisfaction among polyclinic volunteers at the 2002 Winter Olympic and Paralympic Games. *British Journal of Sports Medicine* 39(4), e20.

Saleh, F. and Wood, C. (1998) Motives of volunteers in multicultural festivals: the case of Saskatoon Folkfest. *Festival Management and Event Tourism* 5(1/2), 59–70.

SOCOG (2002) *Official Report of the XXVII Olympiad. Volume One: Preparing for the Games.* Sydney Organizing Committee for the Olympic Games, Sydney.

Treuren, G. and Monga, M. (2002) Does the observable special event volunteer career in four South Australian special event organisations demonstrate the existence of a recruitment niche? In: Jago, L., Deery, M., Harris, R., Hede, A.-M. and Allen, J. (eds) *Proceedings of Event and Place Marketing Conference*, Australian Centre for Event Management, Sydney, pp. 203–231.

Volunteering Australia (2006) *National Survey of Volunteering Issues 06.* Volunteering Australia, Melbourne, Australia.

Walker, M.P. (2002) Going for customer service gold. *T&D* May, 62–69.

Williams, P.W., Dossa, K.B. and Tompkins, L. (1995) Volunteerism and special event management: a case study of Whistler's Men's World Cup of Skiing. *Festival Management and Event Tourism* 3(2), 83–95.

Zarinpoush, F., Barr, C. and Moreton, J. (2004) *Managers of Volunteers: a Profile of the Profession.* Canadian Centre for Philanthropy, Toronto, Canada.

V   Management of People and Work

Contemporary event organizations face continual challenges when managing personnel and the environment where events are conducted. The management of volunteers, of employees at high-risk events and of practices at conferences are examples of these challenges. This part comprises four chapters: the first two concentrate on research that raises awareness of the management of volunteers in sport events; the third discusses the stewarding and security activity of high-adrenalin work environments at events; and the final chapter addresses the need for a country to embrace the global practices of human resource management in order to strengthen the casual approach it has when managing conferences.

The chapter by Hoye and Cuskelly (Chapter 13) explores the psychology of sport event volunteerism. The authors review existing research on volunteer motives, satisfaction, commitment and retention; they highlight how these concepts are interrelated and the importance they have regarding the implications for the management of volunteers in sport events. However, the dearth of literature on this topic indicates the need for research to delve deeper into how to manage volunteer motivation and commitment, and how management practices should be adapted to maximize volunteer satisfaction and retention. In order for sport event volunteer research to agree about the dimensionality of event volunteer motivation, Hoye and Cuskelly emphasize the need for research to move beyond one-off, single-event studies that use cross-sectional research designs.

Continuing the theme of managing sport event volunteers, Auld, Cuskelly and Harrington (Chapter 14) argue that volunteers are an established component of the legacy rationale that surrounds major events. They discuss sport event volunteering and how event volunteers can be managed in order to encourage them to engage in further volunteer activity. At this stage the authors emphasize the need for a broader volunteer participation base, which helps establish links between dissimilar community groups in order to create broader social outcomes. The chapter invites future research to determine the potential for longer-term volunteer legacies.

Kemp (Chapter 15) concentrates on stewarding and security activity in the front-of-house areas in high-adrenalin work environments, such as rock and indie music concerts. Kemp argues that Geller's (1996) event safety triad, which comprises the elements of person, environment and behaviour, is a vital connection between the audience and those working in crowd management at events, and can be instituted if a tight management structure is focused on the outcomes. Five key points evolve from Kemp's chapter, which raises the reader's awareness of managing the conditions and pattern of behaviour evident in high-adrenalin work environments.

Finally, Okech (Chapter 16) focuses on the importance of managing human resources at conferences in Kenya. Statistics highlight the increasing number of conferences conducted in Kenya; however, there is a short-term and fragmented approach to related human resource management practices. Incorporating examples from global case studies, Okech argues that training and portable national competency standards targeted to a variety of hospitality and tourism occupations should strengthen the standard of managing human resources. In return, the quality of conference provision and its value for money will assist with the sustainability of, and continued increase in, conference demand in Kenya.

13 The Psychology of Sport Event Volunteerism: a Review of Volunteer Motives, Involvement and Behaviour

RUSSELL HOYE[1] AND GRAHAM CUSKELLY[2]

[1]La Trobe University, Australia; [2]Griffith University, Australia

Introduction

The reliance of mega sport events, as well as smaller-scale national, regional and local sport events, on volunteers is well documented (ASC, 2000; Cuskelly et al., 2004). Irrespective of the scale (international to local community) of events such as the Olympic, Paralympic and Commonwealth Games or local tournaments, these events utilize the knowledge, skills and expertise of volunteers to officiate at competitions, liaise with visiting teams, support media and security organizations, manage hospitality and catering services, deal with spectators, and provide services for athletes and sponsors before, during and after events.

The purpose of this chapter is to explore the psychology of sport event volunteerism, specifically the motives and involvement of event volunteers and behavioural aspects of event volunteering. This chapter seeks to explore the questions of why people volunteer for sport events, the nature and extent of their involvement, and issues surrounding their commitment and retention. The chapter comprises four parts: first, the extent of volunteer involvement in sport events is briefly described; secondly, the existing research on volunteer motives is reviewed; thirdly, specific aspects of volunteer commitment and retention are reviewed; and fourthly, some conclusions are drawn for future research into the psychology of sport event volunteerism.

Volunteer Involvement

The nature of volunteer involvement in sport events is largely dependent on the scale and complexity of the event. Sport events can be 'held annually or more frequently, conducted on a single day or over a number of days, staged in a single venue or multiple venues, focused on one sport or recreation activity or involve a variety of activities' (ASC, 2000:3) and can be conducted for participants of differing age groups or ability. For the purpose of this chapter, sport events are defined as any event held where organized sporting activity or competition is the primary focus. These include finals or championship games of sporting competitions or leagues, multi-sport events such as the Olympic or Commonwealth Games, or single-sport championships at regional, state/provincial, national or international level (e.g. Rugby or FIFA World Cup Events). Events such as parades, fairs and other community activities are not considered as part of this chapter. The focus of the chapter is therefore on volunteers within sport events, in particular events which require a significant volunteer labour force.

The involvement of volunteers in major sport events is undoubtedly significant. The 2000 and 2004 Summer Olympic Games utilized more than 40,000 and 45,000 volunteers, respectively, while the 2006 Commonwealth Games in Melbourne, Australia, and the 2006 Asian Games in Doha, Qatar, each utilized more than 15,000 volunteers (Cuskelly *et al.*, 2006). The staging of single-sport events at international level, such as the 2007 Rugby World Cup (3000 volunteers) and the 2007 ICC Cricket World Cup (3500 volunteers), is also largely dependent on considerable numbers of volunteers.

The economic contribution of volunteers to major sport events was the focus of a study by Solberg (2003), who explored the value of volunteer labour at the 1999 World Ice Hockey Championship. This event was held over 2 weeks, with 16 national teams playing 49 matches, in front of more than 175,000 spectators. The event involved 800 volunteers, who worked more than 71,000 hours. The majority of these volunteers took paid leave or used their leisure time to volunteer at the event, with the result that the event had little impact on the displacement of goods and services in the formal economy, as volunteers were not financially disadvantaged and they were still spending in the local economy. The study found that the services provided by volunteers had a high market value. Solberg (2003:24) also found that there was 'a net increase in people's motivation to work with other events and other kinds of voluntary work' and that, overall, volunteer involvement in the event did not adversely affect the supply of volunteers for other forms of sporting activity.

Volunteer Motives

Before reviewing the research into sport event volunteer motives we first address the debate over the dimensionality of volunteer motives. The motivation to volunteer can be described as a desire to help others or for personal and social rewards. Stebbins (1996), in his widely cited work, labelled these motives as altruism and self-interest, which, he argued, co-exist within formal organizational settings. Other researchers have developed and argued for volunteer motivation models that comprise a single dimension (Cnaan and Goldberg-Glen, 1991), two dimensions (Smith, 1981), three dimensions (Knoke and Prensky, 1984), four dimensions (Batson *et al.*, 2002) or more complex models with as many as six unique dimensions (e.g. Clary *et al.*, 1992, 1998; Clary and Snyder, 1999; Finkelstein *et al.*, 2005). The lack of agreement on what constitutes volunteer motives was noted by Wang (2004:420), who said that 'despite recent advances in research on volunteer motivations, there is still considerable debate about the underlying structure or dimensionality of volunteer motivations'.

Perhaps not surprisingly the majority of research into the motives of sport volunteers has been in the context of large-scale sport events (e.g. Farrell *et al.*, 1998; Ralston *et al.*, 2004; Wang, 2004; Downward and Ralston, 2005; Fairley, *et al.*, 2007). Relatively few studies have focused on the motives of longer-term or seasonal volunteers operating at the community level of sport, with notable exceptions being Burgham and Downward (2005) and Eley and Kirk (2002). The majority of the research into volunteer motives has been based on scales adapted from the work of Cnaan and Goldberg-Glen (1991) or has taken a qualitative approach.

One of the earliest reported studies of sport event volunteer motives was conducted by Andrew (1996:24), who concluded that 'individuals will be attracted by and expect different material and personal incentives when volunteering for a cause'. The implications from this study were that sport event managers needed to understand the variety of motives held by a diverse volunteer labour force and therefore use a variety of management techniques to sustain these motivations over the duration of an event. In a similar vein, Farrell *et al.* (1998:288–289) identified the importance of sport event organizers understanding volunteer motives so they could 'respond effectively to [volunteer] management needs in the areas of recruitment, retention, and daily operations'. They also argued that managing volunteer experiences appropriately would assist in the 'maintenance of a strong volunteer base in the community for future events' (Farrell *et al.*, 1998:289).

The results of Farrell *et al.* (1998) also suggested that sport event volunteer motives differed from those of sport volunteers in other settings. They found that motives of sport event volunteers could be grouped into four categories: purposive, solidary, external traditions and commitments. Purposive motivation is based on a desire to do something useful and contribute to a society or community. Solidary motivation was based on the need for social interaction, group identification and networking. These two categories matched those originally proposed by Caldwell and Andereck (1994) as incentives for volunteering. The additional factors identified in the study, external traditions (an emphasis on extrinsic motivations) and commitments (expectations from others for volunteering), were the lowest ranking in terms of importance to event volunteers. In other words, Farrell *et al.* (1998) argued that the episodic nature of sport events and the different volunteer experiences they provided relative to longer-term volunteer settings attracted individuals for different reasons.

The uniqueness of a sport event and affinity with the sport are important reasons volunteers continue an association with a sport event over a long period of time. Coyne and Coyne (2001) investigated volunteer motives associated with professional golf events and found that volunteer motives were initially based on identifiable personal rewards but these changed as volunteers remained involved in successive events. In other words, sport event volunteer motives might be considered somewhat 'fluid', in that they may change over time as they experience the event.

The expectations of event volunteers have also drawn the attention of researchers. Ralston *et al.* (2004) investigated the expectations of volunteers prior to the 2002 Manchester Commonwealth Games, an event which utilized more than 10,500 volunteers. Ralston *et al.* (2004:15) reported that sport event volunteering 'tends to be sporadic and episodic and is highly dependent on the availability of tangible and intangible incentives and awards to attract and motivate volunteers'. Other motives identified by Ralston *et al.* (2004) included a feeling of connectedness with something special, an empathy with the spirit or philosophy of the event, a general commitment as local and national citizens, support for an event that leads to the development and image of a local community, region or nation, and volunteers' expectations of the experience itself. Ralston *et al.* (2004) concluded that three factors were involved in volunteer motives: altruism, involvement and the uniqueness of the event. They argued that understanding these motives is important for designing recruitment and training programmes, and that they shape volunteer expectations of the particular roles they may play in an event.

Other investigations of the motives of event volunteers have highlighted the complex nature of this phenomenon. For example, a study by Reeser *et al.* (2005) of the motivations of polyclinic volunteers (medical and allied health professionals) at the 2002 Salt Lake City Winter Olympic Games yielded similar results to Ralston *et al.* (2004), with the highest-ranking motivating factors being a sense of altruism, wanting to be involved in working with a variety of people and elite athletes, and to feel part of a unique event. They concluded that these specialist sport event volunteers were motivated by a complex process described as enlightened self-interest, where volunteer motives were not solely altruistic but based on a sense of reciprocity, with identifiable benefits accruing not just to the event organizers and participants but to the volunteers themselves (Reeser *et al.*, 2005).

The relatively few completed studies of sport event volunteer motives have tended to use different measures without significant efforts to test their dimensionality. One study that has attempted to do this was completed by Wang (2004), which identified five motives held by sport event volunteers, namely altruistic value, personal development, community concern, ego enhancement and social adjustment. Wang (2004:421) provided a strong argument for utilizing a multi-dimensional structure, claiming that 'previous evidence to support the uni-dimensional structure was rather weak' and that the 'overwhelming majority of prior studies have suggested that motivation to volunteer is a multi-dimensional construct'. The altruistic values dimension is based on people choosing to volunteer because of personal values and beliefs, enjoyment derived from helping other people and being a person who likes to be involved. The personal development construct is concerned with motives to volunteer to gain experience, for the challenge and being with people with similar interests. Community concern is focused on volunteering to make a contribution and service to the community. The social adjustment dimension is based on people volunteering because it is important to significant others who support their volunteer activities. Ego enhancement reflects the notion that people volunteer to feel part of a unique experience or event, because volunteering is fun and to feel needed or important. A later study by Fairley *et al.* (2007) of volunteers travelling to the 2004 Olympics identified a similar range of motives.

In summary, from the relatively small number of published studies on the motivations of sport event volunteers, several conclusions can be made. First, the variety of motives held by sport event volunteers suggests that they should not be treated as a homogeneous group but rather as a collection of individuals each with different motives for engaging in volunteering. Secondly, sport event volunteers tend to be motivated for reasons that differ from volunteers involved in voluntary sport organizations (VSOs) on an ongoing basis. In other words, the episodic nature of sport events attracts different people to serve as volunteers. And thirdly, volunteer motives are likely to change over time as volunteers engage in their roles and experience various management strategies and may be involved repeatedly in the same event in successive years. The variety of attempts to develop a robust measure of volunteer motives is matched by efforts to discover how volunteer motives are related to other elements of the voluntary experience such as commitment and retention.

Volunteer Satisfaction, Commitment and Retention

Without reasonably high levels of volunteer satisfaction and commitment, volunteer retention rates are likely to be negatively affected, making it difficult to stage and manage sport events, particularly those that run over many days. As noted by Cuskelly *et al.* (2006), volunteer satisfaction, commitment and retention are complex and interrelated phenomena that have attracted an increasing amount of attention from researchers. One of the earliest studies in this area, in which the focus was event volunteers, was conducted by Elstad (1997), who investigated the determinants of volunteer satisfaction amongst volunteers involved in the 1994 Winter Olympic Games in Lillehammer. Respondents' high levels of satisfaction were based on the opportunity to expand their personal network, to be part of the event and to achieve a desired level of job competence.

In 1998, Farrell *et al.* discovered that volunteer satisfaction was related to the level of communication between volunteers that was facilitated by event organizers and the recognition afforded individual volunteer efforts. Farrell *et al.* (1998:298) concluded that 'volunteer satisfaction with the experience overall is not only a function of fulfilling their expectations, but is also related to their satisfaction with the facilities and the organization of the event'. Thus, the way volunteers are managed is directly related to their level of satisfaction with the voluntary experience. This finding was supported by Reeser *et al.* (2005), who concluded that feedback on performance and recognition of volunteer efforts by event managers has a significant effect on the level of satisfaction felt by volunteers.

While the reported studies of volunteer motives, expectations and satisfaction go some way towards explaining the nature of the volunteer experience within the context of sport events, they do not explain the behaviour of sport event volunteers, in particular their likelihood of returning to volunteer again or to engage in further long-term volunteering roles. Volunteer retention is recognized as a significant problem for the community sport sector as it limits the capacity of sport organizations to deliver services to members and other users (Cuskelly, 2004). However, there is a very limited amount of published research on the retention of volunteers in sport events or even in the wider non-profit literature (Gidron, 1985; Mesch et al., 1998). A study by Mesch et al. (1998) identified that three variables have been reported to affect volunteer retention: motives, meaningful work and satisfaction. The results of various studies using each of these variables are mixed, with arguably only the relationship between volunteer motives and retention being firmly established in the literature. Volunteer motives have usually been identified as altruistic or instrumental, with both motives contributing to volunteer retention. However, Mesch et al. (1998) found that only instrumental motives were predictive of volunteer retention.

One aspect of sport event volunteering that has attracted little research attention is distinguishing between factors that influence individuals' decisions to initially volunteer and those factors that affect volunteers' decisions to continue volunteering. In a study of telephone crisis centre volunteers, Lammers (1991:139) investigated the factors that predicted volunteer service duration and argued that 'predictors of *volunteering* should be different from predictors of volunteer *duration*' (emphasis in original). In other words, volunteers join an organization for a variety of motives, which might well be different from why they would remain within an organization once they had experienced its culture, management system, interactions with other volunteers or undertaken volunteer roles.

This important distinction was the focus of a study by Cuskelly et al. (2004), who investigated the behavioural dependability (i.e. the extent to which the performance and attendance of sport event volunteers meets or exceeds the expectations of event organizers) of sport event volunteers in a number of sport event contexts. They argued that the duration of an event and subsequent expectations placed upon volunteers by event organizers, as well as support from family and friends of event volunteers, were important determinants of the behavioural dependability of sport event volunteers. Importantly, Cuskelly et al. (2004:87) argued that 'understanding and influencing the behaviour of major event volunteers is more complicated than ensuring that the motives of volunteers are satisfied by event organizers'.

The results of Cuskelly et al. (2004) seem to be in direct contrast to earlier work reported by Clary et al. (1992), and later Clary and Snyder (1999), who argued that functional theory suggests that volunteers will be satisfied if their volunteer experience matches their motivations and that this will, in turn, lead to volunteers remaining for longer periods. A study by Clary et al. (1998) concluded that volunteer service organizations should consider matching volunteer experiences to volunteer motives to reduce volunteer turnover (i.e. increase retention). A recent study by Kim *et al.* (2007) of youth sport volunteers concluded that there remains much work to be done to investigate the relationship between volunteer motives and retention.

Conclusion and Future Research Directions

This review of the psychology of sport event volunteering has focused on several core concepts: volunteer motives, satisfaction, commitment and retention. It is clear from the research literature that these concepts are interrelated and that they have important implications for the management of volunteers in sport events of varying scale and complexity. It is important to note that the majority of volunteers involved in special events (including sport events) conducted on a regular or annual basis in the same locale are repeat volunteers (Treuren and Monga, 2002a,b). In addition, because these volunteers are usually sourced from organizations related to the event organization through the social networks of previous volunteers or from prior participants, a 'combination of targeted recruitment and planned training' may substantially increase the effectiveness and efficiency of volunteer recruitment efforts for repeat sport events (Treuren and Monga, 2002b:226). In addition, sport event organizers need to 'recognize that if the majority of their volunteers are repeat volunteers or that their involvement is part of a long term career in volunteering at sport events, then the typical sport event volunteer will be familiar with many volunteer management practices' (Cuskelly *et al.*, 2006:144). Thus, the organizers of sport events held on a regular or annual basis need to adopt innovative recruitment and management practices in order to reduce dissatisfaction amongst their volunteer labour force for potential gains in volunteer retention rates.

Sport event volunteers have also been described as being involved in 'serious leisure' – leisure that takes place in a defined social world, with identifiable social contacts, within lifestyles that accommodate the leisure activity, in association with a variety of small groups, and in some cases focus on a collective activity (Stebbins, 1996). Such long-term involvement in volunteering has been defined as 'career volunteering', where volunteers seek satisfaction through contributing to their own well-being or that of the general community (Stebbins, 1996). In a study of motor sport volunteers, Harrington *et al.* (2000:445) identified volunteers as taking part in 'the collective provision of a mutually-valued phenomenon, the motorsport race', where their volunteer involvement 'makes possible the spectator sport/entertainment that corporate stakeholders invest in and control to profitable advantage'. Volunteers perceived that the rewards they receive from their involvement assist them to sustain their 'career' as an event volunteer, sometimes at great personal cost. Ironically, the study by Harrington *et al.* (2000:445) found that career volunteers 'resent the treatment and lack of appreciation they are afforded by organizers', but they persist in their role based on their intrinsic motivation to be associated with the event. This incongruity could be addressed through improved volunteer management practices, which focus on providing better recognition and organizational support to sport event volunteers. This example highlights the relative lack of understanding of volunteer motives by sport event managers and the requirements volunteers have of management in order to maintain their commitment and enthusiasm for the duration of an event or the subsequent stagings of an annual event.

The rather uninformed management approach to sport event volunteers highlighted here should be understood in light of the quality and capability of most sport event organizations. For example, in an analysis of the broader UK event management industry, Harris (2004:108) contended that 'there remains little coordination, coherence, or understanding about what is required to be fully professionalized'. While there are many examples of successful sport events involving large numbers of volunteers, the major sport event industry is in its infancy (Cuskelly et al., 2006). From the limited research reported in this chapter it is clear that there remains much to be discovered about how best to manage volunteer motivation and commitment in the context of sport events, and how volunteer management practices should be adapted to maximize volunteer satisfaction and retention. This lack of detailed theoretical and applied knowledge of sport event volunteers was highlighted in a review of event management research conducted by Harris et al. (2001), who noted that very few research articles focused on the issue of event volunteers. The unique environment of sport events, in particular their episodic nature and the increasing commodification of some major sport events, has a number of implications for volunteer motivation, satisfaction, commitment, performance and retention (Cuskelly et al., 2006). Thus, there are many opportunities for further research into volunteering within the context of sport events, investigating, in particular, the relationships between volunteer motives, commitment, satisfaction with management practices and contextual influences on volunteer performance and retention.

Our knowledge and understanding is likely to be more fully developed, whether as a scholar or as an event manager, if future research into event volunteers moves beyond the descriptive studies of volunteer motives and satisfaction. Event volunteer research has generally lacked a theoretical foundation and a clearly specified research design, and tended to focus in an evaluative way on single events, using convenience sampling and cross-sectional research designs, and developed measurement tools that are one-off and often event-specific.

A large proportion of sport event volunteer research has taken an empiricist approach, perhaps driven by a desire to explore the motives of event volunteers and the extent to which these motives are satisfied by participating in the staging of an event. Whether through an endeavour to meet the event managers perceived research needs, to gain access to a research population, or through insufficient research planning and design, there has been a tendency to overlook motivation theory. As a consequence, there is almost no agreement about the dimensionality of event volunteer motivation. A lack of agreement on dimensionality is compounded by a penchant for researchers to develop their own measurement scales. The use of exploratory factor analysis techniques to uncover underlying dimensions rather than more rigorous confirmatory analyses weakens research validity in this field. Furthermore, much of the published research has been heavily context specific, focusing on volunteers at a single-sport event or even a particular category of volunteers at a specific event. Coupled with a tendency to utilize convenience and other sampling techniques that lack scientific rigour, the generalizability of event volunteer research is questionable.

The state of event volunteer research and our ability to reliably explain or predict the commitment or retention of sport event volunteers can be improved. Researchers need to be more willing to genuinely engage in the processes of clearly specifying research questions or hypotheses as well as conceptualizing their research and using relevant theory to inform research design. Contextual factors are an important consideration in understanding event volunteers' involvement, motives, commitment, satisfaction and retention. However, researchers need to move beyond one-off, single-event studies, using cross-sectional research designs, if the knowledge base in this field is to be further advanced.

References

Andrew, J. (1996) Motivations and expectations of volunteers involved in a large scale sports event: a pilot study. *Australian Leisure* 7(1), 21–25.

ASC (2000) *Volunteer Management Program: Managing Event Volunteers*. Australian Sports Commission, Canberra, Australia.

Batson, C.D., Ahmad, N. and Tsang, J. (2002) Four motives for community involvement. *Journal of Social Issues* 58(2), 429–445.

Burgham, M. and Downward, P. (2005) Why volunteer, time to volunteer? A case study from swimming. *Managing Leisure* 10, 79–93.

Caldwell, L. and Andereck, K. (1994) Motives for initiating and continuing membership in a recreation-related voluntary association. *Leisure Studies* 16, 33–44.

Clary, E.G. and Snyder, M. (1999) The motivations to volunteer: theoretical and practical considerations. *Current Directions in Psychological Science* 8(5), 156–159.

Clary, E.G., Snyder, M. and Ridge, R. (1992) Volunteers' motivations: a functional strategy for the recruitment, placement and retention of volunteers. *Nonprofit Management and Leadership* 2(4), 333–350.

Clary, E.G., Snyder, M., Ridge, R.D., Copeland, J., Stukas, A.A., Haugen, J. and Miene, P. (1998) Understanding and assessing motivations of volunteers: a functional approach. *Journal of Personality and Social Psychology* 74(6), 1516–1530.

Cnaan, R. and Goldberg-Glen, R.S. (1991) Measuring motivation to volunteer in human services. *Journal of Applied Behavioral Science* 27(3), 269–284.

Coyne, B.S. and Coyne, E.J. (2001) Getting, keeping and caring for unpaid volunteers for professional golf tournament events. *Human Resource Development International* 4(2), 199–214.

Cuskelly, G. (2004) Volunteer retention in community sport organizations. *European Sport Management Quarterly* 4, 59–76.

Cuskelly, G., Auld, C., Harrington, M. and Coleman, D. (2004) Predicting the behavioural dependability of sport event volunteers. *Event Management* 9, 73–89.

Cuskelly, G., Hoye, R. and Auld, C. (2006) *Working with Volunteers in Sport: Theory and Practice*. Routledge, London.

Downward, P. and Ralston, R. (2005) Volunteer motivation and expectations prior to the XVII Commonwealth Games in Manchester, UK. *Tourism and Hospitality Planning and Development* 2(1), 17–26.

Eley, D. and Kirk, D. (2002) Developing citizenship through sport: the impact of a sport-based volunteer programme on youth sport leaders. *Sport, Education and Society* 7(2), 151–167.

Elstad, B. (1997) Volunteer perception of learning and satisfaction in a mega-event: the case of the XVII Olympic Winter Games in Lillehammer. *Festival Management and Event Tourism* 4, 75–83.

Fairley, S., Kellett, P. and Green, B.G. (2007) Volunteering abroad: motives for travel to volunteer at the Athens Olympic Games. *Journal of Sport Management* 21, 41–57.

Farrell, J.M., Johnston, M.E. and Twynam, G.D. (1998) Volunteer motivation, satisfaction, and management at an elite sporting competition. *Journal of Sport Management* 12, 288–300.

Finkelstein, M.A., Penner, L.A. and Brannick, M.T. (2005) Motive, role identity, and prosocial personality as predictors of volunteer activity. *Social Behaviour and Personality* 33(4), 403–418.

Gidron, B. (1985) Prediction of retention and turnover among service volunteer workers. *Journal of Social Service Research* 8, 1–16.

Harrington, M., Cuskelly, G. and Auld, C. (2000) Career volunteering in commodity-intensive serious leisure: motorsport events and their dependence on volunteers/amateurs. *Loisir et Societe/Society and Leisure* 23(2), 421–452.

Harris, R., Jago, L., Allen, J. and Huyskens, M. (2001) Towards an Australian event research agenda: first steps. *Event Management* 6, 213–221.

Harris, V. (2004) Event management: a new profession? *Event Management* 9, 103–109.

Kim, M., Chelladurai, P. and Trail, G.T. (2007) A model of volunteer retention in youth sport. *Journal of Sport Management* 21, 151–171.

Knoke, D. and Prensky, D. (1984) What relevance do organization theories have for voluntary associations? *Social Science Quarterly* 65(1), 3–20.

Lammers, J.C. (1991) Attitudes, motives and demographic predictors of volunteer commitment and service duration. *Journal of Social Service Research* 14, 125–140.

Mesch, D.J., Tschirhart, M., Perry, J.L. and Le, G. (1998) Altruists or egoists? Retention in stipended service. *Nonprofit Management and Leadership* 9(1), 3–21.

Ralston, R., Downward, P. and Lumsdon, L. (2004) The expectations of volunteers prior to the XVII Commonwealth Games, 2002: a qualitative study. *Event Management* 9(1/2), 13–26.

Reeser, J.C., Berg, R.L., Rhea, D. and Willick, S. (2005) Motivation and satisfaction among polyclinic volunteers at the 2002 Winter Olympic and Paralympic Games. *British Journal of Sports Medicine* 39(4), e20.

Smith, D.H. (1981) Altruism, volunteers and volunteerism. *Journal of Voluntary Action Research* 10(1), 21–36.

Solberg, H.A. (2003) Major sporting events: assessing the value of volunteers' work. *Managing Leisure* 8, 17–27.

Stebbins, R.A. (1996) Volunteering: a serious leisure perspective. *Nonprofit Voluntary Sector Quarterly* 25(2), 211–224.

Treuren, G. and Monga, M. (2002a) Are special event volunteers different from non-SEO volunteers? Demographic characteristics of volunteers in four South Australian special event organizations. In: Jago, L., Deery, M., Harris, R., Hede, A.-M. and Allen, J. (eds) *Proceedings of Event and Place Marketing Conference*, Australian Centre for Event Management, Sydney, pp. 275–304.

Treuren, G. and Monga, M. (2002b) Does the observable special event volunteer career in four South Australian special event organisations demonstrate the existence of a recruitment niche? In: Jago, L., Deery, M., Harris, R., Hede, A.-M. and Allen, J. (eds) *Proceedings of Event and Place Marketing Conference*, Australian Centre for Event Management, Sydney, pp. 203–231.

Wang, P.Z. (2004) Assessing motivations for sports volunteerism. *Advances in Consumer Research* 31, 420–425.

14 Managing Volunteers to Enhance the Legacy Potential of Major Events

CHRISTOPHER AULD, GRAHAM CUSKELLY AND
MAUREEN HARRINGTON

Griffith University, Australia

Introduction

The dependence of major events on volunteer labour is well established. Volunteers are an essential component of the success of major events and, moreover, the scale and scope of the event volunteer workforce frequently makes volunteers the most visible element of events and the one with whom most participants and/or spectators interact. For example, the Sydney Olympic Games utilized approximately 47,000 volunteers (SOCOG, 2000) and a further 15,000 volunteers contributed their skills to Sydney's Paralympic Games. Cashman (2006), however, reported that the total volunteer workforce for both events was over 70,000. Cuskelly *et al.* (2006) also indicated that the 2006 Melbourne Commonwealth Games and the 2006 Doha Asian Games each utilized more than 15,000 volunteers and that even single-sport events, such as the 2007 Rugby World Cup (3000 volunteers) and the 2007 ICC Cricket World Cup (3500 volunteers), require considerable numbers of volunteers. Furthermore, there has been a trend of increasing involvement of volunteers in events. This includes the operations of the Olympic Games, where there were around 28,000 volunteers at the 1984 Los Angeles and 1988 Seoul Summer Games compared with an estimated 60,000 at the 2004 Athens Olympics and 100,000 at Beijing in 2008, with the latter two including both Olympic and Paralympic Games volunteers (Karlis, 2003). While the Winter Olympics have fewer volunteers than their summer counterpart, they have also demonstrated a trend towards an increasing level of volunteer engagement (from just under 7000 at Lake Placid in 1980 to an estimated 20,000 in Turin in 2006).

According to Webb (2001), a total of 6 million hours were given by volunteers to the 2000 Sydney Olympics and, in the 4 years leading up to the Games, the

500 'pioneer volunteers' contributed a further 200,000 hours. As indicated by Haynes (2001:5), if:

> SOCOG had paid for the hundreds of thousands of work hours provided by the volunteers, wages would have added AUS$140 million to the cost of the event. Their work went far beyond an economic consideration; the enthusiasm of the volunteers was a huge hit with all. The volunteers were held in such high regard that 100,000 people turned up for a ticker-tape parade for the volunteers after the Games.

However, although Haynes (2001:5) argued that the Sydney Olympics highlighted the role of volunteers and this resulted in 'a great impetus post-Games to see some of the highly regarded volunteers make themselves available for other community projects', it is not evident that this has occurred. Haynes (2001:10) also goes on to quote Hugh Mackay (2001:7), who indicated that: 'Six months on, though, I'm struggling even to recall what the changes were supposed to be. ..... But why search for more than you're ever likely to find? We have acquired some pleasant memories. Shouldn't we leave it at that?'

This view seems to characterize much of the post-event phase. While there is much 'legacy rhetoric' circulating before major events, it appears the commitment to actually rigorously address impacts and legacies of events, especially the more intangible and social aspects of legacy, loses momentum once the event has been concluded. Toohey (2008) argued that it is debatable if there has been a long-term legacy for Sydney and further that there was limited enthusiasm for evaluation of the Olympic legacy in the years immediately following the Games. Toohey concluded that any social impacts appear to have dissipated. Cashman (2002) and Shipway (2007) also noted the dearth of post-Games analysis, and it appears that the lack of ongoing interest in event legacies occurs in other jurisdictions.

Event Legacies

Despite the shortcomings summarized above, event bids invariably invoke and promote the post-event legacy that will result for the host community. Legacies may include such things as facility and transport infrastructure, economic benefits due to increased employment and accelerated economic development, enhanced local and national pride, international profile and visibility, and a more vibrant and sustainable volunteer sector.

Preuss (2007) argued that while much has been written about the legacies of mega sport events, there has been no clear definition of the term 'legacy', and Cashman (2006) adds that the term is elusive. Preuss (2007) indicated that this may be because there is a sense that the term legacy is self-evident and generally assumed to be positive. Shipway (2007:119) suggested that there appears to have been 'an assumption that legacy benefits will flow down to the community at the end of the Games, as a matter of course'. Preuss (2007) argued that some previous attempts to define legacy (e.g. by the International Olympic Committee) have been somewhat narrowly focused on sports facilities and other 'public improvements', ignoring some of the broader and less-recognized intangible event outcomes. He subsequently offered the following definition of legacy: 'Irrespective of the time of production and space, legacy is all planned and unplanned, positive and negative, tangible and intangible structures created for and by a sport event that remain longer than the event itself' (Preuss, 2007:211).

Preuss's definition reinforces the view that a gradual shift to a new paradigm in impact research is becoming evident: one advocating that 'impact' studies adopt a longer-term and more strategic approach, which examines the leveraging of long-term benefits rather than only focusing on short-term outcomes (Chalip, 2006).

While there are mixed data concerning potential legacies, a number of authors (e.g. Austrian and Rosentraub, 2002; Preuss and Solberg, 2006) have argued that the anticipated outcomes from hosting events are frequently not realized or fall well below expectations. Gratton *et al.* (2005) indicated that the quantity and distribution of returns (especially medium and long term) on public sector investment in sport events are uncertain and under-researched, while Swindell and Rosentraub (1998) suggested that, at the very least, there is a need for some scepticism. Furthermore, while evidence suggests that it is possible to assess expenditures during and immediately after sport events, assessment of the longer-term legacy is more elusive (Gratton *et al.*, 2005). This may be partly because the 'stated benefits...are often...vague' (Cashman, 2002:7).

At the same time, there is growing agreement concerning the less tangible social outcomes generated by major events. Gratton *et al.* (2005) and Ritchie (2001) suggested that, for some types of events, the social and psychological benefits can be far greater than the economic impacts, and others (e.g. Swindell and Rosentraub, 1998; Crompton, 2004) have argued that such benefits are becoming more valued by the community. Despite these views, intangible benefits have been reported less frequently in event impact studies (Downward and Ralston, 2006) and, in terms of the specific volunteer legacy, there are scant data. As with economic benefits, anecdotal evidence suggests that claims about social outcomes made prior to the event tend to be overstated, but there is little research to support a conclusion either way. In response to this dearth of information, Crompton (2004) advocated that impact studies should focus more on the 'psychic income' generated by events.

Potential for Volunteer Legacy

Because of the sheer size and the visibility of the volunteer workforce at major events, as well as the 'feel good' factor they engender, volunteers have become an established component of the legacy rationale surrounding such events. According to Karlis (2003), the 'Volunteers, Global Society and the Olympic Movement' conference, hosted by the Olympic Museum in 1999, concluded that the contribution of volunteers to the Olympics extends beyond just the provision of services to enhancing the social and cultural dimension of the Games. Ritchie (2001:156) concluded that 'the strengthened social structure related to the strengthening of community volunteerism' was amongst the most valuable of all the legacies for Calgary after hosting the 1998 Winter Olympics. Shipway (2007:120) indicated that the anticipated benefits outlined in the London 2012 bid documents included 'a mass volunteer recruitment drive that could result in a volunteer culture across Britain'.

However, most of the literature on event legacy has concentrated on economic and infrastructure issues, and even where the focus is on social outcomes, volunteer issues do not always feature prominently. For example, Chalip (2006) strongly endorsed the potential for leveraging social outcomes from major events but did not mention either volunteers as a component in the social enhancement process or indeed the potential for social outcomes for the volunteers themselves.

Furthermore, despite the emphasis given to social legacies prior to events, only a small number of studies have examined the outcomes from volunteers engaging in major sport events (despite frequently stated intentions to do so). For example, Solberg (2003:24), in a study of volunteers at the 1999 World Ice Hockey Championship, found that there was 'a net increase in people's motivation to work with other events and other kinds of voluntary work' and that involvement in the event did not have a detrimental impact on the supply of volunteers for other sports. Cashman (2006:39) argued that a web site for volunteers established just prior to the Sydney Olympic Games, and still active in 2006, 'was sustained by a broader commitment to volunteering', and although used as a vehicle to promote other sport event volunteer opportunities, was also utilized by non-sport groups for volunteer recruitment. Cashman (2006:39) concluded that more than 4 years after the Games, there was a 'clear and continuing volunteer legacy'.

Despite this conclusion, it appears that even if volunteers involved in major events subsequently increased their level of volunteer engagement, if their volunteer activities are restricted mainly to involvement with sport clubs, it is questionable how much social benefit may be produced (e.g. Coffé and Geys, 2007). Weisinger and Salipante (2005) argued that much of the activity in community organizations was exclusionary, and there is some evidence to indicate that unless the post-event volunteers broadened their involvement to a wider range of third-sector agencies, then the potential social capital outcomes may be somewhat constrained. Auld (2008:154) suggested that:

> Despite the focus on sport and the intuitive and widely held comforting sense that it must be good for communities, it is not axiomatic that social capital results from the actions of community organizations or indeed that social capital always has positive impacts on communities. On the other hand, such organizations may actually have deleterious impacts on their members and those with whom they interact, especially in the context of inner and outer groups.

This view reinforces that of Coffé and Geys (2007), who suggested that membership of voluntary associations does not necessarily produce positive outcomes for communities. They concluded that the development of strong bonding ties may create in-group bias, which can lead to out-group hostility. Reinforcing this, Tonts (2005) reported that, in some rural areas in Australia, sport participation was divided according to class, ethnicity and status, and Paxton (2002) also found that sport clubs were less likely to develop external connections than some other types of voluntary associations. Thus, unless sport event volunteering results in a broader volunteer participation base that helps establish links between dissimilar community groups, there is likely to be little long-term and systemic legacy effect, at least in terms of social capital. However, it is possible that event volunteers can be managed in such a manner that they are more likely to want to engage in further volunteer activity and thus enhance the potential for broader social outcomes.

Event Volunteers – Motivations and Satisfaction

To manage volunteers in a way that may assist in any potential community legacy, it is crucial that event managers understand the motivations of their volunteers as well as the factors that influence the perceptions of volunteers about their experience. Diminished satisfaction of event volunteers may impact upon the operational success of future events if they are less likely to participate again or because, through word of mouth, they discourage other potential volunteers. Furthermore, volunteers may be less likely to seek further volunteer opportunities in other community organizations if their participation as an event volunteer was not positive. Thus a poor event management experience may not only result in a minimal legacy impact but in fact could have a negative influence on legacy; dissatisfied event volunteers may not only choose not to take up other volunteer opportunities but also similarly influence the opinions/actions of other volunteers.

Meeting the expectations of volunteers and maintaining high levels of volunteer satisfaction are therefore significant challenges for event organizers, especially as a number of researchers have argued that event volunteers and regular seasonal (e.g. winter or summer) sport volunteers are different. For example, Treuren and Monga (2002a) concluded that the demographic features of event volunteers can vary significantly from those suggested by the volunteering literature. Farrell *et al.* (1998) suggested that the motivation of sport event volunteers was different from other types of sport volunteers, owing to the nature of sport events and the associated volunteer experience. Both Slaughter (2002) and Coyne and Coyne (2001) found that event volunteer motivations changed over time, shifting from a focus on more personal reasons (e.g. social interaction) to a more altruistic basis, as volunteers remained associated with successive events. One of the challenges, then, for event organizers is to ensure that they manage their volunteers in such a way that the experience is a rewarding one and they are able to regularly re-engage volunteers so that volunteer motivations become based more on altruistic interactions.

More recent research has tended to reinforce these findings. Ralston *et al.* (2004:15) reported that sport event volunteering 'is highly dependent on the availability of tangible and intangible incentives'. Both Ralston *et al.* (2004) and Reeser *et al.* (2005) found that sport event volunteers were motivated by three main factors: altruism, a sense of involvement (e.g. working with a variety of people and elite athletes) and the uniqueness of the event. Reeser *et al.* (2005) concluded that the motivations of the volunteers in their study were complex and mainly involved self-interest factors as well as altruism and reciprocity, in which benefits accrued not only to the volunteers but also to event organizers and participants. Cuskelly *et al.* (2006:140) concluded from the relatively small number of studies on the motivations of sport event volunteers that:

> First, the variety of motivations held by sport event volunteers suggest they should not be treated as a homogeneous group; second, sport event volunteers tend to be motivated for reasons that differ from volunteers involved in VSOs [voluntary sport organizations] on an ongoing basis; and third, these motivations may change over time for volunteers involved repeatedly in the same event.

The findings from studies that have focused on volunteer satisfaction are not inconsistent with those from the motivation research. Elstad (1997) found that event volunteer satisfaction was due to opportunities to expand personal networks, to be part of the event and to feel a sense of job competence. Similarly, Farrell *et al.* (1998:298) found that volunteer satisfaction was based on the recognition received by volunteers as well as the amount of communication between volunteers, and concluded that volunteer satisfaction is related to both fulfilling their expectations and the organization of the event. Kemp (2002:115) concluded 'that internal factors seem to be important to avoid dissatisfaction among the volunteers, but are not sufficient to explain satisfaction. To increase satisfaction, the external context of being part of the Olympic celebratory atmosphere and involvement in a unique event is critical.' Reeser *et al.* (2005) also found that the management of volunteers by event organizers impacted on volunteer satisfaction.

However, some authors (Auld and Cuskelly, 2001; Auld, 2004; Cuskelly *et al.*, 2004; Rundle-Thiele and Auld, 2009) have argued that many of the elements that influence event volunteer behaviour and satisfaction are frequently not under the direct control of sport event organizers and thus volunteer managers should focus on those managerial elements on which they can have some impact. Auld and Cuskelly (2001) found that while some reasons that influenced people to discontinue volunteering were not controllable by sport organizations, many of the factors associated with retention were related to both the nature of the organization and the volunteer work itself. They found significant relationships between management practices and retention issues. This is a crucial issue in the often stressful, 'pressure cooker' environment of sport event operations. For example, Cuskelly *et al.* (2004) reported that, while over a 12-month period sport volunteers in community settings completed a median of 60 hours of volunteer work, volunteers at the Sydney Olympic Games completed a minimum of 80 hours of volunteer work over 16 days. Therefore event organizers, if they are to influence the likelihood that volunteers will have a positive experience and thus may become more likely to engage in other volunteer experiences, need to focus on those aspects of the event volunteer experience over which they have some degree of managerial control. These may include, for example: the nature, quality and frequency of communication with volunteers; matching volunteers with roles that reflect their interests; avoiding excessive workloads; and providing mentoring support for less experienced volunteers.

There is a well-developed theoretical basis for this view through the work of Penner (2002). Penner argued that very little research had examined the relationships between personal dispositions and the contexts in which volunteers work, despite the recognition that it is the experiences of volunteers in organizational and sport system settings, in combination with their personal dispositions, that influence whether they become long-term volunteers. Penner and Finklestein (1998) and Penner (2002) argued that *in situ* variables such as organizational commitment and job satisfaction are central to understanding why people remain engaged as a volunteer. Penner (2002) subsequently developed a 'model of sustained volunteerism' that incorporates the personal and organizational factors that may influence both the initial decision to volunteer and subsequent decisions to either continue or discontinue.

Managing Volunteers to Enhance the Legacy Impact

Cuskelly *et al.* (2006) argued that owing to the differences between sport event and VSO volunteers' motivation, satisfaction and commitment, sport event volunteers should be managed differently from volunteers with ongoing responsibilities with a sport club. Some studies have specifically addressed the sport event volunteer context.

Hanlon and Jago (2004) argued that event managers should utilize specific retention strategies for each operational stage of their events and should start with the induction process, which is somewhat problematic in the 'pulsating' context of sport events (Hanlon and Cuskelly, 2002). Hanlon and Jago (2004) recommended that in the pre-event stage, the status of the event, timing of the event, recognition schemes and the development of a sense of ownership among volunteers should be emphasized. During the conduct of the event, they advocated debriefing sessions concentrating on volunteer roles and the nature of volunteer support, while for the post-event stage, event managers should focus on recognition initiatives. In the longer term, Hanlon and Jago suggested that organizers should maintain regular contact with the volunteers so that other volunteer opportunities could be communicated.

Treuren and Monga (2002b) argued that the majority of volunteers involved in special events (including sport events) run on a regular or annual basis in the same geographic locale are repeat volunteers. They also suggested that these volunteers are associated with organizations related to the event via the social networks of previous volunteers and/or participants, and consequently are familiar with volunteer management practices. Furthermore, Harrington *et al.* (2000) found that such 'career' event volunteers in the commodified motorsport setting resented the lack of appreciation and the manner in which they were treated by organizers. Cuskelly *et al.* (2006:144) argued that, overall, these findings suggest that 'organizers of sport events that are held on a regular or annual basis need to be innovative in how they manage volunteers to avoid dissatisfaction with volunteer management and support practices'.

In a related study, albeit focusing on regular-season volunteers, Auld and Rundle-Thiele (2007) utilized Penner's model to examine the retention of junior coaches in Australian Rules Football (AFL). They found that the club culture and context (especially the social atmosphere) and the nature and level of support provided to volunteers were key ingredients in the decision of coaches to stay on for another season. They also argued that providing an opportunity to build relationships within the club is crucial in encouraging coaches to continue and that the development of close relationships may counteract negative perceptions relating to time pressures and burnout. The authors recommended that to enhance coach retention, local AFL clubs should:

- Support the logistical elements of the volunteers through timely and accurate communication.
- Regularly recognize efforts of volunteers (i.e. not just at the conclusion of the season).
- Develop strategies (e.g. formal and informal mentoring) to integrate first-year volunteers into the network of established volunteers. More experienced and/or retired volunteers who may still want to stay involved in the club could be used as mentors.
- Provide opportunities for regular informal social, networking and mentoring interactions as well as formal development sessions.

However, the main focus of these studies has been on improving the volunteer experience in order to increase retention, rather than how this might help develop the longer-term and social legacy outcomes of major events facilitated through volunteers. Further analysis of the data from the Cuskelly *et al.* (2004) study sheds additional light on strategies for enhancing the event volunteer experience in order to build potential legacy effects. As indicated, much of the previous work on sport event volunteers has focused on their individual characteristics and dispositions, motivations and satisfaction levels. Increasingly, however, more contemporary approaches to volunteer research have incorporated measures of the organizational context in which volunteers work, in particular the manner in which they perceive they are managed.

This later analysis of the data from the earlier Cuskelly *et al.* (2004) study concentrates on the relationship between management policies and processes impacting on sport event volunteers and their perceived satisfaction with their volunteer experience. A pre-event and post-event survey protocol was used to gather data from volunteers (n = 391) at five different sport events in Australia. The events included in the study covered a wide array of event types, including single- and multi-sport, annual and one-off, and events organized by all three industry sectors. A total of 842 operational-level volunteers were sampled and 649 (77%) returned the pre-event questionnaire and 443 (52.6%) returned the post-event instrument. A total of 391 respondents provide sufficient information for this analysis.

Respondents were predominantly male (58%), Australian-born (80%), had completed at least a high-school education (36%) and were employed full or part time (70%). The mean age was 41.2 years. The participants were rostered for a mean of 36 hours during their events and actually completed a mean of

42 hours. The overall satisfaction mean was 4.3 and ranged from 4.2 to a high of 4.6 across the five events, although ANOVA revealed no significant differences between the satisfaction scores for each of the events.

Further analysis using mainly correlation and regression revealed that, despite anecdotal evidence to the contrary, the satisfaction of event volunteers was not related to such factors as long hours, availability of uniforms, reimbursement for out-of-pocket expenses and access to meal breaks. It may be that these types of volunteer management factors act in a similar fashion to Herzberg's hygiene factors and only serve to reduce dissatisfaction (Robbins, 2001). Alternatively, satisfaction was significantly related to appropriate orientation and training, choice over rosters (but not over the number of hours worked), having sufficient free time, car parking and the matching of their skills with appropriate volunteer roles. Taking these findings together suggests that volunteers:

- want to feel that they can commit and contribute to the event (even if it means long hours), especially when they are supported by effective training;
- desire some control over their work environment; and
- don't want to feel overly inconvenienced or taken for granted.

Given concerns about retention of event volunteers, many event managers tend to over-recruit volunteers. This tactic may actually be deleterious to any potential volunteer legacy as many volunteers may be underworked, subsequently perceive that they have not been able to make a real contribution to the event and hence feel less than satisfied with their volunteer experience. This potential outcome may be ameliorated by providing more control over the work environment to the volunteers.

Concluding Comments

It seems that many event organizers still tend to manage volunteers based on the assumption that volunteers are extrinsically motivated. This approach ignores a body of theoretical and empirical research that has found that volunteer rewards are in the main derived from participation in the activity itself (see Pearce, 1993). The evidence indicates that event organizers who overemphasize extrinsic rewards may ignore the importance of intrinsically rewarding factors such as the enjoyment of using their skills to enhance event delivery; making a contribution to the event; interacting socially with other event volunteers, participants and patrons; and contributing to the community (Cuskelly *et al.*, 2004). These outcomes can be facilitated through appropriate management practices.

Maximizing satisfaction appears to stem from effective pre-recruitment and orientation processes, extending through to a small number of perceived and actual working conditions experienced during the event. It is crucial that the volunteers be appropriately inducted into their event roles and responsibilities, subsequently feel they are allowed the freedom to actually carry out these roles and feel valued when doing so. Furthermore, event managers must also focus on ensuring that volunteers develop self-confidence in their skills and abilities through training and orientation programmes as well as sensitive management protocols.

While such management behaviours and policies do not guarantee that a volunteer legacy will be created, they do lay the foundations for a rewarding event volunteer experience and thus may encourage broader post-event volunteer engagement. However, this issue is a challenge for future research: determining the extent to which satisfied event volunteers continue to volunteer and, if so, the degree to which this realizes systemic community benefits. In particular, future research could determine the potential for longer-term volunteer legacies through the examination of a wider range of volunteer, as well as temporal and event, contexts. These studies could include, for example, the investigation of the relationship between volunteering for the same event at another time or location, volunteering for a range of other sport events (i.e. different sizes and types), seasonal sport volunteers, and volunteering in community/third-sector organizations other than sport and the spreading of positive messages to other community members and the extent to which they are encouraged to volunteer for events, sport clubs or other community sector organizations.

References

Auld, C.J. (2004) Behavioural characteristics of student volunteers. *Australian Journal on Volunteering* 9(2), 8–18.

Auld, C.J. (2008) Voluntary sport clubs: the potential for the development of social capital. In: Hoye, R. and Nicholson, M. (eds) *Sport and Social Capital*. Elsevier, London, pp. 143–164.

Auld, C.J. and Cuskelly, G. (2001) Behavioural characteristics of volunteers: implications for community sport and recreation organizations. *Australian Parks and Leisure* 4(2), 29–37.

Auld, C.J. and Rundle-Thiele, S. (2007) Retention of AFL community coaches. Unpublished report, Australian Football League, Melbourne, Australia.

Austrian, Z. and Rosentraub, M. (2002) Cities, sports, and economic change: a retrospective assessment. *Journal of Urban Affairs* 24(5), 549–563.

Cashman, R. (2002) Impact of the Games on Olympic host cities: university lecture on the Olympics. Centre d'Estudis Olímpics (UAB) International Chair in Olympism (IOC-UAB), Barcelona, Spain. Available at: http://olympicstudies.uab.es/lectures/web/pdf/cashman.pdf (accessed 25 March 2008).

Cashman, R. (2006) *The Bitter-sweet Awakening: the Legacy of the Sydney 2000 Olympic Games*. Walla Walla Press, Sydney.

Chalip, L. (2006) Towards social leverage of sport events. *Journal of Sport and Tourism* 11(2), 109–127.

Coffé, H. and Geys, B. (2007) Toward an empirical characterization of bridging and bonding social capital. *Nonprofit and Voluntary Sector Quarterly* 36(1), 121–139.

Coyne, B.S. and Coyne, E.J. (2001) Getting, keeping and caring for unpaid volunteers for professional golf tournament events. *Human Resource Development International* 4(2), 199–214.

Crompton, J. (2004) Beyond economic impact: an alternative rationale for the public subsidy of major league sporting facilities. *Journal of Sport Management* 18(1), 40–58.

Cuskelly, G., Auld, C., Harrington, M. and Coleman, D. (2004) Predicting the behavioural dependability of sport event volunteers. *Event Management* 9, 73–89.

Cuskelly, G., Hoye, R. and Auld, C.J. (2006) *Working with Sport Volunteers: Theory and Practice*. Routledge, London.

Downward, P.M. and Ralston, R. (2006) The sports development potential of sports events volunteering: insights from the XVII Manchester Commonwealth Games. *European Sport Management Quarterly* 6(4), 333–351.

Elstad, B. (1997) Volunteer perception of learning and satisfaction in a mega-event: the case of the XVII Olympic Winter Games in Lillehammer. *Festival Management and Event Tourism* 4, 75–83.

Farrell, J.M., Johnston, M.E. and Twynam, G.D. (1998) Volunteer motivation, satisfaction, and management at an elite sporting competition. *Journal of Sport Management* 12, 288–300.

Gratton, C., Shibli, S. and Coleman, R. (2005) Sport and economic regeneration in cities. *Urban Studies* 42(4/5), 985–999.

Hanlon, C. and Cuskelly, G. (2002) Pulsating major sport event organizations: a framework for inducting managerial personnel. *Event Management* 7, 231–243.

Hanlon, C. and Jago, L. (2004) The challenge of retaining personnel in major sport event organizations. *Event Management* 9, 39–49.

Harrington, M., Cuskelly, G. and Auld, C. (2000) Career volunteering in commodity-intensive serious leisure: motorsport events and their dependence on volunteers/amateurs. *Loisir et Societe/Society and Leisure* 23(2), 421–452.

Haynes, J. (2001) Socio-economic impact of the Sydney 2000 Olympic Games. Centre d'Estudis Olímpics UAB, Barcelona, Spain. Available at: http://olympicstudies.uab.es/pdf/wp094_eng.pdf (accessed 25 March 2008).

Karlis, G. (2003) Volunteerism and multiculturalism: a linkage for future Olympics. *The Sports Journal* 6(3). Available at: http://www.thesportjournal.org/article/volunteerism-and-multiculturalism-linkage-future-olympics (accessed 25 March 2008).

Kemp, S. (2002) The hidden workforce: volunteers' learning in the Olympics. *Journal of European Industrial Training* 26, 109–116.

Mackay, H. (2001) The Games that changed us forever? Not quite… *The Age*, March.

Paxton, P. (2002) Social capital and democracy: a cross-national study. *American Sociological Review* 67, 254–277.

Pearce, J.L. (1993) *Volunteers: the Organizational Behavior of Unpaid Workers*. Routledge, London.

Penner, L.A. (2002) The causes of sustained volunteerism: an interactionist perspective. *Journal of Social Issues* 58, 447–467.

Penner, L.A. and Finkelstein, M.A. (1998) Dispositional and structural determinants of volunteerism. *Journal of Personality and Social Psychology* 74(2), 525–537.

Preuss, H. (2007) The conceptualization and measurement of mega sport event legacies. *Journal of Sport and Tourism* 12(3/4), 207–227.

Preuss, H. and Solberg, H.A. (2006) Attracting major sporting events: the role of local residents. *European Sport Management Quarterly* 6(4), 391–411.

Ralston, R., Downward, P. and Lumsdon, L. (2004) The expectations of volunteers prior to the XVII Commonwealth Games, 2002: a qualitative study. *Event Management* 9(1/2), 13–26.

Reeser, J.C., Berg, R.L., Rhea, D. and Willick, S. (2005) Motivation and satisfaction among polyclinic volunteers at the 2002 Winter Olympic and Paralympic Games. *British Journal of Sports Medicine* 39(4), e20.

Ritchie, J.R.B. (2001) Turning 16 days into 16 years through Olympic legacies. *Event Management* 6, 155–165.

Robbins, S. (2001) *Organizational Behavior*. Prentice Hall, Upper Saddle River, New Jersey.

∪ndle-Thiele, S. and Auld, C.J. (2009) Should I stay or should I go? Retention of junior sport coaches. *Annals of Leisure Research* 12(1), 1–21.

Shipway, R. (2007) Sustainable legacies for the 2012 Olympic Games. *The Journal of the Royal Society for the Promotion of Health* 127(3), 119–124.

Slaughter, L. (2002) Motivations of long term volunteers at events. In: Jago, L., Deery, M., Harris, R., Hede, A.-M. and Allen, J. (eds) *Proceedings of Event and Place Marketing Conference*, Australian Centre for Event Management, Sydney, pp. 232–252.

SOCOG (2000) About volunteers. Sydney Organizing Committee for the Olympic Games, Australia. Available at: http://www.sydney.olympic.org/content/volunteers.html/about_volunteers (accessed 26 October 2000).

Solberg, H.A. (2003) Major sporting events: assessing the value of volunteers' work. *Managing Leisure* 8, 17–27.

Swindell, D. and Rosentraub, M. (1998) Who benefits from the presence of professional sports teams? The implications for public funding of stadiums and arenas. *Public Administration Review* 58(1), 11–20.

Tonts, M. (2005) Competitive sport and social capital in rural Australia. *Journal of Rural Studies* 21, 137–149.

Toohey, K. (2008) The Sydney Olympics: striving for legacies – overcoming short term disappointments and long term deficiencies. *The International Journal of the History of Sport* 25(14), 2098–2116.

Treuren, G. and Monga, M. (2002a) Are special event volunteers different from non-SEO volunteers? Demographic characteristics of volunteers in four South Australian special event organizations. In: Jago, L., Deery, M., Harris, R., Hede, A.-M. and Allen, J. (eds) *Proceedings of Event and Place Marketing Conference*, Australian Centre for Event Management, pp. 275–304.

Treuren, G. and Monga, M. (2002b) Does the observable special event volunteer career in four South Australian special event organisations demonstrate the existence of a recruitment niche? In: Jago, L., Deery, M., Harris, R., Hede, A.-M. and Allen, J. (eds) *Proceedings of Event and Place Marketing Conference*, Australian Centre for Event Management, Sydney, pp. 203–231.

Webb, T. (2001) *The Collaborative Games*. Pluto Press, Annandale, Australia.

Weisinger, J.Y. and Salipante, P.F (2005) A grounded theory for building ethnically bridging social capital in voluntary organizations. *Nonprofit and Voluntary Sector Quarterly* 34(1), 29–55.

15 High-adrenalin Work Environments at Events

CHRIS KEMP

Buckinghamshire New University, UK

Introduction

This chapter focuses on a range of working environments in which those employed are exposed to a high-level risk interface linked to a series of micro- and macro-environmental factors which modify normal working practices. In the majority of these working environments, those employed have a reliance on others to provide them with the correct training, briefing and de-briefing opportunities to enable them to feel comfortable in such environments. This chapter will deal with stewarding and security activity in the front-of-house areas at rock and indie music concerts, as it is in these areas that such working environments can be found.

Although Plucker (1999) states that people's internal mental processes, which cannot be measured, should be excluded from scientific study, it is felt that there is sufficient recent research and contemporary studies in risk management to enable a paper which focuses on this area to be formulated. By utilizing a number of small adaptations to Geller's (1996) safety triad, it is possible to identify what conditions and patterns of behaviour need to be focused upon to ensure that some kind of interfacing safety culture can be created between those governing the movement and behaviour of the crowd from a work perspective and those in the crowd from a play or recreational perspective.

Geller (1996) identifies that in the development of long-term behavioural changes there is a requirement for people to change internally as well as externally. In many past crowd disasters, where injuries and fatalities have been caused, it is only in hindsight that research has identified that people in these environments modify their behaviour only in the aftermath of a disaster, as it is only then that they are aware of the disruption or instability that has been generated. However, human nature is such that the crowd soon reverts to similar behaviour, as the memory of such incidents dims and the 'live for now' behaviour reasserts itself.

From research carried out since the early 2000s by the Centre for Crowd Management and Security Studies, it is clear that the majority of crowd management interface is reliant on influencing the environment, managing the crowd and understanding the individual. These three elements agree unreservedly with an adapted 'safety triad model' (Geller, 1996) and are supported by it.

To enable the reader to understand the type of environment identified for this chapter, the following appraisal of the environment has been created.

The Event Environment

The environment features both extremes of heat and cold: heat from the close proximity of upwards of 75,000 people packed closely together with several banks of lights focused on the artist and audience, and cold from the drop in temperature caused by the setting of the sun. This is further exacerbated in many instances by limited cloud cover during the summer months. The situation is also compounded by rising body temperatures during the day (caused by a range of activities including dancing, pogoing, crowd surfing and circle dancing) and the concomitant decrease in heat once the temperature starts to drop and the heat starts to evaporate from the mass crowd during periods of inactivity between artists in the evening. This is further compounded by the audience in general failing to bring warmer clothes for evening activities.

Factors Affecting the Event Environment

The audience moves in specific patterns – forward, backwards, laterally and up and down – and practises antisocial behaviour, including crowd surfing, stage diving and moshing (dancing in a violent manner that involves deliberately colliding with other dancers), and the noise level vacillates between 85 and 140 decibels. Owing to the close proximity of those working at such events to the audience, machinery and/or fencing and barrier constructions, it is clear that the understanding of the importance of the human–machine interface is key (Mill, 1992). Where workers are in contact with audiences alone (e.g. at marches and protests, and in city centres, pubs and clubs), the concentration of the worker is solely on the way that the crowd behaves, moves and utilizes any given physical props. However, where large-scale machinery, barriers or other construction elements, including temporary demountable structures, are concerned, this type of environment adds another dimension to the delivery of the service expected. Thus, the importance of behavioural occupation safety and the need to understand its effect on the reduction of accidents, compared with a range of other approaches, is of paramount importance.

Guastello (1993) ranked a series of ten approaches to safety improvement by analysing data from 53 reports on safety programmes. The findings identified that behavioural-based and ergonomic improvements were the most effective approaches when considering accident prevention. This validates both the work of the Centre and other work carried out by researchers including Krause (1995),

McSween (1995), Geller (1996) and Humphrey (1996). McSween (1995) concurred with Guastello's results, identifying that between 80 and 90% of accidents taking place in the workplace were the result of behavioural aspects rather than environmental conditions. Wozniak (1994) identifies that behaviour has a dual functional route, which has a combinational effect by stimulating conditions in the environment and characteristics within the human. In the concert environment, a stimulation origin for behaviour related to the event can be found throughout, and within such an environment the subcultural or cultural characteristics of the attendee are related to the given values and norms assimilated by the musical subculture being observed, enjoyed or participated in.

To understand the way in which these working environments have developed, a short precis of the types of behaviour practised by those attending the event has been analysed through a range of macro-environmental factors.

By examining the cultural environment within the rock and indie concert, one can comment on the way in which those working for the promoter/venue manager/crowd management company and spectators interface. An understanding of the cultural environment associated with the event is of paramount importance for those working in the pit or at front of house. In the past, the relationship between the front-of-house/pit stewards and the audience has been, at best, fraught. However, with the delivery of a new work ethic, training/education and the pivotal work of stewards at events where there have been disasters or near misses, the role and reputation of those working in these areas has changed. From an early standpoint of a policing culture, there has been a modification to a supportive culture, and this has also been mirrored at football grounds, where the roles of the police and stewards have changed owing to the animosity shown to the uniform and the support given to stewards who are facilitating the enjoyment of the crowd.

In the working environment where face-to-face, body-to-body delivery is found, it is clear that those working in such environments are exposed to risk from a number of avenues. The first is one of substances, which include needles, dangerous weapons and drugs/alcohol, which are all readily available either outside or within an event, and as such the worker here is exposed to an environment containing far more risk than a normal event environment and they need to be attuned to the type of behaviour or audience activity that accompanies the specific type of music. The risks can be manifold, from being struck by a syringe or by a weapon/missile during cultural activity such as moshing or crowd surfing to being abused by someone under the influence of drugs or alcohol. Although it is fairly easy to identify what drugs members of the audience have been exposed to, and it is also clear that some genres of music are synonymous with certain types of drugs, there are still some drugs that are difficult to spot and employees who have not been exposed to those drugs in the past. Owing to this element, it is clear that teams of new employees must be placed with a team of well-rehearsed and mature event workers to ensure that any risk to new recruits is minimized.

It is clear from the way in which an event is organized that audience members entering the arena are protected to some extent by those working at the event, and it is these workers the audience turns to in the face of problems.

It is clear that those within the arena are less likely to cause disturbances that would harm those working as there is a symbiotic reliance framework built into the system, which is underpinned by the level of cooperation between the audience and workers.

Furthermore, the facilities within which employees are expected to operate and the number of hours that they are required to stay focused are different from those for the audience. As a self-regulating community, it is clear that the audience are expected to regulate their behaviour when utilizing the free facilities provided. However, this is often not the case, and as the use of alcohol and drugs escalates during the event, the state of the facilities becomes less and less savoury. At the start of the event, employees are provided to clear facilities, change toilet paper and remove waste. However, as the event develops it is clear that, owing to the way in which the facilities are treated, it becomes less possible to keep them in a premium state, and they soon degenerate into an unusable state, which has an impact on all facilities on the site and the general behaviour of the audience. Through fatigue, the focus of workers at an event begins to lose momentum as the event progresses, thereby exacerbating the lack of effective facility management. The environment found at the event is an alien one to newcomers.

Willis (1990) identifies in *Moving Culture* that the event or festival really is an adventure from start to finish. It is the expansion of your living room, to the local pub and then on to a club, stadium, hall or festival. As the event expands, the way in which the audience interfaces with it also changes. This expansion takes place as the social values or norms concerning the individual's involvement in the event become modified as the event takes on a new and evolving set of norms and values specific to the event itself. Linked to the set of norms and values evolving during an event, Goffman (1963:37) states that:

> The involvement that an individual sustains within a particular situation is a matter of inward feeling. Assessment of involvement must and does rely on some kind of outward expression….Since the involvement idiom of a group appears to be a learned conventional thing, we must anticipate one real difficulty in cross-cultural or event cross-subcultural studies. The same general gathering in different cultures may be organized on the basis of different involvement obligations.

It is clear from this that the outward expression at a particular gathering, in a particular cultural setting, has preordained norms and values, which become apparent and are learned by those working so that they can be dealt with accordingly. In cases where those working at an event expect differing behaviours from an audience, this interface reliance breaks down, and those managing the event begin to lose control of the audience. Thus, being in tune with the event from a worker's viewpoint is important in the delivery of the service to the customer. This is one reason why crowd profiling and the coaching of the audience in advance of the show are so important.

The individual's relationship to an event may tell us something about their relationship to broader units of social life, and, as such, this is far easier to deal with. Thus, it is clear that a socio/psychological crowd-profiling system would aid the way in which an audience is dealt with. The more information forthcoming, the more able those managing the event are to associate behaviour with given attitudes and genres. In the definition of 'safe behaviour', Mill (1992) defines behaviour as safe only when the subject exhibiting the behaviour reacts to a given situation or compensates for a hazardous situation in a way that minimizes risk or injury to people, equipment or the process taking place. In the situation created by the event crowd, the individual is rarely capable of minimizing risk or injury in the environment already outlined. Coupled with this, in many cases individuals' senses may have been either heightened or deadened by alcohol, drugs or other substances, which may increase the risk to others in the concert or event environment. In addition, loud music, freedom from work and access to recreational activities also changes the interface that the audience has with aspects of an event. Thus, it is those who are stewarding or supervising that have the most capacity to stop such disasters or injuries taking place, as they are in a position to spot, identify, regulate and change the behaviour of those at the event.

One example of such behaviour takes place at the Roskilde Festival, Denmark, where the type of behaviour required by the organizers is instilled in the audience well in advance of the event through the web site, at the event through big screens and leaflets, and also during the event through careful management of the audience. An example of this can be found in Kemp *et al.* (2007), where research at the Roskilde Festival into pressure at the front-of-stage barrier identifies that Roskilde has a system of pre-coaching the audience from the initial purchase of the ticket. Members of the audience are requested to visit the web site to view a series of videos and also a series of messages that identify what type of behaviour the management of the event requires from those attending. First, they give warnings about excessive drinking and the abuse of drugs. Secondly, as there was a disaster at the festival in 2000, when nine people lost their lives, the audience is asked to refrain from antisocial behaviour. As well as these messages, others can be seen on big screens during the festival, and spotters and stewards are constantly reiterating messages to the audience. Also the barrier configuration for the event and the queuing system employed for the pens at the front of stage all link into a carefully constructed management strategy that creates a safe haven for those who wish to practise more boisterous behaviour close to the stage. These pens are strictly manned and managed by a team of workers employing a three-tier system. The first tier observes and points out people under stress; these are then attended to or removed to safety by the stewards. The crowd managers or supervisors constantly control the stewards and the situation to ensure that the strategies employed are working in accordance with the plans created for the event. In this way those working in this high-adrenalin environment are able to be in control of the norms and values adopted by those attending the event.

In the UK, the advent of the Private Security Act (2001), the new licensing act and the way in which the legal framework related to the concert environment has changed has completely revolutionized the way in which the worker is expected to behave and perform. The knowledge needed to participate in this type of working environment has been upgraded and it is the employer's responsibility to ensure that those working in such environments are au fait with the laws governing them. In this way, the ignorance-pleading of former years is not an issue as both parties have a liability, which *should* ensure that at least one of the parties is certain to guarantee that everything is covered. In many countries across the world, this type of legislative cover is essential to the smooth running of events. However, some countries do not have specific laws governing health and safety at such events and this causes an added stress factor to those working.

In places that are highly governed by such laws, these laws and *appropriate* guidance are often created by bureaucrats rather than those with direct knowledge of the event environment. In these cases, the law or guidance is often created utilizing mathematical/quantitative judgement without qualitative underpinning, and this has caused added stress to crowd managers, who do not believe that such laws and guidance are based on practical knowledge of the event environment. The Corporate Manslaughter Act, which came into force on 6 April 2008, is another law that adds to the stress surrounding such working environments. For those involved with the delivery of an event, this new act underpins the way in which everyone working at events can be held accountable for each other's actions.

The incidence of stress in situations where an alien environment enables an audience to exhibit behaviour that is not normally found in general society is high for people working at such events. These workers have an end-user interface very different from employment in a nine to five office job. In an office, stress is identified by different social and micro-/macro-environmental factors that focus on deadlines and social interaction concerning business. However, in the concert or event environment, the interface with the end-user is very different. The end-users have a reliance on the worker that relates to a sympathetic and often symbiotic existence. In this way, the employed becomes, in many cases, a life saver, a rule institutor or a legal or guidance identifier. Through these activities, the interface between worker and audience has a very different dynamic. Allied with this, the level of stress articulated by the worker is increased through noise levels, the environment, threat of conflict and the transitory nature of the work. As the work is of a high-octane level and takes place in a short time-frame, the reliability of the workers, and the way in which they apply themselves under stress, is key to the success of the operation, and thus the level of stress on the individual is extremely high.

The issues of noise, heat, change in temperature, mass bodies and crowd dynamics have a tremendous effect on those working in these areas, and it is key that the welfare rights and needs of these workers are supported to enable them to carry out their jobs to the highest standards possible.

Geographical factors

The very nature of this work is changeable for many of those practising it. Often such work takes place in an indoor or outdoor alien environment. In many cases those working may have to camp in tents and are on the road for many months at a time and away from their 'home' environment. The site chosen may be open to the elements, and thus changes in climate may mean the changing of clothes at a moment's notice. The area, if outside, is often open to the use of temporary, demountable structures, which again causes a stress factor as these structures have to be trusted. Climate changes can also change the reliability of such structures, and this, in turn, can affect those working at events.

Demographic factors

In the normal office environment the demographic structure of the customer is usually well documented. However, unless profiling is carried out, the customer base for events is rarely well known. Thus, the worker can be interfacing with a range of ages and differing sex characteristics. The difficulty with many of these events is that working with children, youth and old people is far more stressful than working with the ordinary 25- to 45-year-old. In addition, through the increased dependency on alcohol and drugs by audience members, a support mechanism focusing on welfare should be present at all events to deal with those in the audience who have problems related to this area. In this way, the emphasis for this is taken off the steward and the crowd manager, releasing them from this task. It is clear from participant observation (Kemp and Hill, 2004; Kemp *et al.*, 2007) that the steward is the first point of contact with any member of the crowd. If he/she has a fluorescent jacket on, the audience perceives that he/she can answer any question posed. However, having someone to direct the questions or issues to in this area reduces the tension/stress markedly for the steward, spotter or crowd manager.

Environmental

Environmental factors that impact on those working at the event are many and varied. One factor not often considered is the constant build-up of litter at the event, and the inability to move it or to clear it away causes a difficult issue. Once litter starts to build up, it can become an obstruction for those working in the pit. In many cases, a build-up of paper and/or plastic can cause suffocation possibilities at the front of stage if a crowd collapse or lateral crush takes place in this area.

The constant noise level causes a change to the environment; a once-peaceful site can turn into a different environment owing to the constant beat of music from a large number of stages. Smoke from smoke machines and illicit fires can also cause a problem, and the arrival by car of so many people can cause a pollution nightmare for asthmatics from the large amount of CO emitted from the vehicles.

The climate also affects the working practices of those employed at events and interfacing with the audience. A prime example of this was during the Donnington Park Monsters of Rock (UK) incident in 1998. During this event high winds caused a serious problem, resulting in the collapse of the assembly for a day screen being used at the event. Only a steel fence in the backstage area was preventing the screen assembly from collapsing on a section of the crowd, as related by Upton in Kemp *et al.* (2007) and Upton (2007). In this case, the supervisor had to move a vociferous crowd from the danger area and a rigging crew had to be sent in to retrieve the damaged screen. The crew was continually frustrated by a small group of attendees who insisted on standing under the suspended rig as the screen was still showing pictures of the live act on stage. In this case, more staff had to be deployed in the front-of-stage pit to secure the danger area, cut the power to the screen so it no longer held the attention of the crowd and secure the damaged screen so that it would not fall. It was thus not necessary to stop the show. To do this may have caused rioting or antisocial behaviour, which may have affected more of the audience.

Such cases are called 'near misses' and happen at every event. The key to a near miss is to register it, analyse it and then to ensure that you have contingencies to deal with it. In many cases in the past, near misses have been ignored. In the Watson Walker (1997, cited in Charles, 2003) accident triangle, the examination of both near misses and behaviours forms the base of the triangle, supporting the notion that observation of these areas, which happen most frequently at events, must be identified, as they are potential learning experiences that enable us to monitor and improve our control of events. A wide range of event controllers still rely on accident statistics to create performance indicators for work-related and crowd-related incidences. However, each event that takes place is different, and, although comprising the same overall characteristics and physical development and delivery, all have a multitude of problems, which can occur at any time. This whole area is related to cause and effect. It is the effect of human behaviour that causes near misses, which contribute to the risks and hazards at all events. It is clear from such incidences that risk assessment has to be fluid and, as well as assessing the risk, it must be analysed and then managed.

Clarity of Operational–Tactical and Strategic Developments

The majority of events that take place in the working environment being studied are identified by Alexander and Berlonghi (1993:15-16) as 'cohesive or spectator' motivated. However, the crowd at specific events can become an 'expressive or revelous crowd' and an 'aggressive or hostile crowd', and can also be, from time to time, 'an escaping or trampling crowd' or a 'violent crowd'. It is clear, however, that the crowd changes in relation to a number of elements that change within the event environment. There are, of course, a number of standard elements involved with event employment, but in addition there are also those that are fluid and changeable. The site of the event and the hardware associated with it, the geographical terrain and the legal aspects governing it all stay relatively unchanged throughout the show. However, the climate, the socio/psychological and the environmental aspects are in constant flux, and it is these aspects that govern the change in behaviour of the audience and thus govern the way in which the workers have to deal with the audience.

As identified by Soane (1993), the majority of spectators are relatively immobile (that is they stay in the same place) during the performance of an artist.

However, during the breaks between the artists a high level of migration is seen. At a one-off event this is more pronounced (Kemp *et al.*, 2004). However, at a large festival where more than a handful of bands are playing on any given day, there is a caveat to this. The fans of the band will be relatively immobile, but those who are there for other artists may migrate during the time when bands they do not wish to see specifically are on the stage. At an event like Glastonbury (UK), where there is a wide range of activities taking place over the timeframe of the event, the way in which audience members act can be very different. From research carried out in 2001 (Kemp *et al.*, 2004), it was found that at least 5% of the audience does not specifically visit this festival to see the artists performing. This audience forms part of a ritualistic visit where they feel in community with others, and the focus of their visit to the festival is a range of other activities, which does not include watching the artists perform. Those involved in this group will spend time interfacing with others, family groups and individuals, away from the concert areas. Thus, there is a complex interrelationship between the artist playing and the audience *in situ* on the site. This uncertainty, as regards how many people will be interfacing with the artist at any one time, initiates a lack of knowledge regarding the size of the crowd and the way in which the crowd will behave.

The very nature of crowd mass militates against 'front to back communication' (Fruin, 1993:102). Fruin also states that members of the audience do not have a broad view of what is occurring in the crowd. This may be a positive or negative development: positive if the crowd is able to be moved against its will as members are unsure of what behaviour is taking place in any one area, but negative if the movement of the crowd, or within the crowd, militates against movement by those overseeing the management of that crowd. In such cases, panic, fight response or survival instinct may be the strongest impulses, and in these cases the delivery of instructions to move the crowd is virtually impossible and thus a physical response must be taken to ensure that participants within the crowd are made safe from harm. It is clear from this notion that the stress levels on the individual workers are as high as on those in distress in the audience, and an inability to enhance an escape mode and being drawn into the melee in a concert causes possible post-traumatic stress, leading to illness and a destabilization of the working life.

Au *et al.* (1993) focus on the actions of the collective crowd, identifying that the actions taken by a small number of individuals lead to a larger group of people copying and following what they do. This is especially important in the practice of antisocial behavioural aspects of concert attendance, such as moshing, crowd surfing, etc., which can cause devastating effects for the audience and workers alike. The delivery of such behaviour is clearly driven by the artist or the genre of music practised and, through this behaviour, it is clear that such actions can have a devastating effect on both individuals and the crowd itself. Whilst some people are enjoying their own behaviour, others suffer. Moshing and crowd surfing often cause injury to those working where an audience member has been surfing and then disappears below the headline of the crowd. Once this happens and the audience member does not reappear, the worker has to move into the crowd to rescue the surfer. Once this takes place, he/she is open to two reactions.

The first is an adverse reaction from the crowd, feeling that the worker is trying to spoil their fun, and, secondly, a reaction from others enjoying their form of antisocial behaviour, who perceive that the worker is trying to stop them enjoying what they do at every concert.

It is clear from a number of working sources that when a promoter or venue manager has tried to stop this behaviour from taking place by banning or throwing out those that have participated, the audience has voted with their feet and attendances have fallen in some areas in response to such actions. Thus a model of behaviour needs to be understood before taking any actions whatsoever.

In work carried out by Alexander and Berlonghi (1993) into risk at events, the top five risks were identified as:

- sale and consumption of alcohol;
- size of crowds;
- overcapacity of crowds;
- inexperienced organizers; and
- poor communication.

However, in similar research carried out by Kemp *et al.* (2007), the risk factors are entirely different, and although people are still aware of the risks of alcohol and other risks at an event, the five major risks are:

- crushing;
- fighting;
- mass bodies;
- not being able to get out; and
- lateral movement.

It is clear from this that, since the late 1990s and with the resultant range of high-profile crowd disasters, two things have taken place. First, the crowd seems to be a great deal more aware of the physical dangers of any crowd activity and is not so focused on other elements. Also the audience perspective towards those working at events has shifted from one of mistrust to one where those participating realize the importance of the workers to their enjoyment and safety. The reduction of the major risk issues from 1991 can be seen as being due to a change in the law and the professionalization of crowd management and security since the late 1990s.

Sale and consumption of alcohol has been regulated by law, and the way in which this takes place, where the onus is put on the point of sale and the licensee, has reduced the perceived effect. However, in truth, there are still as many people drinking at events, but the consumption of alcohol is seen as a secondary risk factor to the events (which may be caused by it). The size of the crowd at an event has, in many cases, been reduced by the stringent attitudes of the licensing bodies, ensuring that a correct capacity rating has been attributed to each venue. Prosecutions for overfill and the stringent legal attitudes to those causing offences, where promoters and venue managers no longer seem to abide by the law of chance but are now motivated by the law of profit, have reduced the number of offences in these areas. In today's society a new blame culture has arisen, where the first thought after an accident is 'Who do I sue?' However, overcapacity is still an issue, maybe not in the industry as a whole but in certain sectors, and many of the respondents to the questionnaires carried out in the research in 2007 link many of the hazards and risks associated with an event to there being too many bodies in a range of locations at an event, and especially in the front-of-stage pit area.

Inexperienced organizers have almost all been eradicated at mass events, with the major promoters staging the vast majority of large- and super-scale events. It is clear from this move, that it is virtually impossible now, with the kind of money it takes to stage such an event, that any smaller or new promoters can enter the industry at that level. Those entering have come from the larger companies and started up new businesses in the area. There is now no excuse for poor communication, as new technologies have created a range of communication developers. It must, however, be remembered that at the last two major event disasters the communication systems failed at the vital moments.

Conclusion

It is clear from the aforementioned research that Geller's (1996) model can be utilized in the examination of the interface between the audience and those working in a crowd management scenario at events. The elements of person, environment and behaviour are inextricably connected to this interface, and it is clear that the behaviour of the audience is associated with the environment within which they find themselves. The support prescribed by those trained, and with the knowledge to keep them safe in the environment itself, is again an important aspect of this symbiotic relationship. In addition, information about the audience is key, and the correct briefing delivery and knowledge transfer is an important factor in ensuring that those working in, and those attending, specific concert environments are as safe as they possibly can be.

From this chapter the following key points can be deduced:

- High-adrenalin work environments benefit from knowledge of the proposed crowd and the ability to manage the crowd in all situations.
- The coaching of the audience and the careful management of the physical environment are synonymous with the reduction of stress in crowd management activities.
- The audience/crowd management relationship has changed from one of antithesis to one of mutual benefit since the late 1990s.
- The audience is far more aware of the dangers to themselves and workers at events than ever before.
- The person, environment and behaviour triad adaptation can be instituted if a tight management structure is focused on the outcomes from its use.

References

Alexander, E. and Berlonghi, M.S. (1993) Understanding and planning for different spectator crowds. In: Smith, R.A. and Dickie, J.F. (eds) *Engineering for Crowd Safety*. Elsevier, London, pp. 239–247.

Au, S.Y.Z., Ryan, M.C. and Carey, M.S. (1993) Key principles in ensuring crowd safety in public venues. In: Smith, R.A. and Dickie, J.F. (eds) *Engineering for Crowd Safety*. Elsevier, London, pp. 133–143.

Charles, C.K. (2003) Integrating behaviourism and cognitivism: a paradigmatic reconciliation of occupational safety. Presentation at the Technical Seminar on Occupational Safety. The Hong Kong Institution of Engineers, Hong Kong, 30 June 2003.

Fruin, J.J. (1993) The causes and prevention of crowd disasters. In: Smith, R.A. and Dickie, J.F. (eds) *Engineering for Crowd Safety*. Elsevier, London, pp. 99–108.

Geller, E.S. (1996) *The Psychology of Safety: How to Improve Behaviours and Attitudes on the Job*. Chilton, Radnor, Pennsylvania.

Goffman, E. (1963) *Behaviour in Public Places: Notes on the Social Organization of Gatherings*. Free Press, New York.

Guastello, S.J. (1993) Do we really know how well our occupational accident prevention programmes work. *Safety Science* 16, 445–463.

Humphrey, M.A. (1996) Safe behaviour: California-based company emphasises action to achieve safety. *On Workers Compensation Magazine*, December 1996.

Kemp, C.M. and Hill, I. (2004) *Health and Safety Aspects of the Live Music Industry*. ETP, Cambridge.

Kemp, C.M., Hill, I. and Upton, M. (2004) *A Comparative Study of Crowd Behaviour at Two Major Music Events*. ETP, Cambridge.

Kemp, C.M., Hill, I. and Upton, M. (2007) *Case Studies in Crowd Management*. ETP, Cambridge.

Krause, T.R. (1995) *Employee-driven Systems for Safe Behaviour*. VNR, New York.

McSween, T.E. (1995) *The Value Based Safety Process: Improving your Safety Culture with a Behavioural Approach*. VNR, New York.

Mill, R.C. (1992) *Human Factors in Process Operations: a Report of the Human Factor Study Group of the Loss Prevention Working Party of the European Federation of Chemical Engineers*. Institute of Chemical Engineers, Southampton, UK.

Plucker, J. (1999) *Behaviourism: Educational Psychology Resource*. Indiana University. Available at: http://indiana.edu/~edpsych/topics~/behaviour.html (accessed 1 September 2007).

Soane, A.J.N. (1993) The Grand National. In: Smith, R.A. and Dickie, J.F. (eds) *Engineering Safety*. Elsevier, London, pp. 27–34.

Upton, M. (2007) *From Ancient Rome to Rock 'n' Roll*. ETP, Cambridge.

Willis, P. (1990) *Moving Culture*. Gulbenkian, London.

Wozniak, R.H. (1994) *Reflex, Habit and Implicit Response: the Early Elaboration of Theoretical and Methodological Behaviourism 1915–1928*. Routledge, London.

16 Human Resources Perspectives on the Management of Conferences as Events in Kenya

Roselyne N. Okech

Memorial University of Newfoundland, Canada

Introduction

The UN Climate Change Conference may have been a scientific event but it was also a tourism event for Kenya. Indeed, any conference and event is. Conference tourism is not only the largest subsector in the business but it is also the fastest growing. For a long time, tourists were destined for leisure, wildlife safaris, sand and sea, and cultural tours – basically attractions of a traditional variety (Muriuki, 2006). This tourist is typically known as *mtalii* in the Swahili language. However, other forms of tourism are emerging. For instance, there is the transit tourist, a traveller stopping over for a day or two en route to another destination. The visitor finds himself in the country and samples the fauna, flora and culture. The domestic tourist is the citizen who travels in the country for leisure, business or both. Then there are the trendsetting business travellers, who are key to countries that look to generate revenue from tourism. In recent times, the definition of who a lucrative business traveller is has expanded to include those who attend conventions, seminars, conferences and other meetings. Therefore, this is the fastest-growing industry and there is a need to give it serious thought, commensurate with its contribution to the economy.

The World Tourism Organization's Tourism: 2020 Vision forecasts that tourism movement to Africa will increase to 47 million arrivals by 2010 (UNWTO, 2001). This represents an average annual growth rate of 5.5%, in contrast to the global forecast rate of 4.1%. Africa's market share of global international tourism is projected to be 5% by 2020 (Ministry of Tourism, 2008). Given this background, with time, cities are expected to absorb the growing numbers of international travellers, the bulk of them at conferences. They must prepare for the massive growth and position themselves to meet the needs of business travellers. Looking at the numbers at the climate conference in Kenya in 2006 and other similar events, it is important to ponder what the delegates meant for the economy in terms of revenue. This was through private sector goods and service providers, and the government also obtains its rightful share in taxes. Conference tourism is a public–private partnership, since the primary beneficiaries of conference tourism are tour operators, hotels, transport providers, restaurants, curio dealers and technical equipment dealers, among others. At the second tier are secondary winners, such as extra staff hired at conferences, farmers whose products fetch better prices, private security firms, translators and many more. There are many ways of boosting tourism earnings. Kenya must be promoted as a magical destination, where tourists spend as much as possible.

In conference tourism, Kenya is ranked fourth in Africa, after South Africa, Egypt and Morocco. This is an improvement from 2004, when it was fifth (Wekesa, 2006). Revenue from conference tourism is also growing, due to several factors. For instance, the rehabilitation of Kenyatta International Conference Centre (KICC) has played a crucial role and it has hosted many international meetings. With modernization and aggressive marketing, KICC will be the nectar that attracts bees to the honey that is Kenya's tourism. Provision of first-class service is needed so that the visitors return after meetings. However, it is important to note that all that is required to kiss the lucrative business goodbye is for one or two international conferences to go wrong – conference organizers will avoid Kenya. It is therefore important to entrust coordination and running of conferences to professionals, such as destination management companies to take care of logistics, human resources, transport, accommodation and tours. Other skills required are translation, event organization and venue management.

Services should be sought from destination management companies in the tourism business. However, the destination management company concept is still very much underdeveloped in Kenya. Conferencing is about business over and above the meetings and technical sessions. There is a need for the public and private sectors to join hands with the government to manage key events. Events should boost the economy of host cities, countries and the private sector. It is also important to extend shopping hours, to have 24-hour streets, outdoor entertainment and traditional dances, and to exploit the cultural heritage by encouraging street marketing in an organized way for traders to take artefacts to travellers. Safety and security are paramount, as is good infrastructure, including easy access to toilets, resting benches and recreation facilities. South Africa's city of Durban is the number one events and, indeed, conference venue in Africa. This is attributed to conference facilities of international standards and back-up services. Aggressive marketing and good weather complete the picture. In Kenya, other than KICC and the UN complex, large conference facilities that can accommodate thousands of delegates are lacking.

Overview of Conference Tourism in Africa

The meetings and conventions industry is perceived as a 'red-hot' industry (Shure, 1993; Ja Choi and Boger, 2002) and one of the healthiest and most growth-oriented sectors within the tourism industry (Abbey, 1987). While the term 'meetings' covers all forms of meetings, conventions, conferences, exhibitions and special events (Crouch and Ritchie, 1998), the term 'conventions' is described as the entire membership meetings of the sponsoring organization or association (Rockett and Smille, 1994) and a form of annual meetings (Astroff and Abbey, 1998). A relatively new concept in the tourism industry, conference tourism is a niche market subsector that revolves around service provision to business travellers attending seminars, workshops, conferences and conventions. In the recent past, huge numbers of interest groups have been travelling to various destinations to attend global meetings. Conference tourism in Kenya reached its peak when the Youth Entrepreneurship Summit and the Africities 4 Summit took place (Wekesa, 2006). In 2 weeks, Nairobi's population soared, with more than 10,000 delegates as the two conferences converged in the city. Other conferences included the International Parliamentary Union (IPU) Conference and the Media Conference in the same year. These two conferences exemplify the ascendancy of this specialized form of tourism, which is a mix of business and leisure.

Worldwide, the tourism subsector nets US$672 billion annually, of which Africa's share is 10%. Africa accounts for 2% of the global conference tourism market share. According to the International Congress and Convention Association (ICCA, 2005), the subsector regulator, it is also estimated that conference tourism will double by 2013, with a predicted growth rate of 4% per annum in the coming years (ICCA, 2005; Wekesa, 2006). According to ICCA figures, there were approximately 5315 conferences of a large magnitude in 2005 worldwide, with Europe accounting for 58% of the market share. Although Asia followed Europe with a huge dividing margin at 18%, it is worth pointing out that the continent recorded the fastest-growing figures, thanks to the rise in importance of the free port city of Dubai as a conference tourism destination, coupled with the rise in importance of Asian tiger cities. North America – the USA and Canada – had a 10.5% share, while South America held on to 7% against Australia's 4%, as Africa trailed with a paltry 2.5% or 132 meetings (Wekesa, 2006).

Recognizing the importance of conference tourism, the apex organizers of the Africities 4 Summit, the United Cities and Local Governments of Africa (UCLGA), held a stakeholders' meeting that discussed strategies through which African cities can benefit from the meteoric rise in conference tourism. In Kenya, Mombasa city is ideal for holding large meetings because it already has sufficient bed capacity, augmented by a warm climate and a variety of tourist attractions. The missing link for Mombasa is that it lacks international-level conference facilities that can cater for thousands of delegates. Out of the 2.5% of Africa's share of the global conference tourism, South Africa had a clear lead according to last year's figures, which placed the country at 43.8% or 56 meetings. Egypt was number two on the continent, with 15 large meetings, accounting for 11.7% of the continent's total. Morocco came third, with 11 meetings, which translated to 8.6%, while Kenya was ranked fourth, with eight international-scale meetings, accounting for 6.3%.

Kenya improved from position five in 2004 to number four in 2005 and has great potential for moving up the ladder if a strategic plan is implemented to specifically train focus on conference tourism (Muriuki, 2006). Conference tourism involves other sectors of the economy – stationery providers, translators, food and catering service providers, drivers and many more. Also benefitting from conferences are suppliers of equipment such as overhead projectors, photocopiers and various ICT services (Wekesa, 2006). Indeed, with a good strategy, attracting more business travellers to attend high-profile meetings in Nairobi, Mombasa or other cities and towns could have a multiplier effect in more than one way. Because conference tourism hinges on the convergence of hundreds of people on one location, many Kenyans with a professional background in tourism or conference support services could get employment.

Nature of the work

Events bring people together for a common purpose, and event planners work to ensure that this purpose is achieved seamlessly. Event planners coordinate every detail, from the speakers and meeting location to arranging for printed materials and audio-visual equipment. Event planners work for non-profit organizations, professional and similar associations, hotels, corporations and government. Some organizations have internal meeting-planning staff, and others hire independent meeting and convention planning firms to organize their events. Organizations also have to put up all forms of electronic communication needed for the meeting or convention, such as e-mail, voice mail, video and online communication. Logistics management of meetings and conventions, such as labour and materials, is another major component of the job. Planners register attendees and issue name badges, coordinate lodging reservations and arrange transportation. They make sure that all necessary supplies are ordered and transported to the meeting site on time and that meeting rooms are equipped with sufficient seating and audio-visual equipment. All these have implications for human resources management. There is a wealth of literature that explores the relative costs and benefits of the conference industry (Dwyer and Forsyth, 1997; Mistilis and Dwyer, 1997), with Leask and Spiller (2002) identifying direct and indirect advantages and disadvantages of conference centre development. The fragmented nature of the conference business and a competitive environment has spawned a number of marketing consortia, which operate to attract businesses of specific categories to venues.

Conference tourism trends in Kenya

According to the Kenya National Bureau of Statistics, 2002–2007, the following are the numbers of local as well as international conferences in Kenya. In 2006, there was a total of 2120 local conferences and 209 international conferences in Kenya (Table 16.1). This is a significant increase from 754 (local) and 115 (international) in 2002. This shows the major role of human resources in management of conferences in Kenya.

Table 16.1. Conferences in Kenya, 2002–2006. Data source: Kenya National Bureau of Statistics (see Ministry of Tourism, 2007).

Year	Local	International
2002	754	115
2003	805	126
2004	912	145
2005	1553	186
2006	2120	209

Management practices in human resource management

Recruitment and selection

Taylor (1947, cited in Brown, 1990) identified the importance of selecting the right people for each job in his recommendations on the recruitment of first-class men. Despite the sexism, few human resource managers in event management in Kenya appear to undertake comprehensive human resource planning, although pre-opening strategies no doubt include some degree of labour market analysis. It is, however, important that human resource specialists maintain strategic approaches to labour demand and supply projections, including an examination of turnover/wastage levels, in order to ensure effective, and cost-effective, utilization of their employees to accountably contribute to the productivity of their establishments.

Flexible employment practices

One distinguishing feature of the event industry in Kenya is that it is heavily influenced by consumer demand, which is not always easy to predict accurately in advance. Some event management employers now maintain two groups of staff: one group forming the core staff and employed full time, with another group available employed on a fixed part-time or casual basis, to meet the peaks of demand as they arise. Whilst not an example of job redesign acceptable to the academic purist, the development of flexible practices, such as casual staff banks, self-employed staff, split-shift working and mobile relief teams, is evidence of practical responses to the need to cover peaks in consumer demand or shortfalls in the supply of full-time or committed part-time staff. Such practices have proved successful in meeting the short-term needs of event employers for staffing coverage.

Measurement of performance

Many areas of public sector service provision have been required to develop performance indicators so that they can provide some better estimate of their efficiency and their effectiveness. Many service managers, therefore, have had to draw up satisfactory measures of their resource use and to identify measures which could validly evaluate their effectiveness in achieving key objectives. These changes have directly affected the public sector in particular, through the government-imposed requirement for competitive tendering. Hence the responsibility lies with event organizers to come up with ways of improving the performance of their employees.

Methods of rewarding employees

Despite the focus on financial rewards by some management, employees may also be experiencing enhanced motivation through the setting of management targets. Locke and Latham (1979) presented the intuitively appealing goal-setting theory that people are more motivated to perform when set specific goals and when feedback is given on performance. Accumulating evidence lends support to this theory, and since the present emphasis upon measurable performance requires the setting of specific goals, there is scope for improved employee motivation within event management, provided they are involved voluntarily in the process.

Training and development of staff

Perhaps the one enduring lesson which practitioners have drawn from theory in the human resources management field is that training is necessary both for self-development and for improving organizational effectiveness. As a consequence, there has been widespread growth in training activities in the event industry, as the industry tries to develop managers for the future and to shape the behaviour of the employees needed for the present. Customer care programmes have been introduced into many event organizations to develop both their staff and their organization. Telephone technique training has been used to create positive attitudes towards the clients, while service delivery training has ensured that new clients will wish to return. The development and maintenance of positive staff attitudes and behaviours through such programmes have demonstrated their efficacy, if commercial success is used as the evaluation criterion. More diverse proxy measures, such as reduced staff turnover, improved cooperation and fewer grievances, have also been claimed as evidence of their success in motivating employees.

Employee relations

Perhaps the most significant changes in managerial practices within human resource management have occurred on the issue of industrial relations. 'Industrial relations' has traditionally referred to situations where trade unions have regulated the relationships between employer and employees. Where good industrial relations prevail, the unions have usually been granted legal recognition and its attendant rights to organize the workforce, to represent its members within procedures and to participate in collective bargaining on their behalf. In Kenya, the staff hired during events is not unionizable as most of them are on contract.

Cross-cultural transfers

Among the best examples of cross-cultural transfer is that of customer care programmes, which were pioneered in the leisure industry by US organizations such as McDonalds and Disneyland. Another transfer is that of the quality circle, a practice common in Japanese organizations, where a supervisor leads open discussions with employees on how best to achieve quality and production targets. The quality circle meets on a regular basis to review past difficulties and to pool ideas for future improvements. Implicit in the process is the proposition that quality is a shared responsibility and that everyone should strive to ensure quality in their individual efforts. The approach has a long and successful history within Japanese industry, notable for its high levels of cultural consensus and commitment, lifetime employment and respect for seniority and status. This method can prove effective for event managers and their employees.

Methodology

A review of the Kenyan literature highlighted the need for research in this particular area. Owing to the dearth of literature specifying selection and quality attributes, a qualitative study was carried out to augment a range of attributes for inclusion in the proposed questionnaire. Qualitative research allows the subjects being studied to give much 'richer' answers to questions put to them by the researcher and may give valuable insights that might have been missed by any other method. Not only does it provide valuable information to certain research questions in its own right but there is a strong case for using it to complement quantitative research methods. For example, if the area of interest has not been previously investigated, such as this one on events management in Kenya, then qualitative research may be a vital forerunner to conducting any quantitative research. In this research, the exploratory exercise included interviews with two event organizers and, owing to a request for anonymity, Company A and Company B shall be used to discuss the results.

Results and Discussion

The number of conferences organized by the respondents varied from one to five in the previous 12 months (2007), and the average number of delegates ranged from 50 to more than 100. Conference duration was fairly evenly split between daily and residential, with 48% and over 50%, respectively. The majority of the conferences organized were corporate conferences (70%), and this would explain the fact that most conference fees and residential accommodation were paid for by the employer. City centre hotels and lodges were the most popular venue location. Star ratings and crown ratings played an important part in venue selection, with over 70% often/always influencing venue choice. A major influence could be the introduction of a classification and grading scheme for conference venues, as the organizers indicated that if one was available it would often/always influence venue selection.

Company A was established in the year 2003 and has 15 permanent staff. They host different types of events, including business luncheons and workshops, national exhibitions, international expos, and corporate as well as social events. Company B was established in the year 2000 and has 12 permanent staff. Their annual turnover is over 30,000,000 Kenyan shillings (£238,753, as of 26 October 2008). They host different types of events, such as sports, regional corporate meetings, annual corporate events and annual general meetings for companies. At the moment, destination management companies do not play any role in preparation of events in Kenya. In terms of remuneration of staff, both Company A and Company B paid their staff well and kept a re-employment roll for future reference, in order to reduce labour turnover and absence.

The research was also based on the following variables with regard to human resource management of the two companies A and B. They include: (i) benefits and compensation; (ii) employment regulation and policy; (iii) managing employees; and (iv) personnel administration.

Benefits and compensation
In Company A, the manager and owner earns 85,000 Kenyan shillings (£675), sales representatives earn on commission and event designers earn 30,000 Kenyan shillings (£238). The company pays for outpatient care in terms of health and there are no retirement plans. Company B employees have average earnings of 15,000 Kenyan shillings (£119), and benefits and perks are for only three members of management. There are no health insurance or retirement plans.

Employee regulation and policy
Company A keeps all the basic required employment regulations, and ethics are upheld in all areas, while Company B meets all statutory requirements and has workman compensation, although the employees are not unionized.

Managing employees
Company A has 70% of their staff outsourced, and their average daily rate of pay is 350 Kenyan shillings (£3). Recruitment is based on need, although training is a challenge as employees are not permanent. Company B staff report to the events operation manager and the company awards an annual bonus to motivate staff. They do not have external training.

Personnel administration
Company A has no privacy policies and they make use of temporary employees. They have no employee handbook. Company B has no privacy policy and does not make use of interns. They make use of standard operating procedures.

Both companies identified the positive impacts of events as a way of developing the economy, and enhancing personal profits and multicultural sharing in running events. On the negative side, the impact of events causes cultural erosion, negative social behaviours and environmental degradation. The challenges and problems the companies face as event operators are: (i) the high cost attached to hosting events, which can be disastrous if one is not careful; and (ii) the companies also have to keep training staff, as most of the employees are part time or hired only when there is an event, although preference is usually given to staff used previously. According to the companies, the trend that international tourism is taking is that people want to meet and visit parks or attractions, and so very soon many conferences and meetings in Kenya will be held in parks. Both

Companies A and B think that the Kenya Tourism Board (KTB) should play a huge role in marketing conferences and events in Kenya.

It is important that the conference industry develops a partnership between the various stakeholders in the industry. Doing so could help satisfy the requirements needed to provide a balanced range of facilities to meet the needs of the conference delegate. The development of the conference industry should be a partnership between the private and public sectors. Where the line is drawn in this partnership depends on the prevailing economic, political and social policies of the country. It is suggested that the government needs to intervene, assist and regulate this partnership. The complex nature of the conference industry means that it is unlikely that the private sector will satisfy the industry needs on its own, for example by providing adequate infrastructure for the conference industry.

Attribute analysis

Location and image
Good standard of décor and facilities and accessible road links are rated as extremely important. Previous satisfactory experience is another relatively important attribute with regards to location and image of the venue. Managers need to maintain a detailed guest history and consider using this as a tool for database marketing if they are to attract customers with previous satisfactory experience. The respondents also stated that a good standard of décor and facilities is fairly easily maintained and that funds should be spent in this area as it would be a productive investment. Accessible road links to the venue are extremely important, with clear location signs within the venue.

Competence
Cleanliness of facilities was very important to organizers, and arrangements should be carried out as requested by clients. Good taking and delivering of messages by staff, convenient and free parking, and a flexible menu all require competent staff. Management can review the process of taking and delivering of messages to ascertain whether it is effective. Convenient or free parking is extremely important, but for some venues this is not possible, so venue managers need to consider the alternatives available. Management should also ensure that flexible menus are available and requests for specific diets could be taken in advance. These results highlight the necessity of recruiting and training enthusiastic and professional staff who are friendly and helpful, to enhance the overall quality of the experience.

Conclusion

The research identifies that Kenya does not yet have a mature and extensive event industry. However, there is evidence that the industry is being developed at a high rate. Research into human resource management and other aspects of events management is also lacking. The market is not saturated as yet, and hence the future of the market depends on matching the needs of the organizers with the provision of appropriate venue facilities and services. This chapter has explored the nature of the Kenyan event industry, and in particular its human resource management practices. Using the minimal literature in the area, the chapter argues the case for a comprehensive and integrated human resource management strategy, encompassing innovative recruitment, selection, training, development and performance management techniques, which will effectively contribute to the events industry productivity and profitability.

The event industry in Kenya appears to be characterized by: a culture of 'casualization', like its international competitors; significant gender imbalances; and a largely transient workforce, which is relatively underpaid and under-represented by industry unions. As a highly labour-intensive industry, it is also disproportionately expensive, at times less productive or profitable than its counterparts. Human resource management practices remain fragmented and short-term oriented, and without direct significance to overall events productivity. Recent developments in the establishment of a plethora of tourism training institutions and colleges, coupled with portable national competency standards for a variety of hospitality and tourism occupations, will no doubt ensure a skilled pool of potential employees in the area of concern.

Linking such training to individual occupational criteria and supplementing it with thorough orientation programmes, on-the-job training modules and appropriate supervision will no doubt fill this previous gap in human resource management for the event management industry. These developments parallel the findings of a previous study in the UK and Germany (Prais et al., 1989), which found that Germany's productive edge was at least partly due to its nationally accredited vocational training system (Nankervis, 1993). Studies of some of the best US and Australian hotels (Gray, 1992, cited in Nankervis, 1993) also suggest that the cement that binds skilled and motivated employees to their organization, and who are thus more enthusiastic, more committed and potentially more productive than their competitors' employees, is clear and ongoing communication between managers and their employees. The 'messages' sent through the host of human resource activities, strategies, policies and procedures need to be congruent and consistent, and might include promotion of mission statements, the nature of the physical working environment, management by walking around, staff–supervisor meetings, active (and positive) use of guest feedback, and grievance mechanisms. Owing to the continued growth of conference and meeting events in Kenya, the organizing clientele will have to become more experienced and, as a result, demand more specific responses to their needs. The quality of provision and value for money are, therefore, key factors that event organizers in Kenya must recognize if they are to sustain and increase their market share.

Acknowledgement

The author would like to thank the valuable contribution of Dr Joseph Wadawi, Strathmore University, to the collection of parts of the research.

References

Abbey, J.R. (1987) The convention and meetings sector – its operation and research needs. In: Ritchie, J.R.B. and Goeldner, C. (eds) *Travel, Tourism, and Hospitality Research*. John Wiley and Sons, New York, pp. 265–274.

Astroff, M.T. and Abbey, J.R. (1998) *Convention Sales and Services*, 5th edn. Waterbury Press, Cranbury, New Jersey.

Brown, R.J. (1990) The management of human resources in the leisure industries. In: Henry, I.P. (ed.) *Management & Planning in the Leisure Industries*. Macmillan Publishers, London, pp. 70–96.

Crouch, G.I. and Ritchie, J.R.B. (1998) Convention site selection research: a review conceptual model, and prepositional framework. *Journal of Convention & Exhibition Management* 1(1), 49–69.

Dwyer, L. and Forsyth, P. (1997) Impacts and benefits of MICE tourism: a framework for analysis. *Tourism Economics* 3(1), 21–38.

ICCA (2005) The international meetings market 2005. International Congress and Convention Association. Available at: http://www.iccaworld.com/spps/sitepage. cfm (accessed on 7 January 2008).

Ja Choi, J. and Boger, C.A. (2002) State association market: relationships between association characteristics and site selection criteria. *Journal of Convention & Exhibition Management* 4(1), 55–73.

Leask, A. and Spiller, J. (2002) UK conference venues: past, present and future. *Journal of Convention & Exhibition Management* 4(1), 29–54.

Locke, E. and Latham, G. (1979) Assigned versus participative goal setting. *Journal of Applied Psychology* 60, 299–302.

Ministry of Tourism (2007) Update on tourism statistics. Available at: http://www.tourism. go.ke/ministry.nsf/doc/Facts 2007.pdf (accessed 24 November 2008).

Ministry of Tourism (2008) Facts and figures. Available at: http://www.tourism.go.ke/ ministry.nsf/pages/facts_figures (accessed 19 June 2008).

Mistilis, N. and Dwyer, L. (1997) Capital cities and regions: economic impacts and challenges for development of the MICE Industry in Australia. In: Bushell, R. (ed.) *Tourism and Hospitality Research Conference Proceedings: Building a Better Industry*. Bureau of Tourism Research, Canberra, pp. 390–408.

Muriuki, D. (2006) Conference tourism is the new fad in business. *Standard Newspaper* 27 November.

Nankervis, A.R. (1993) Enhancing productivity in the Australian hotel industry: the role of human resource management. *Research & Practice in Human Resource Management* 1(1), 17–39.

Prais, S.J., Jarvis, V. and Wagner, K.J. (1989) Productivity and vocational skills in services in Britain and Germany: hotels. *National Institute Economic Review* November, 52–72.

Rockett, G. and Smille, G. (1994) Market segments: the European conference and meetings market. *Travel and Tourism Analyst* 4, 36–50.

Shure, P. (1993) Annual spending of $75 billion supports 1.5 million jobs. *Convene* 8(6), 36–41.

UNWTO (2001) *Tourism: 2020 Vision - Africa*. UNWTO, Madrid.

Wekesa, B. (2006) Kenya takes a large bite of the growing conference tourism pie. *Standard Newspaper* 10 September.

Conclusion

It is an exciting time in the events and conventions sector. We have witnessed in recent decades the emergence of events as an experience phenomenon that is clearly differentiated from tourism and hospitality while having close links, both conceptually and organizationally, to these areas. It is a sector that is emerging as a separate domain of study, with a growing education and research agenda. Events and conventions are also a major area for various forms of work within the emerging, post-industrial experience economies of many countries. This work provides opportunities for people to meet a wide variety of personal and organizational needs, in many ways encapsulating the crossover between public and private domains in terms of motivation.

This book offers a synthesis of current understanding relating to people and work opportunities that comprise events and conventions. In reviewing the breadth and depth of research that is being conducted, it is clear that the status of events and conventions as a sector or industry is growing at a global level but at differential rates. This book offers a unique insight into this growth, afforded by the range of collaborators and the scope of research undertaken in Australia, the USA, the UK, Hong Kong, Hungary and Kenya. The book is not intended as a 'how to' text; rather it seeks to redress the dearth of current understanding regarding human resource management issues in light of the operational complexities surrounding the events and conventions industry. It is an industry that is often fragmented, highly temporal and seasonal, with weak career paths and high turnover. The research insights afforded by this book fundamentally aim to enhance management practice so as to overcome these issues and ensure the sustainability of event and convention employment. This conclusion offers a summary of the way forward as suggested by our collaborators, setting the scene for a continued research agenda relating to human resource management in the events and conventions sector.

Setting the background for this book, Part I highlights the emergence of the events industry, examining, in particular, workplace issues. As Mair rightly points out in Chapter 1, many of the areas that now comprise the events industry have traditionally been part of established sectors such as tourism and hospitality. Arcodia (Chapter 2) notes that further research is required to catalogue the skills and attributes required of people working in the emerging events industry.

Building on Arcodia's work, Part II examines in detail career development in the events and conventions sector. Beaven, St George and Wright (Chapter 3) look at embedding employability in cultural event education. One gap in the research that they recognize is employer perceptions of the value of some aspects of experiential learning (e.g. student projects) as a means of providing students with adequate industry experience. As the authors go on to suggest, a greater dialogue is needed between educators and industry in order to promote the benefits of project work as a means of enhancing graduate employability. In Chapters 4 to 6 Ladkin and Weber, McCabe, and Jago and Mair all focus on aspects of career theory; the first two chapters apply this theory in the context of the conventions industry in Hong Kong and Australia, whereas the third chapter uses major event employment as its research context. Noting the general dearth of research on careers in the convention sector, Ladkin and Weber's findings (Chapter 4) go on to support Mair's contention in Chapter 1 that the career paths of a large number of people working in the events sector, in this case business events or meetings, incentives, conferences and exhibitions (MICE) in Hong Kong, begin outside of the industry. Ladkin and Weber argue that more research is required to assess whether this lack of a clear career route into and around the industry is a structural feature caused by the relative immaturity of the industry and whether it is a deterrent to people considering a career in the convention sector. They also note that further research is needed to ascertain the value of education to the convention industry. Ladkin and Weber's research evidences the notion of boundaryless careers in the convention sector. Extending this perspective, McCabe's research (Chapter 5) suggests the careers in the convention sector follow a 'butterfly' pattern, of people flitting or shifting between sectors and between jobs in order to gain expertise in areas of functional responsibility which enhance overall career progression. Mirroring Ladkin and Weber's call for more research, McCabe suggests that work is needed to understand more fully the format and structure of careers in the convention sector.

Rounding out the examination of career theory, Jago and Mair (Chapter 6) move away from business events to explore the other main component of the sector, major events. The authors rightly suggest that investigation is needed, given that business events often provide more stable employment options in terms of full-time, ongoing employment, compared with the more temporal nature of major event employment. Jago and Mair suggest the existence of an internal labour market (ILM), with key staff rotating between different major event organizations in order to secure year-round employment. The authors suggest the full potential of an ILM will not be realized until the major event sector becomes less fragmented and adopts a sectoral approach to staff development. Given the infancy of this concept, more research is required. Jago and Mair also touch on the implications of Generation Y and their changing needs and expectations in the context of event employment. More research is needed across all facets of the sector to examine the characteristics of Generation Y and what implications these have for employers in terms of managing staff and providing sustainable careers for this generation of future workers.

Adding another dimension to the book's discussion of education and career development, Formádi and Raffai (Chapter 7) chart the developing professionalism of the event sector in Hungary. The authors refer to the establishment of an education agenda relating to event management, the work of associations in having event management formally recognized as a profession in Hungary, and the development of and adherence by association members to ethical codes of professional behaviour. The authors note that the field of event management is under-researched in Hungary, and the same can be said for many other countries. Future research might incorporate cross-cultural comparisons to chart the various life cycle stages of the industry globally.

Moving on, Part III explores themes surrounding the flexibility of work in the events sector. Noting the pulsating nature of major sporting event organizations, and the degree of flexibility required by rapid shifts in staff numbers, Hanlon and Jago (Chapter 8) examine the unique human resource challenges associated with managing staff in these organizations. Akin to the findings of Jago and Mair (Chapter 6), Chapter 8 hints at the possibilities of an ILM operating in this sector, which has potential benefits for enhancing the continuity of employment associated with major sporting events. Hanlon and Jago's chapter supplements the few studies that have examined the application of generic HR practices to the events sector. In doing so, it makes a case for why staff selection, induction, team management and staff retention issues are different in the context of pulsating organizations such as those structured around the management of major sporting events. Hanlon and Jago note, however, that there is a growing need for clear and formalized guidance concerning best practice in HR management and suggest that replication of their study in other pulsating event organizations may offer a way forward to achieving this goal.

Hanlon and Jago touch on the management of volunteers in relation to major sporting events. The episodic or infrequent nature of these involvements in the event sector in general is the specific focus of Lockstone and Smith (Chapter 9). They explore the application of flexible work practices to the management of episodic or short-term volunteers to gain a better understanding of how and when event organizations are required to meet the flexibility needs of their volunteers in order to ensure positive recruitment and retention outcomes. This application highlights various gaps in our knowledge of volunteers and volunteer management in the event sector. Lockstone and Smith suggest that a worthwhile topic for future research would be examining whether episodic event volunteers crossover to take up volunteering opportunities on a more continuous basis. Their findings suggest that event volunteers are likely to be more accepting of less flexible working conditions if they perceive this is tied to the operational constraints of running temporally based events. Lockstone and Smith note that more research is required to assess when and why volunteers choose to accept or reject the flexible work options (in terms of rosters and choice of volunteer assignments) on offer in event organizations. The authors also suggest that a longitudinal replication of their study, accounting for constructs relating to volunteer commitment and performance, would provide for a more complete picture of how flexibility practices can be used to maximize the contribution volunteers make to their event organization(s) of choice.

Part IV provides a more focused discussion of recruitment and retention issues affecting the events and conventions industry. Deery (Chapter 10) focuses across the gamut of business and leisure events in her examination of recruitment and retention strategies for the event management sector, drawing on lessons from the related tourism and hospitality sectors to do so. Once again, the role of volunteers in the event sector is highlighted, with Deery noting that the limited research undertaken on retention strategies in the events industry has focused on volunteer labour. This represents a significant research gap, and efforts need to be directed to exploring issues that impact on the retention of paid staff in the leisure and business events sectors. Deery suggests the inclusion of job satisfaction as a research construct should be a focal point for this agenda. Goldblatt and Matheson (Chapter 11) continue the spotlight on the involvement of volunteers in the events sector, offering an Australia and USA comparison of the issues surrounding the recruitment and retention of these unpaid workers in both countries. Their research suggests that there is a need for a comprehensive quantitative study of volunteer supply and demand, inclusive of all elements of the events sector, including conventions, music, sport and other events. This could ensure the sustainability of these offerings in light of the expansion of the global events industry and the static, and in some cases declining, numbers of volunteers. Smith and Lockstone (Chapter 12) continue the research tradition of recruitment and retention surrounding volunteers; however, the authors extend the contextual boundary of this work to examine cultural festivals as a counterbalance to the dominance of work focusing on sporting and mega-events. In doing so, the authors highlight several worthwhile areas for future effort, including the potential disadvantages of certain recruitment methods. Smith and Lockstone suggest that research is yet to investigate whether the dominance of volunteer recruitment through word-of-mouth channels leads to a homogeneous volunteer cohort, which over time could stifle the necessary creativity and innovation associated with cultural festivals. The use of associative groups as a conduit for volunteer recruitment also warrants research, to assess whether volunteers recruited to events in this manner are more committed to the club or group (e.g. sporting club, employer or education institution) that sourced them rather than the event itself, with which these volunteers may only have a temporary involvement. Smith and Lockstone touch on the importance of return or bounce-back volunteers to annual events. The authors encourage more research to discover what encourages this unique form of retention and focused attention on the motivation, satisfaction, commitment and turnover intentions of bounce-back event volunteers. This call lends itself to Smith and Lockstone's final plea for comparative research involving newly recruited and veteran volunteers, to assess their opinions, expectations and subsequent volunteering experiences in the events sector.

Part V widens from recruitment and retention to the management of people and work in the events and conventions sector. The first two chapters continue the focus on volunteers, with Hoye and Cuskelly's review of the psychology of sport event volunteerism (Chapter 13) and Auld, Cuskelly and Harrington's insight into the legacy impacts of volunteering in relation to major events (Chapter 14). Mirroring Deery's call in Chapter 10 for more research on the job satisfaction of paid events staff, in Chapter 13 Hoye and Cuskelly suggest that there is still much to be discovered about how volunteer management practices should be best operationalized to maximize volunteer satisfaction and retention outcomes. The authors go on to recommend that this research agenda should move beyond merely descriptive studies of volunteer motivation and satisfaction to encompass multiple-event evaluations, using probability sampling techniques and longitudinal research designs. Hoye and Cuskelly also suggest there should be greater emphasis on motivation theory and confirmatory analyses with which to assess the dimensionality of event volunteer motivation. Motivation and satisfaction also feature in Auld, Cuskelly and Harrington's exploration of the legacy impacts associated with event volunteering (Chapter 14). The authors suggest that the challenge for future research is to examine the extent to which both factors act as precursors for realizing systemic community benefits as a result of positive event volunteering experiences. Akin to Lockstone and Smith's appeal in Chapter 9 for research to examine whether episodic volunteers crossover to more sustained forms of volunteering, Auld, Cuskelly and Harrington recommend that research should take into account a wide range of temporal and event contexts to assess the continuance of event volunteers with the same event over time and the take-up amongst volunteers of opportunities to work for other sporting events and/or non-sport-related community volunteering.

Kemp (Chapter 15) offers a distinct break in perspective from the preceding chapters to examine the implications for people working in and dealing with the extremes of high-adrenalin event environments. He suggests that crowd profiling offers a way forward for a better understanding of audiences and how they can be dealt with in high-adrenalin environments. The author cautions that without a thorough understanding of behavioural models governing these environments, management action to control crowds can sometimes be hasty, with negative impacts for event attendance. Rounding out the book and the various cultural insights that have been presented in relation to event management, in Chapter 16 Okech explores the management of conferences in Kenya. As with Formádi and Raffai's Hungarian insight (Chapter 7), Okech also laments that the field of event management is under-researched in Kenya. The author makes the case for a comprehensive human resource strategy for driving industry growth and supplementing the dearth of current knowledge of human resource management issues affecting the conference industry in Kenya. This chapter adds weight to the call for cross-cultural comparisons of the status of the global events industry.

The future of events and conventions is largely dependent on the management practices of people working in the industry. The wealth of research provided by the collaborators in this book signifies a range of practices that can be incorporated to enhance the future of the sector. In addition, a research agenda has been established to provide stimulus for future study in this area.

Research is needed that catalogues the skills and attributes required of people working in the events and conventions industry. This would assist with the respective training and education sectors and further strengthen the link between industry and education. Following on from this, study is required on how to increase the confidence of employer perceptions of educational experiential learning as a means of providing students with adequate industry experience. In addition, future study in the convention industry is needed to determine the value of education and the format and structure of careers.

In relation to employment, more research is needed into the internal labour market to determine how key staff can rotate between different major event organizations in order to secure year-round employment. In addition, research that explores the issues that impact on the retention of paid staff, in particular incorporating job satisfaction as a research construct, is also required.

There is a range of research opportunities regarding volunteers. These include when and why volunteers choose to accept or reject flexible work options, and determining how flexible practices can be used to maximize the contribution volunteers make to their events organization of choice. Study is required into the potential disadvantages associated with the recruitment strategies of volunteers, and when retaining volunteers, research is needed to determine what encourages volunteers to return to annual and other reoccurring events, and comparative research is required into the newly recruited and veteran volunteers to assess their volunteering experiences in the events sector. There is a need to incorporate multiple-event evaluations, using probability sampling techniques and longitudinal research design. Greater emphasis is required on motivation theory and confirmatory analysis in order to assess the dimensionality of event volunteer motivation. Finally, there is a need for research to examine the legacy aspects of event volunteering and realizing the potential benfits of positive event volunteering experiences. Research opportunities also extend into cross-cultural comparisons to chart the various life cycle stages of the industry globally, and the need to determine what formalized guidance is required for best practice in HRM within the event sector.

In many respects, the growth of events and conventions and the maturation of employment paradigms within the area mirrors that which was codified with respect to tourism some 30 years ago. This is certainly true in the context of educational provision. Looking forward some 30 years, we can see a world in which demographic change has imposed a very different environment upon us, particularly in developed world countries. We will be older, more dependent on a smaller pool of employment-active taxpayers, and focused on health care rather than education. At the same time, we will be reaping the rewards of a far more highly educated, mature population, interested in stimuli and experiences that far outstrip the agenda of today's population. Events and conventions will play a major role in providing such stimulation, whether in the form of specialist activities within the closed social worlds of music, sport or collecting, or open-to-all events such as mega sporting occasions. Events will continue to demand high levels of human engagement to support delivery and mediation of the experiences. Therefore, the imperative is to understand the dynamics of events and conventions work and the people who engage in it, in order to both meet contemporary needs and plan for the events and conventions workforce of the future.

Index

Page numbers in *italics* indicate information in figures and tables.